God in Eisenhower's Life, Military Career, and Presidency

God in Eisenhower's Life, Military Career, and Presidency

A History of the Influence of Religion in His Life and Leadership as WWII Supreme Allied Commander and President of the United States

JERRY BERGMAN

Foreword by Paul Jungmeyer

PREFACE BY GENERAL ANDREW GOODPASTER

WIPF & STOCK · Eugene, Oregon

GOD IN EISENHOWER'S LIFE, MILITARY CAREER, AND PRESIDENCY
A History of the Influence of Religion in His Life and Leadership as WWII Supreme
Allied Commander and President of the United States

Wipf & Stock
An Imprint of Wipf and Stock Publishers
199 W. 8th Ave., Suite 3
Eugene, OR 97401

www.wipfandstock.com

PAPERBACK ISBN: 978-1-5326-6067-2
HARDCOVER ISBN: 978-1-5326-6068-9
EBOOK ISBN: 978-1-5326-6069-6

Manufactured in the U.S.A.   MARCH 3, 2019

To Andrew J. Goodpaster, without whose encouragement I would have never completed this project. General Goodpaster was a close friend of Ike and the White House staff secretary under President Eisenhower. He earned a PhD at Princeton and during the Eisenhower administration was the White House military adviser to the president. He ended his career as Supreme Allied Commander in Europe, the commander of all NATO forces.

And to Carlo D'Este, who reviewed the manuscript, providing numerous suggestions, concluding that "you must get this book published!"

Contents

Foreword

*"Dwight Eisenhower was the most religious president
in the twentieth century."*[1]

DWIGHT DAVID EISENHOWER IS a revered figure in American history,
emerging perhaps as the most popular figure of the World War II era. Ike, as
he was called, ultimately became a popular president in 1952. Eisenhower's
personality and character have been described in numerous ways. He was
modest, humble, a team player, relaxed, expressive, genial, optimistic, and
trusting. His smile could charm anyone who met him.

Scholars have invested much time in relating the stories of presidents.
The life of Dwight David Eisenhower has been inscribed in the pages of
literally dozens of books and an untold numbers of articles. His important
role as Supreme Allied Commander and General of the Army, directing
the Normandy (or D-Day) Invasion, would by itself attract the attention
of those who chronicle such events. His presidency would obviously be
the focus of historians and political scientists. One would wonder if any
remaining aspects of Ike's life and character exist to study.

An interesting aspect of Eisenhower's life, while it has not been ignored (but has garnered little attention), is his religious beliefs. The importance of faith and prayer in the life of Ike during his military career,
especially during World War II, has been discussed by historians. Less
attention, however, has been devoted to the antecedents of Eisenhower's
religious background, views, and how his stance on religion was shaped
and manifested throughout his life.

1. Holl, "Dwight D. Eisenhower," 119.

ix

God in Eisenhower's Life, Military Career, and Presidency, written by Jerry Bergman, PhD, examines in detail the religious life of Eisenhower from childhood throughout his life. It traces his upbringing in a strict fundamentalist family from Abilene, Kansas through his journey in honing a religious set of principles and beliefs that would guide him. Dr. Bergman's careful study of the Eisenhower family dispels misunderstandings, misinterpretations, and myths that have become a part of Eisenhower folklore. The author also provides persuasive evidence that religion and faith were essential elements in Eisenhower's life.

Dr. Bergman's work expertly chronicles the forces in his family and his surroundings which shaped Eisenhower's religious beliefs. The book clearly illustrates the story of Ike's rejection of his parents' Jehovah's Witness background, but it also shows that many of the values and beliefs Ike learned as a young lad would be reflected in living his life as a military figure and president.

As a soldier, Eisenhower's use of biblical imagery and his familiarity with Scripture are well documented by Bergman. The statement of one of Ike's aides that Eisenhower could "quote Scripture by the yard" and that he used scriptural quotations in his speeches provides only one indication that Ike was not the non-religious person thought by some. The glimpses of Eisenhower's prayers witnessed or recorded during World War II manifest a depth of faith and belief that was unknown or unacknowledged by many.

The Eisenhower presidential era was an interesting period in our nation's history. It was a time when the United States was experiencing significant population and economic growth. The country witnessed the beginning of the construction of the Interstate Highway System. It was a time of civil rights unrest. It was also a time when Eisenhower was faced with many foreign policy challenges besides the Cold War. The challenges confronting the United States from newly emerging nations at times bedeviled the Eisenhower administration. America was troubled by Russia's emergence as the leader in the field of space technology. Yet, it was also a time of relative peace. There was no "hot" war that involved the country after Eisenhower negotiated a conclusion to the Korean War.

Historians and political scientists enjoy ranking American presidents, and Eisenhower is no exception. In early assessments of his presidency, Ike fared poorly, often being called a "do-nothing" president, placing him alongside presidents like Chester Arthur and perhaps even Herbert Hoover. As time passed, as the pundits gained new perspectives on Eisenhower, and as new records become available, a fresh evaluation of Eisenhower's leadership and impact on the country has witnessed a significant rise in his popularity, ranking him in the top ten presidents.

Dr. Bergman's book reveals several dimensions of Eisenhower's faith. Through numerous initiatives, Ike demonstrated the essential role of religion in the life of the country. Some believe that his baptism into the Presbyterian Church as president was motivated out of political consideration rather than from sincere religious convictions. However, the institution of prayer breakfasts, opening cabinet meetings with prayers, the unprecedented inclusion of prayer before his first inaugural address, his role in placing the words "under god" into the Pledge of Allegiance, and his invitation to Nikita Khrushchev to attend worship services with him reflect more than a superficial adherence to the importance of faith and religion in his own and his country's life. He firmly believed that the nation's conscience is the church.

Dr. Jerry Bergman's book is an important contribution and represents a significant resource for scholars and students who want to gain a more balanced understanding of the life of President Dwight David Eisenhower.

PAUL JUNGMEYER, PhD
Professor of History,
Columbia College,
Jefferson City, Missouri

Preface

HAVING KNOWN AND WORKED closely with Dwight Eisenhower for several decades, I have reviewed this book with much interest. Dr. Bergman has done a masterful job in accurately chronicling Eisenhower's religious life and beliefs. This book fills in a very important, but often neglected, part of Ike's life—a part of his life that was critical in Eisenhower's military career and presidency. I commend him for his meticulous research and for correctly arriving at a detailed picture of this important aspect of his life. Indeed, his spirituality, faith in God, and God's role for him on earth were all central to what Eisenhower achieved, and he achieved a great deal in his life.

GENERAL ANDREW GOODPASTER
White House Staff Secretary October 1954–January 20, 1961. Served as NATO's Supreme Allied Commander, Europe and Commander in Chief of the United States European Command from May 5, 1969 until his retirement on December 17, 1974. He earned an MS in engineering and an MA and PhD in international affairs, all from Princeton University.

Acknowledgments

AMONG THE SCORES OF people to whom I am grateful for input on this book, some for whom I relied on extensively include the staff at the Dwight Eisenhower Presidential Library in Abilene, Kansas, for their help and encouragement in this research. I must also thank the Eisenhower Room staff at Defiance College in Defiance, Ohio for their critical research assistance. Defiance College's interest in Eisenhower's religious activities stems from the fact that the college is a denominational school, and a former Defiance College president, Dr. Kevin McCann, was an Eisenhower speechwriter. Furthermore, the bond between the college and Eisenhower resulted in the college's archive having fairly good holdings of material on Eisenhower.

I also wish to express my thanks to doctoral student Craig Keller for providing several of the documents quoted in this book. I also thank both Dr. Morris Sider and Gloria J. Stonge of the Brethren in Christ Church Archives at Messiah College, Grantham, Pennsylvania. Many primary sources about Eisenhower's religion were stored in their archives. A special thanks also to Robin Lesher, Director of Adams County Library, for use of the treasure trove of material at the Gettysburg Library, 140 Baltimore Street, Gettysburg, Pennsylvania. Ms. Lesher gave me full access to the Eisenhower room, which was used by Eisenhower for official governmental work when he lived in Gettysburg. In this room was a goldmine of Eisenhower books and papers.

And, too, critically important was the help of Gladys Dodd, who used extensive primary sources to produce the definitive and valuable study of the Eisenhower family's religious background. Last, I wish to thank Dwight Eisenhower's son, General John Eisenhower, and the late General Andrew J. Goodpaster of the Eisenhower World Affairs Institute for their encouragement and insight. Any shortcomings that may remain in this historical study are not due to the helpful feedback from these many persons and

Acknowledgments

the many others who kindly honored me with their time and experience in reviewing the many drafts of this manuscript. These persons included historian Dr. David Herbert, Carlo D'Este, Marilyn Dauer, and especially Eric Smith, who did a masterful job helping to get this book ready for publication. And of course my loving wife, Dianne Bergman, who was there for me for most of this project. Any errors that remain are solely the author's responsibility. Some minor grammar errors in the quotes were corrected rather than using "sic" to indicate their existence.

Introduction

HUNDREDS OF BOOKS AND journal articles have been published on President Eisenhower but surprisingly little attention has been given to the major importance of religion in his life and presidency.[1] This work was designed to lay the foundation to help further clarify the historical role of religion in the American government.[2]

Although the focus of this work is on President Dwight David Eisenhower and the role that religion played in his life, his family's religious background will also be discussed in some detail. Specifically, my goal is to understand the importance of religion in Eisenhower's role as a U.S. General, as Supreme Commander of the Allied Forces during World War II, and as President of the United States.

Many myths exist about Dwight and the Eisenhower family, not the least of which relate to their religion.[3] I have striven in this work to dispel some of the more common myths, some even accepted by Eisenhower scholars—no easy task several decades after Dwight's funeral. For example, claims have been made in the literature that Dwight was raised as (or became) a River Brethren, a Mennonite, a Jew (his U.S. Military Academy yearbook called him the "Swedish Jew"), a Roman Catholic, an agnostic, or as a part of the group now known as the Jehovah's Witnesses, commonly called the Watchtower.[4]

As will be documented, although Dwight eventually ended up a baptized and committed Presbyterian, he was reared in the Watchtower sect in which both parents were active for many years.[5] Much of the misunder-

1. Keller, *Intellectuals and Eisenhower*, 33.

2. DiCianni, *Faith of the Presidents*.

3. See D' Este, *Eisenhower*, 22.

4. Smith, *Faith and the Presidency*, 235.

5. Wirt, "Faith of Dwight D. Eisenhower."

standing about the religion of Dwight's childhood and youth has resulted from an inadequate knowledge and understanding of the Watchtower, including both their history and their teachings. In completing this study, I had the advantage of being reared a Jehovah's Witness, a requirement to fully understand Dwight and the nuances of his religious background. I have also published widely about the Witness movement.[6] Many of the common misconceptions about the Witnesses, their history, and their core teachings will also be covered in this book. See Appendix II for a detailed discussion of the Watchtower.

A second goal is to direct attention to the long-neglected role of religion in Dwight's life.[7] Most of the many books about him and his presidency largely, or totally, ignore this factor—at best a few paragraphs are devoted to his religious beliefs. This work also raises the topic of the place of religion in government—an issue that gives every indication of growing more important.

MY INTEREST IN EISENHOWER

I have been interested in Eisenhower's religious background for several decades, partly because I am a distant relative of Dwight by marriage.[8] My connection with Kansas and my memories of discussions about Dwight since I was a child have also motivated my interest in his life.

My research on Dwight's life agrees with Jameson's conclusions in chapter 14 of *Heroes by the Dozen*, titled "Praying President from Abilene." He wrote that the more one studies Dwight D. Eisenhower's life and achievements, both his military career and as President of the United States,

> the more obvious it becomes that he was an exceptionally devout man who believed in prayer and who quite regularly prayed publicly or privately before making many of the major decisions which might hold the world together or blow it apart . . . the part the

6. See Bergman, "Adventists and Jehovah's Witnesses," "Jehovah's Witnesses' Experience," "Modern Religious Objection," "Steeped in Religion," *Jehovah's Witnesses*, "Influence of Religion," "Jehovah's Witnesses" (2005), ""Jehovah's Witnesses" (2006), "Dwight Eisenhower," "Toledo Dentist Charles Betts."

7. Holl, "Dwight D. Eisenhower," "Dwight D. Eisenhower Religion."

8. My mother was originally from Meade, Kansas. The daughter of Eisenhower's brother Roy, Patricia, married Thomas Fegan. Their son, T. Michael Fegan, married Eulonda Beck, who was part of the Eckholf family branch, as was my maternal grandmother (Eckholf and Eckholf, *Eckhoff Family History*, 112).

Bible played in his eventful life was so pronounced—and so often overlooked in the day to day reporting—that it seems quite appropriate it should be highlighted.[9]

The role of Dwight's parents, especially his mother, was also a critical factor in his enormous military and political success. His parents instilled in all of the Eisenhower boys "the beliefs and principles that shaped their lives. Deepest of these was a religious sense."[10] Dwight's parents divided the world into good and evil, and "Ike never lost the language of right and wrong," which becomes very obvious in his struggle against the Nazis.[11]

I have dedicated this work to Andrew Goodpaster for several reasons. When obtaining grants to help finance this research, the Eisenhower foundation obtained a copy of my early articles on this topic, which were passed on to Andrew Goodpaster for his evaluation. He read my study and, as a result, phoned me at the college where I then taught. Goodpaster strongly encouraged me to continue researching this topic because, he stressed, my thesis was clearly important. I have now published several articles, including my first article on Eisenhower's religion, published in *Kansas History*, which earned the Edgar Langsdorf Award, and a chapter in a book published by Columbia University Press. I value Goodpaster's wisdom and advice on Eisenhower because he worked closely with Dwight on various projects on and off since 1947.[12] He also has a deep understanding of Eisenhower's person.[13] Goodpaster stressed that Dwight's religious values guided him in most everything he did.

Goodpaster also noted that Dwight had much charisma, writing, "No one could meet with him without really being lifted, without coming out just bubbling with enthusiasm . . . when he was ill . . . President Nixon asked each of his Cabinet officers and senior appointees to go out and see President Eisenhower and cheer him up. And his comment was that they all came back with the same response, 'We didn't cheer him up; he cheered us up.' That was true throughout his administration."[14]

---

9. Jameson, *Heroes by the Dozen*, 149.

10. Morin, *Dwight D. Eisenhower*, 11; See also Fairbanks, "Religious Dimensions of Presidential Leadership."

11. Thomas, *Ike's Bluff*, 102.

12. Nelson, *Life and Work of General Andrew J. Goodpaster*, 2016.

13. Thomas, *Ike's Bluff*, 42.

14. Tompson, *Portraits of American Presidents*, 73.

Goodpaster's association with Eisenhower goes back to when Dwight was Army Chief of Staff and Goodpaster was serving in the Operations Division of the War Department. In 1954 Goodpaster became Eisenhower's Staff Secretary and Defense Liaison Officer, a position in which he worked closely with Dwight. Goodpaster was a key Eisenhower aid and oversaw the entire U.S. operations in Europe in the early 1970s as Supreme Allied Commander. He also was the 51st Superintendent of the United States Military Academy at West Point and a senior fellow at the Eisenhower Institute when he contacted me.

It was because of his encouragement that I continued researching this topic to document the fact that Dwight's Witness background had a profound influence on his life and presidency. Since then I have, in the words of Professor Jack Holl, documented beyond question the fact that Eisenhower's "religious values shap[ed] the Eisenhower administration's domestic and foreign policy."[15]

15. Holl, "Dwight D. Eisenhower," 120.

I

Ike's Mystery Religion

ALTHOUGH MUCH HAS BEEN written about Eisenhower's life, many biographers have concluded we actually know very little about his personal life and the various factors that influenced him to achieve what he did. We do know the problems he faced during World War II were Herculean and the fact that "he was equal to the task is now virtually taken for granted."[1] The focus of most writers tends to be on his decision-making process in the battlefield, and the contingencies that impinged on his life as an adult.

Interestingly, Dwight's religious background has been discussed by many writers, but most contain much misinformation or largely ignore the whole topic of his religion. The fact is that Dwight Eisenhower was raised under a strong influence of the Bible Students, renamed Jehovah's Witness in 1931, and Watchtower literature. The misinformation about the religion is compounded by the fact that many Eisenhower biographies, and even writings by the Eisenhower children, often declined to fully acknowledge their parents' religious affiliation and the extent of Ida's (his mother) involvement.[2]

Many authors referred to the Watchtower faith only as a "fundamentalist" sect, "Bible Students," or "Russellites"—the latter a term few persons likely understood.[3] Lyon even stated, "The specific nature of the religion is uncertain. The parents appear to have left the River Brethren for a more

1. D'Este, *Eisenhower: A Soldier's Life*, 4; Keim, *John Foster Dulles.*
2. Fleming, *Ike's Mom*, 1; A. Eisenhower, "Eisenhower: Soldier of Peace."
3. Beschloss, *Eisenhower*; Holl, *Religion, Politics, and the Evils of Communism*, 384.

primitive and austere sect, something referred to as the Bible Students, and they would later gravitate to the evangelical sect known as Jehovah's Witnesses."[4] Lyon fails to note that the Bible Students morphed into the Jehovah's Witnesses. Another Eisenhower biographer, Stephen Ambrose, said about this topic only that Ida was "a deeply religious woman" and a pacifist.[5]

Accounts of the Eisenhower family history also commonly repeat the erroneous claim that Dwight's parents were River Brethren or were not directly involved with the Watchtower. Miller included a whole chapter on Ida in his book, and often noted her religious faith in this chapter, but never once mentioned what it was.[6] One does get some hints, but nothing more.

Another example is a *Time Magazine* article stating only that Ike's "parents were members of the River Brethren, a Mennonite sect," adding "along with their piety, the Eisenhowers gave their sons a creed of self-starting individualism."[7]

After claiming Eisenhower's parents were members of the River Brethren, another account noted they "brought up their children in an old-fashioned atmosphere of puritanical morals. Prayer and Bible reading were a daily part of their lives. Violence was forbidden, though in a family of six boys the edict was a bit hard to enforce."[8]

An article titled "The President's Religious Faith," by Paul Hutchinson, contained nine paragraphs on the Brethren in Christ Church, implying Dwight was reared in this denomination. Long correctly writes, "throughout his youth Dwight Eisenhower had attended [the Brethren in Christ Church in Abilene] with his parents and brothers."[9]

Even President Eisenhower's spiritual mentor and close friend, Billy Graham, was led to believe that Eisenhower's parents "had been River Brethren, a small but devoutly pious group in the Mennonite tradition."[10] Graham added Ike had made a personal commitment to Christ as a boy and reaffirmed it publicly after becoming president.[11]

---

4. Lyon, *Portrait of the Hero*, 38.

5. Ambrose, *Ike: Abilene to Berlin*, 16.

6. Miller, *Eisenhower, Man and Soldier*, 86–101.

7. *Time*, April 4, 1969, 20.

8. Whitney, *American Presidents*, 311.

9. Long, *Stalwart Faith*.

10. Graham, "General Who Became," 190.

11. Pierard, *Billy Graham and the U.S. Presidency*, 117; Pierard, *Billy Graham—Preacher,*

In her book about Mamie's and Dwight's lives, John Eisenhower's daughter, Susan, managed to almost completely avoid the subject of religion, noting only that Dwight's parents were very religious, didn't smoke or drink or play cards, read the Bible daily, held prayer meetings in their home, and believed in the brotherhood of mankind.[12] No hint was provided as to what that brotherhood of mankind religion might be, but the book inferred they were Mennonites. She then devoted an entire page to their Mennonite background.[13] Even their family friend, *Time Magazine* magnate owner Clare Booth Luce, claimed Dwight Eisenhower told her his family were Mennonites.[14]

Official Eisenhower biographer Bela Kornitzer mentions only that the Eisenhowers were "Bible Students," had "fundamentalist religious beliefs," and studied "the writings of 'Pastor Russell,'" ignoring the fact that Pastor Russell was the Watchtower founder.[15] (When Russell died in 1916, his writings were soon replaced by those of the new president, "Judge" J. F. Rutherford, resulting in several major schisms in the movement and their transformation into the Jehovah's Witnesses.) The group morphed dramatically after Russell's death (including the name change), but the literature and much of the doctrine was unchanged.

Even works that included extensive discussions of Dwight Eisenhower's religious upbringing, such as the aforementioned Bela Kornitzer book, primarily discuss the River Brethren background that had influenced Dwight mostly during his preschool years.

Others, such as Gerald L. K. Smith, claimed Dwight was Jewish, a group which Smith evidently did not think much of (but he thought even less of Jehovah's Witnesses). When confronted with the Jewish question, Milton tactfully answered, "I always wish I did have some Jewish blood in me."[16]

An even more common practice of Eisenhower biographers is to totally omit the predominant religion in which Dwight was reared and its importance in the Eisenhower boys' formative years.[17] Other examples to illustrate how common misinformation is about Ike's religion are in Appendix II.

Pierard, *One Nation under God.*

12. S. Eisenhower, *Mrs. Ike*, 27.

13. J. Eisenhower, *General Ike*, 23.

14. Keller, "Intellectuals and Eisenhower," 238.

15. Kornitzer, *Great American Heritage*, 14, 22, 32.

16. Keller, "Intellectuals and Eisenhower," 235–36.

17. For example, see Larson, *Eisenhower; The President.*

2

Growing Up in the
Wrong Side of Town

"The churches of America are citadels of our faith in individual freedom and human dignity. This faith is the living source of all our spiritual strength. And this strength is our matchless armor in our world-wide struggle against the forces of godless tyranny and oppression."[1]

UNDERSTANDING DWIGHT EISENHOWER AS a man requires an examination of his childhood, the source of much that allowed him to accomplish the following: (1) become the soldier that successfully commanded the Allied victory in Europe, (2) direct the American occupation forces in Germany, (3) become Army Chief of Staff, (4) become President of Columbia University, (5) achieve best-selling author status, (6) become President of the United States of America, and (7) be re-elected for a second term as president. Dwight himself repeatedly attributed his many achievements to his upbringing in Abilene, Kansas, especially due to the influence of his mother.

The making of the man lies in the early years that mold him into the person that interacts successfully with the adult world. How one deals with this world depends heavily on their experiences during their formative years. Although this study focuses primarily on the religious aspects of

1. Dwight D. Eisenhower, Message to the National Co-Chairmen, Commission of Religious Organizations, National Conference on Christians and Jews, July 9, 1953.

those years, Ike's social, intellectual, and psychological world as a young child and youth were also all critically important. This chapter summarizes what is known about his childhood and adolescence in an attempt to understand the facts and dispel the many myths about his early life.

DWIGHT'S EARLY LIFE

Dwight was born in Denison, Texas on the evening of October 14, 1890. He was the third son of David and Ida Eisenhower.[2] Some have speculated his birth during a violent Texas thunderstorm was prophetic of his role in the most violent war the world had ever faced, then or since. Because the physician arrived too late to help with the delivery, the baby was birthed with the assistance of neighbors.[3] Dwight was named after Dwight Moody, the famous Christian fundamentalist who founded Chicago Moody Church, Moody Press, Moody Bible Institute, and the Moody Science Institute that produced many creation science films.[4]

His birth name was David Dwight (the name printed in the family Bible), but the family reversed the names to avoid his being confused with his father, David.[5] Ida was originally born Elizabeth Ida and also reversed her name as she later did for David Dwight—thus, he became Dwight David Eisenhower.[6] His two older brothers gave him the nickname "Ike," which stuck and became an ideal political name that produced the "I like Ike" slogan widely used when Dwight campaigned for president.[7]

About a year after Dwight was born, the family moved to Abilene, Kansas. In 1898, after the Eisenhowers' sixth son was born, the family moved into the modest two-story, white, wood-sided house on South Fourth Street in the southern edge of Abilene, where the family lived until Ida died. The house belonged to David's brother, Abraham,[8] and rent was affordable only because Abraham allowed his brother David to live in the house at a bargain price if their father Jacob could live with them. The house was actually part of a small three-acre farm that had a smokehouse,

2. Ambrose, *Ike: Abilene to Berlin*, 12.

3. D'Este, *Eisenhower: A Soldier's Life*, 22.

4. D'Este, *Eisenhower: A Soldier's Life*, 22.

5. Gullan, *Faith of Our*, 224.

6. D'Este, *Eisenhower: A Soldier's Life*, 15.

7. Greene, *I Like Ike*.

8. Johnson, *Nazi Terror*, 13.

a large barn with a steep roof, and enough land to grow a large garden and fruit trees, plus room to keep a few cows, pigs, and chickens.[9]

Dwight and his four brothers that survived to adulthood (Arthur [b. 1886], Roy [b. 1892], Earl [b. 1898], and Milton [b. 1899]) were all raised in Abilene. One son, Paul (b. 1894), died as an infant—a tragic event in the lives of the Eisenhowers.

When the Eisenhower family moved to Abilene in 1891, it was hardly a town as we know the meaning of the term today. It lacked paved roads, sewers, and most parts of the town even lacked a water supply. Public transportation consisted of a single mule-drawn streetcar. The one-man police force's function was to collect a two-dollar "tax" levied on all adult males.[10] Although Abilene had a lurid past and boasted a famous sheriff named "Wild Bill" Hickok, when the Eisenhowers moved there it was a much tamer town of around four thousand residents.[11] At this time Abilene, Kansas in many ways fit the common stereotype of an 1800s Middle America small town.

Ida, a frugal, hard-working woman, planted a large vegetable garden on their three acres to grow many of the family's produce needs. The Eisenhower family rarely had any spare cash, never took a vacation, had no savings, and luxuries were unknown, but they never went without the necessities.[12] When the Eisenhowers arrived in Abilene, their sole material assets amounted to a few family possessions and twenty-four dollars.[13] Soon David had a steady job, a house, a small farm, and the basic necessities of life.

David, even though he was very much a loner, did miss his family enormously when he was away from them during his twelve-hour workday which rarely even allowed him to come home even for lunch. He usually arrived home at six in the evening just in time to say grace at the start of supper, and was silent through much of the family supper time. When the meal was finished, he often left to go to his room and read. Dwight noted his father was largely absent from his life as a result of his long workday at a physically demanding job.[14]

9. Neal, *Eisenhowers*.

10. D'Este, *Eisenhower: A Soldier's Life*, 26.

11. Gullan, *Faith of Our*, 224.

12. Ambrose, *Ike: Abilene to Berlin*, 12.

13. D'Este, *Eisenhower: A Soldier's Life*, 22.

14. Eisenhower, *At Ease*, 37.

For many years David's annual salary was close to 350 dollars a year for a twelve-hour day of hard manual labor required to maintain the machinery and steam equipment. The family could survive only if they were very frugal and self-sufficient. Even though the work was backbreaking and long, David Eisenhower evidently never complained—although when the opportunity arose in 1916 for a similar position at the local gas plant, he left the creamery and was soon promoted to general manager at his new job, where he stayed until he retired in 1931. The Eisenhowers remained in Abilene because of their desire to stay close to their family and friends, even though David probably could have done much better where more opportunities existed. He never made more than a 150 dollars a month during his entire thirty-nine years of toil at work in Abilene.

One event about David that is likely false is the report he "was fired from the Belle Springs Creamery in 1916 after attending a Jehovah's Witness convention in Washington, D.C." In fact, not "only had David long since lost interest in the Watchtower at this time, but the authoritative history of the Witnesses reflects no such events held in 1916 anywhere in the United States. Moreover, Witness conventions did not occur with regularity until the 1920s."[15]

ABILENE CULTURE

The Eisenhower family's religiousness was not all that unusual for Abilene citizens during the early 1900s generation. Author Broadwater wrote Dwight was reared in a "series of austere fundamentalist sects" where "Ike was sure to learn a great deal about decency and honesty but was far less likely to develop a tolerance of political 'dissenters or a recognition of the value of intellectual debate.'"[16] I was unable to locate any evidence that supported this later claim.

Most of Abilene's adult citizens had "strong religious beliefs" as well as the values of determination and hard work—and they believed these traits would bring them success.[17] Only one small area of the town called "The Herd" contained most of the non-believers, or at least the non-churchgoers, of Abilene.[18] One reflection of the town's "strong religious beliefs" was

---

15. D'Este, *Eisenhower: A Soldier's Life*, 714.

16. Broadwater, *Eisenhower & the Anti-Communist*, 17.

17. D'Este, *Eisenhower: A Soldier's Life*, 26.

18. Eisenhower, *At Ease*, 67.

the fact that Abilene's numerous churches were regularly filled on Sunday. Dwight observed social life in Abilene also centered around the churches.[19] Even the name Abilene is biblical—it comes from Luke 3:1, which says, "In the fifteenth year of the reign of Tiberius Caesar—when Pontius Pilate was governor of Judea, Herod tetrarch of Galilee, his brother Philip tetrarch of Iturea and Traconitis, and Lysanias tetrarch of Abilene."[20]

Evidence of this religiousness includes the fact many of the letters Dwight received from home after he left Abilene contained expressions of religious piety. For example, Art Hurd, an attorney, a former mayor of Abilene, and friend of Dwight since childhood, wrote "we are, of course, praying for you and your men."[21] A letter from Frances Curry that explained how the war had impacted her life closed with the advice that "Honor has its own place as a just reward; but, Dwight, it is a lot more than worldly honor for which I know you are working so hard. And that is the way we all pray for your safety, guidance and success in God's name—and that is the reward. The girls all send their best wishes and prayers."[22] Abilene culture and religious social environment is also indicated by the fact Eisenhower stated he never knew anyone from a divorced family until he went to West Point.[23]

In spite of being reared in what is today often derisively called a "fundamentalist" religion, as a child Dwight seemed to have had what most people consider fairly normal interests. General horseplay, baseball (his boyhood hero was the great Pittsburgh Pirates hall-of-fame shortstop Honus Wagner), and all manner of sports were his steady youthful diet. Dwight's childhood actually closely "resembled the quintessential depictions of rural American youth in the paintings of Norman Rockwell."[24]

However, like many Witnesses (who were called Bible Students until 1931), Dwight Eisenhower was from the "poor side" of the tracks in a town physically (and socially) divided in half by the Union Pacific Railroad. The south side contained mostly blue-collar workers who lived in small wood-framed houses such as the Eisenhowers. In contrast, the "other side"

19. Eisenhower, *At Ease*, 68.

20. Jameson, *They Still Call Him Ike*, 19.

21. Irish, *Hometown Support*, 21.

22. Irish, *Hometown Support*, 33.

23. Eisenhower, *At Ease*, 37.

24. D'Este, *Eisenhower: A Soldier's Life*, 23.

of town contained the "fine Victorian homes of the well-to-do" lawyers, doctors, and successful businessmen.[25]

The Eisenhowers woke at 5:30 in the morning and, during the winter, had to dress under the covers while still in bed to stay warm in their poorly heated house. In the summer, their house was unbearably hot—at times the heat rose up to over a 100 degrees. For many years the house lacked running water and indoor plumbing. Bathing involved filling a large tub in the kitchen with water that was heated on the stove. The weekly bath, as was common then, was shared by the whole family, the youngest first and the oldest last.

Being poor did have some advantages, though—all of the Eisenhower boys developed a healthy respect for work, a smart frugalness (even mending their own clothes), and learned the value of money and possessions. What few material things they owned were not only appreciated, but treasured. Dwight learned to work hard; in addition to his daily chores, he became an able gardener and a shrewd business entrepreneur, enabling him to make a profit from peddling vegetables, usually cucumbers and sweet corn.[26] David encouraged all of his sons to earn their own spending money—this gave them a strong incentive to work and rewarded them for a job well done. Dwight's other chores included cooking and cleaning. He also shared in taking care of his younger brother, a task he evidently strongly disliked.

Being poor had other advantages as well—unable to afford toys during most of their childhood, the Eisenhower boys manufactured their own toys from whatever materials they had on hand. As a result, Dwight evidently developed some mechanical skills—no doubt influenced by both his father's interest and skills. Recreation typically involved activities that did not cost much and were simple, such as water fights or, because they could not afford bathing suits, swimming in a nearby creek in the buff.

Foremost, while growing up Dwight learned the "religious values of self-discipline and self-sacrifice," values that guided him throughout his entire life.[27] As a young man, Dwight developed many friendships that lasted for his lifetime, including Everett Hazlett and Mark Clark, the latter who would also become a general in the Army.[28] As an adult, Dwight regularly

25. D'Este, *Eisenhower: A Soldier's Life*, 26.

26. D'Este, *Eisenhower: A Soldier's Life*, 28.

27. Chernus, 2002, 91.

28. Holt, *An Unlikely Partnership*.

corresponded with many people he had known as a youth, often until death separated one or the other. People were drawn to Dwight, and he was able to successfully motivate people to want to support him.[29]

29. Holt, *An Unlikely Partnership*, 149.

3

Lessons in Childhood

WHEN SEARCHING FOR THE experiences that prepared Dwight for his future role in the world, one receives hints, but no clear signs, of his early greatness, except an unusual level of boundless energy and a seemingly insatiable drive to learn.[1] Although clearly bright, little in Dwight's youth indicated he would become a future world leader. He was in many ways an ordinary boy, even in school, involving himself in the typical boy's activities. He was of average size and was an average student in grade school, although he did display his legendary bad temper rather early in life.[2] As a youth it appeared he would be much more likely to teach history than to make it.

One experience that served Eisenhower well occurred when he was almost five. While visiting his uncle, he encountered a bad-tempered aggressive male goose in the barnyard. His uncle took pity on Dwight because he was obviously intimidated (and frustrated) by the goose's untamed aggression. The uncle stripped an old broom of its straw and showed the child how to protect himself. A smack on the goose's fanny reversed the pecking order—and the goose never bothered Dwight again. Eisenhower later recalled, "I quickly learned never to negotiate with an adversary except from a position of strength."[3]

1. Gullan, *Faith of Our*, 225.
2. Eisenhower, *Dwight David Eisenhower*, 12.
3. Eisenhower, *At Ease*, 30.

Some idea of Dwight's sensitivity (and compassion) was revealed in an accident involving his younger brother Earl. One day Earl was playing near a butcher knife that Dwight was using. The butcher knife fell and injured one of Earl's eyes and, several years later, while rough housing with Milton, he totally lost his sight in the injured eye. Although Ida attempted to comfort her children to help them deal with the accident, Dwight was "remorseful for the remainder of his life" about his part in the unfortunate accident.[4] This sensitivity to the feelings of others remained with him until his last days—he was even bothered when his grandchildren were in a situation where their eyesight *could* be threatened.

BOYHOOD FIGHTING

In one way, Eisenhower did not fit the stereotype of a religious youth from a good family. According to Ike's boyhood friend John E. Long, an unusual number of undisciplined boys who lived in Abilene offered ample opportunity for fighting, of which Dwight Eisenhower was involved in his fair share.[5] Because he was small for his age, Dwight often lost the fights he was involved in, but evidently rarely gave up. Many interpret this fact as a sign of normalcy for the time.

In what may seem to be a contradiction, both Edgar and Dwight were evidently regarded as "the best bare-knuckles fighters in the tough south side."[6] One reason was they had to earn a reputation to survive in their "other side of the tracks" community. The world was not kind to them, or at least their part of it, and they dealt with it the only way they believed they could—by prevailing in physical conflicts.

The brothers also fought amongst themselves—especially Dwight and his older brother Edgar.[7] In the cramped quarters of their small house, one would expect that friction would be common, and it was—rivalries abounded; however, Dwight's son, John, suspected the stories of combat passed down to him were exaggerated.[8] That the frequency and intensity

---

4. Eisenhower, *At Ease*, 84.

5. D'Este, *Eisenhower: A Soldier's Life*, 26.

6. D'Este, *Eisenhower: A Soldier's Life*, 39.

7. Edgar was named for Edgar Allen Poe, a fact that surprised the Eisenhower boys because of Poe's well-known problems with alcoholism. Ida replied to this concern by stating "I still liked his poems" (Jameson, *They Still Call Him Ike*, 44).

8. D'Este, *Eisenhower: A Soldier's Life*, 31.

of these fights may have been exaggerated is supported by statements of family friends who remembered the Eisenhower home as a happy place, largely free of friction. Milton once said he never once heard a cross word pass between his parents.

One fight involving Wesley Marrifield occurred in October of 1903 when Ike was only thirteen.[9] Evidently, neither boy had much inclination to fight, but a howling mob egged them on, intimidating them into entertaining the crowd. Eisenhower claimed that the two went at it for about an hour (other accounts claim this claim was embellished to draw attention to the exploit). The fight was said to be a draw, but Dwight left the fight with a black eye among other injuries. One result was a strong reprimand from Ike's parents, who as punishment kept him out of school for several days. Both parents disapproved of fighting, except in David's view it was justified in certain self-defense situations. Ida realized there was not a lot she could do to stop the fighting, and for this reason she tended to turn a blind eye to her son's youthful altercations.[10]

Although it is often alleged the boys were not conscious of their poverty, they could not help but be aware of it at some level because this fact was partially behind some of their fighting. They knew they were from the wrong side of the tracks, but as hard-working, proud people, poverty likely motivated them to succeed in their tangles with their tormenters—which they often did.[11]

DISCIPLINE

David Eisenhower strongly believed that to spare the rod would spoil the child—and his beatings were sometimes considered excessive, even by the Eisenhower boys. Dwight once hotly responded to a beating his brother Edgar experienced for skipping school to earn some extra money working for a doctor by stating, "I don't think anyone ought to be whipped like that, not even a dog."[12]

Ida took a very different approach than David to disciplining the children. When Dwight lost his temper because he was not allowed to go trick-or-treating with the other kids because he was considered too young,

9. Cannon, *War Hero and President*, 19.

10. D'Este, *Eisenhower: A Soldier's Life*, 37.

11. Netty Stover Jackson, *Oral History*, electronically filed at the Eisenhower Library.

12. Eisenhower, *At Ease*, 36.

he repeatedly hit an apple tree with his fists until they bled. As a result, Dwight ended up with a severe thrashing from his father, who ordered him to bed.[13] Once in bed, Ida Eisenhower soon arrived with a washcloth to clean up (and then wrap) Dwight's bleeding hands. She calmly explained, using Bible verses to support her point, that by losing his temper in this situation he was only harming himself and nobody else.

Eisenhower later recalled this was "one of the most valuable moments of my life."[14] The Bible verse that impressed him the most was "he that conquereth his own soul is greater than he who taketh a city."[15] Dwight acknowledged his temper did not disappear after that event, but he was better able to both control it or at least hide it from others.

GUNS

A favorite childhood game the Eisenhower boys played was reenacting Wild West heroes, including Wild Bill Hickok, Jesse James, and others. Shooting guns was of special interest in the family, and Dwight was considered the best shot in the family.[16] His shooting paid off handsomely—in high school he inherited a sixteen-gauge pump-action shotgun from his older brother, and his hunting brought a good supply of meat to supplement the family's vegetable garden. Everything from jack rabbits to coyotes was fair game. Dwight's interest in guns and war was opposed by his mother, of course, but his imagination stimulated in him a desire to involve himself in the excitement of the military. Ida rarely interfered with their games, but the game of war was one she did object to due to what D'Este described as her "extreme passivism," which motivated occasional lectures on the "wickedness of war."

DISEASE

An example of religion's influence in the family involved what at first appeared to be a minor knee abrasion Dwight sustained that became badly infected. Both Ida and the family doctor concluded the leg was in an advanced

13. Eisenhower, *At Ease*, 51–52.
14. Eisenhower, *At Ease*, 52.
15. Eisenhower, *At Ease*, 51–52.
16. D'Este, *Eisenhower: A Soldier's Life*, 25.

stage of blood poisoning and, consequently, must be amputated. Dwight was adamantly against amputation. The family united behind Dwight and prevented this from happening. Soon the "fever miraculously abated, and the ominous black line gradually disappeared. That Dwight's life and his leg had been saved was viewed by the family as nothing less than God's will."[17]

Physicians who have studied his case concluded the problem was likely a streptococcal infection of the skin and soft tissues. Although it was assumed during this time that Dwight was in a coma, recent medical evaluation considered it more likely his condition was delirium brought on by high fever. Whether it was healed by God is debatable, but the fact the family *believed* it was healed by God is not: this incident left a strong and lasting impression on Dwight Eisenhower and his family. Dwight later stated the common claim that constant prayer occurred throughout his ordeal was exaggerated,[18] but Edgar insisted there was a great deal of prayer by everyone. Dwight added his parents did not believe in "faith healing," but did believe God could heal the sick. He "grew up with faith in the power of prayer," and this would have a profound influence on his entire life.[19]

LOVE OF READING

The Eisenhower boys felt their home religious training—Bible reading and study, for example—greatly helped them to achieve in school. They read the Bible aloud until a mistake was made and caught by someone else—then the privilege ended. As a result of their Bible reading they felt their reading abilities in front of their teachers and classmates were superior to many of their peers.

Dwight Eisenhower's Bible reading was not a task merely performed solely to please his parents, but he delved into the Scriptures with so much passion he "could recite passages from memory by the hour."[20] He also would often quote Scripture in his everyday life, and he once said that "to read the Bible is to take a trip to a fair land where the spirit is strengthened and faith renewed."[21] He reportedly read the entire Bible twice, once by age twelve and again before he left for West Point.[22]

17. D'Este, *Eisenhower: A Soldier's Life*, 41.

18. Eisenhower, *At Ease*, 97.

19. Morin, *Dwight D. Eisenhower*, 13.

20. D'Este, *Eisenhower: A Soldier's Life*, 46.

21. *American Bible Society*, 1969.

22. D'Este, *Eisenhower: A Soldier's Life*, 33.

Dwight was always a voracious reader; he even neglected household tasks to read to the extent that Ida locked up his books in a cabinet to prevent him from continuing to indulge in reading at the expense of his household duties. Dwight soon found the key to the cabinet and, when he had an opportunity, retrieved a book to fill his time.[23] Dwight's favorite books were history and Western pulp novels, a habit that stuck with him at least until World War II, when he regularly wrote to his wife requesting Western novels, preferably those that were full of six-shooters and barroom brawls.

DWIGHT EISENHOWER'S EDUCATION

Dwight entered Lincoln Elementary School in 1896 at the tender age of six. He termed his first day of school as cataclysmic, and it didn't get much better after that. The focus was on rote memorization, and boredom dominated the school day. Although the school was near the family's home on Abilene's south side, it lacked indoor plumbing and lighting. Consequently, it was dark and uncomfortably cold during the winter season. The students used stone slates to write on, and paper was supplied only when the students reached sixth grade.[24]

HIGH SCHOOL

Eisenhower was one of the few persons in his town that attended high school—if you could properly call the school he attended a high school! Dwight's graduating class consisted of only thirty-four students.[25] The school was situated in makeshift rooms on the second floor of the old city hall. In one room was the chapel, and teachers took turns leading devotional services and giving lectures on the Bible and various Bible scriptures.[26] Since Dwight Eisenhower had little expectation of going to college—few young people even completed high school then—there was not much incentive for him to do well in school.

In contrast to today, school was usually not the route to success in the early 1900s and often was, at times, actually an impediment. The outside

23. Eisenhower, *At Ease*, 39.
24. D'Este, *Eisenhower: A Soldier's Life*, 38.
25. Eisenhower, *Dwight David Eisenhower*, 20.
26. D'Este, *Eisenhower: A Soldier's Life*, 40.

world was run by males, and the schools were run by females. In Abilene High, girls outnumbered boys two to one, and by the time graduation was reached the ratio was twenty-five girls compared to only nine boys.[27]

Eisenhower as a teenager taken in 1907 when Ike was 17

Nonetheless, Dwight did very well in most of his school subjects, including not only history but also spelling, arithmetic, and the proper use of words, which reflected itself in his penchant for precision and following rules (at least the rules he wanted to follow). In spite of his insistence on proper word usage, his penmanship was atrocious—so bad that occasionally he could not read his own writing. The foreign language choices available in his school were only Latin or German—Dwight chose Latin even though his father spoke fluent German.[28]

Dwight's high school grades were above average, and he was seen as somewhat of a scholar and intellectual—it was even predicted in his yearbook that he would end up as a professor of history at Yale University.[29] His grades were particularly good during his last two years of high school when he attended the new Abilene High School. He scored high in every subject except Latin.[30] One quality that clearly helped him in his future was his

27. Eisenhower, *At Ease*, 99.

28. Lee, *Soldier and Statesmen*, 19.

29. Curry, *Class Prophecy*.

30. D'Este, *Eisenhower: A Soldier's Life*, 43.

uncanny ability to remember not only virtually everything he read, but also that which was shown or told to him. He also listened well and often asked perceptive, penetrating questions, which helped him to better understand complex situations.

Of all subjects, though, ancient history was first in Eisenhower's list of interests, especially historical events related to war.[31] Eisenhower's love of history was partially related to his great interest in the study of the triumph of good over evil.[32] No doubt he was influenced in this area by his religious background—at its core, Watchtower theology is essentially the triumph of good over evil, culminating in the great battle of Armageddon where all evil will be destroyed, and the righteous people will inherit the earth to live therein forever in paradise. As with most other millennial religions, this theme has dominated Watchtower theology from their beginning down to today.[33]

COLLEGE

After high school, Dwight was determined to attend college, but knew he could not afford this luxury. One solution was for his older brother Ed to go to college first and for Dwight to help him finance his education. Then, when Ed graduated, he would work and help Dwight to attend college. Ed enrolled at the University of Michigan and, to help Ed, Ike worked at the creamery where his father worked. He worked there from June 1906 to 1910, first as an "ice puller," then as an "operator in charge of the fireman."[34] This proved to be a difficult solution because his twelve-hour (6 p.m. to 6 a.m.), seven-day-a-week job paid him a mere fifteen dollars a week. Not much money was left over to pay for Ed's University of Michigan tuition.

Encouraged by his close friend Everett "Swede" Hazlett, Dwight attempted to secure an appointment at the U.S. Naval Academy at Annapolis.[35] It was not difficult to convince Ike to try for an Annapolis slot.[36] Dwight realized the only way he could afford to go to college was to attend a military academy financed by the government. He initially did not want to

31. Eisenhower, *At Ease*, 40; Eisenhower, 1996, 29.

32. Eisenhower, *At Ease*, 46.

33. Penton, *Apocalypse Delayed*.

34. Brubaker, *Ike and the Brethren*.

35. Eisenhower, *General Ike*, 29.

36. Griffith, *Ike's Letters*, 3.

have a military career, but he did want an education, and he did not know how else to get it. Once he was in West Point, he ended up spending most of his entire career in the military. It turned out that by the time he applied to Annapolis he was not eligible because he would be past the age limit (he would be twenty-one at the start of the school term), so Dwight applied to West Point, where he could still be accepted at age twenty-one.

During this time, he also made time to study for admission into West Point—successfully, as it turned out. One Ike biographer opined that he was successful because at West Point he was judged on his academic skills and not on his "income, religion, [or] previous social background" as was true in European officer training schools of the time.[37] Although clearly capable, at West Point he was a good student but somewhat "easygoing" about his studies—his main interest then was still sports.[38]

In some ways, Dwight's Watchtower background probably helped to prepare him for life at West Point. For example, at West Point, as in the Watchtower Society, obeying authority was paramount, and too much independent thinking was not only discouraged, but could result in punishment.[39]

IDA'S OPPOSITION TO DWIGHT'S ATTENDING WEST POINT

When first accepted to West Point, Dwight wrote, "this was a good day in my life" and the

> only person truly disappointed was Mother. She believed in the philosophy of turn the other cheek. She was the most honest and sincere pacifist I ever knew, yet at the same time she was courageous, sturdy, self-reliant. It was difficult for her to consider approving the decision of one of her boys to embark upon military life even though she had a measure of admiration for West Point because one of her instructors at Lane University, a favorite of hers, had been a West Point cadet . . . But when I went off, no one thought of war. I can hardly imagine any time when we were so free from talk of war or seemed so far from it. Even that could not change things appreciably for my mother. But, she said, "It is

37. Field, *Mister American*, 10.
38. Eisenhower, *At Ease*, 7.
39. D'Este, *Eisenhower: A Soldier's Life*, 63.

your choice." She saw me off, and then went back home to her room. Milton told me later that for the first time in his life he heard Mother cry.[40]

Alden Hatch, after recounting the consternation Ida had over Dwight attending West Point—to the extent that she hoped he would fail the entrance exam—claims the reason for her opposition was her "abhorrence to war."[41] In June of 1911, when Dwight was leaving for West Point, Ida and Dwight's twelve-year-old brother Milton were seeing him off. Milton remembered, "I went out on the west porch with mother as Ike started uptown, carrying his suitcase, to take the train. Mother stood there like a stone statue and I stood right by her until Ike was out of sight. Then she came in and went to her room and bawled."[42]

Although it is often claimed the major reason Ida opposed Dwight's attending West Point was her "pacifism" and outspoken opposition to war, which is commonly also given for her opposition to Ike's military career, D'Este accurately stated the reason "had less to do with pacifism than it did with Witness theology."[43] Ida's opposition likely involved several reasons and, consequently, she hid her "weakened faith" and "grief" that resulted from Ike's pursuing a military career. Family friend Donald Kimball wrote the following:

> Ike showed the appointment to his mother who verbally approved and then retired to her room to cry. The whole idea of Ike's becoming a soldier displeased David and Ida Eisenhower but they chose to leave the choice to Ike's conscience. The Lord would surely guide him. Ida's influence was strong with the young Ike and he probably had some misgivings in his own heart. She felt that Ike would make a final decision and he would have to live with it. Not only Ida, however, disapproved but many of the other River Brethren considered that Ike's ostensibly choosing a military career would not be "wholly respectable."[44]

Some of Ida's other concerns about Dwight attending West Point relate to her beliefs about the potential negative influence the secular world would have on her son—a common concern of fundamentalist religions.

40. Eisenhower, *At Ease*, 106, 108.

41. Hatch, *General Ike* (1st ed.), 21.

42. Pickett, *American Power*, 8.

43. D'Este, *Eisenhower: A Soldier's Life*, 58.

44. Kimball, *I Remember Mamie*, 42.

Her concerns were partly justified. While at West Point, Dwight started smoking, drinking, swearing, and playing cards—all behaviors condemned both by the Watchtower and the River Brethren—as well as the Eisenhower household.[45] Dwight smoked, often heavily, until 1949 when he quit under doctor's orders. His forty years of smoking took a severe toll on Dwight's health, contributing substantially to his cardiovascular troubles and, ultimately, to his death at age seventy-nine.[46]

In spite of her son's violation of these Watchtower norms, Ida never shunned him as is obvious from her continual contact with her son. Since no record exists that Dwight was baptized, he would not have been formally disfellowshipped, but many Witnesses would have shunned him. For example, after attending a 1913 Watchtower convention in Washington and spending a week at the Watchtower headquarters in Brooklyn, Mr. and Mrs. Eisenhower visited their son at West Point.[47]

Nor is there evidence Ida Eisenhower experienced problems with the Watchtower because of associating with a son who obviously violated a major Watchtower policy.[48] In fact, she may have received special treatment from the Watchtower. It is true under the then president of the Watchtower, C. T. Russell, the policy was more flexible. Nonetheless, even after Watchtower policy firmed up, no evidence existed that Ida shunned her son.

Eisenhower often stated that he felt God's hand was directing his career and the numerous fortunate contingencies that all worked together to allow him to attend West Point were not a result of chance, but were instead due to God's help and guidance.

IKE'S RELIGIOUS FAITH AT WEST POINT

When he arrived at West Point in 1911, Dwight developed "almost a religious perspective" on how he viewed himself and his country.[49] Not everything went well for him, though. Once when at West Point, he went through a period of depression—a few times even becoming despondent: "Life seemed to have little meaning" and his need to "excel was almost gone."[50] Some speculate part of Dwight's problem was the period of reli-

---

45. D'Este, *Eisenhower: A Soldier's Life*, 105.

46. D'Este, *Eisenhower: A Soldier's Life*, 103.

47. Fleming, *Ike's Mom*, 1.

48. See Dodd, "Religious Background."

49. Eisenhower, *Personal Reminiscence*, 31.

50. Eisenhower, *At Ease*, 16.

gious doubt he went through while at West Point. Although other factors, such as homesickness and his knee injury that prevented him from playing sports, were also likely involved. For a time at West Point, it seemed sports were more important to Dwight than either education or a career.[51] After a serious knee injury occurred when playing football, though, he settled on a military career, partly because he saw it as the most realistic solution to his career problem.

This was the first time in his life Dwight was away from his family. As he adjusted to West Point, he was eventually able to deal with his depression and became more interested in a military career. Historian Holl opined that after Dwight left home, his mother's critical importance in the family's religious and moral upbringing was still present—actually "the outward signs of his religious faith were often dramatically evident."[52]

Dwight soon actively involved himself in several religious activities at West Point. He joined the YMCA, which at the time had as a "principle function . . . Bible study," and he attended at least once a week on Sunday evening to hear a different sermon.[53] Eisenhower also taught a Sunday school class for the children of West Point personnel and apparently used the teaching materials supplied by the YMCA to instruct his class.[54]

Dwight graduated from West Point in 1915, placing 61 in his class of 164.[55] At his graduation his mother presented him with a copy of the American Standard Version of the Bible, used by the Watchtower at the time because it consistently used the term "Jehovah" for God. The book "became a treasured keepsake" and was the version of the Bible Dwight used when he was sworn in as President on January 1953.[56]

The foundation of Dwight's religion rested on three conclusions that were "well established by the time he graduated from West Point: the dignity of individuals was warranted by God, American democracy was established on that faith, and each generation was called to fight its own crusade to defend freedom against godless forces."[57] These ideals would serve him well in his military career.

51. Eisenhower, *Personal Reminiscence*, 31.

52. Holl, *Civil Religion*, 120.

53. D'Este, *Eisenhower: A Soldier's Life*, 80.

54. D'Este, *Eisenhower: A Soldier's Life*, 80.

55. Cohen, *Gettysburg's First Family*.

56. D'Este, *Eisenhower: A Soldier's Life*, 85.

57. Holl, *Religion, Politics, and the Evils of Communism*, 284.

4

Ike's Mother Ida

We are essentially a religious people. We are not merely religious, we are inclined, more today than ever, to see the value of religion as a practical force in our affairs.[1]

IDA ELIZABETH STOVER (MAY 1, 1862 to September 11, 1946) grew up in Virginia's Shenandoah Valley in a family with seven brothers.[2] The Stovers' extended family were of German background reared in the Brethren in Christ Church. Although some members of her family left this denomination as adults,[3] as a girl Ida attended a Lutheran church and showed a "deep interest in religion from her earliest years,"[4] and "the Bible spoke to her needs as no other voice could."[5]

While still a schoolgirl, Ida studied the Bible extensively and quoted freely from it, once memorizing 1,365 Bible verses in six months, a fact later cited with pride by several of her sons.[6] Her Bible memorizing record is

---

1. Dwight D. Eisenhower. Address at the Second Assembly of the World Council of Churches, Evanston, Illinois, August 19, 1954.

2. Faber, *Mothers of American Presidents.*

3. Lee, *Soldier and Statesmen*, 4; Hertzler, *1879 Brethren in Christ.*

4. Hutchinson, "President's Religious Faith," 364.

5. Faber, *Mothers of American Presidents*, 35.

6. Neal, *Eisenhowers* (2nd ed.), 13.

included in the Sunday school records in the Lutheran church at Mount Sidney near Staunton, Virginia.[7] The Civil War affected the Stover family greatly, evidently hastening the death of both of Ida's parents. This fact was one reason for Ida's lifelong opposition to war.[8]

An intelligent woman and a good student, Ida was determined to obtain an education. So she could go to high school, she moved in with a family willing to provide room and board in exchange for cooking and cleaning.[9] A star pupil, Ida did so well that she taught school after she completed high school.[10] With the financial and other help of her older brother, Ida eventually enrolled in Lane University. It was one of the few colleges that accepted female students. Lane was a small United Brethren college in Lecompton, Kansas, named after Kansas's first U.S. Senator, James Henry Lane (1814–1866).[11] Lane University had ten part-time instructors and about two hundred students.[12] Ida was a good student and studied math, history, and English in college.[13] Ida was also a vibrant, vivacious, young lady—always optimistic, at least on the outside.[14]

IDA MEETS HER FUTURE HUSBAND

Ida met David Eisenhower when they were both students at Lane University. David, an engineering student, was described as a quiet, very serious young man. David's ancestors had immigrated from the Bavarian province of Germany to the United States in the 1740s to escape religious persecution.[15] The family name was originally "Eisenhauer," German for "iron hewer" or ironworker, such as a blacksmith.[16] David's parents were Jacob, a farmer and River Brethren minister, and Rebecca, a housewife. One of fourteen children, David was born shortly after the Battle of Gettysburg.[17]

7. Dodd, "Religious Background."

8. Gullan, *Faith of Our*, 221.

9. Gullan, *Faith of Our*, 222.

10. Angelo, *First Mothers*, 86.

11. Eisenhower, *At Ease*, 78.

12. Smith, *Eisenhower in War*, 5.

13. Lovelace, *"Ike" Eisenhower*, 8.

14. Hatch, *General Ike*, 6.

15. Hatch, *General Ike*, 5.

16. Gullan, *Faith of Our*, 220.

17. Gullan, *Faith of Our*, 221.

The Civil War had much less of a negative effect on David than on his wife (as noted, Ida believed that the war hastened the death of both her parents, partly because the war destroyed their farm and livelihood). It is commonly believed that, as a result, David was less opposed to war than his wife. He was also more independent than Ida and was less of a joiner. By all accounts, David was raised in a very religious family, and this fact influenced the home environment in which he reared their children.

The couple was married on September 23, 1885 in front of twenty guests by the Rev. E. D. Slade, the college pastor and a River Brethren minister. Professor Galampos described Ida as a savior because she was exactly what David needed. David "was almost gruff and grumpy," and in contrast "Ida was indefatigably cheerful and patient."[18] Galambos added David's marrying Ida, a woman "above all dedicated to her religion . . . was the single best decision he ever made."[19]

Soon after they married, they both dropped out of college.[20] Although accounts differ, David and Ida each probably completed only about one year of college. Nonetheless, their desire for education persisted and reflected itself in their strong support for all of their sons' educations.[21]

When David's brother, Abraham, a self-taught veterinarian, decided to become an itinerant preacher, he rented his house at 201 South Fourth Street to David and his family on the condition his father, Jacob, a Brethren pastor, could also live there.[22] David Eisenhower and his family then moved into Abraham's house, where David and Ida lived for the rest of their lives.

The Eisenhower Presidential Library contains some of the Abilene Congregation of Jehovah's Witnesses records, copies that were donated to the library in 2002 by Witness Richard A. McIntyre. When the donation was made, Mr. McIntyre was a Jehovah's Witness circuit overseer from Topeka, Kansas. The 230 pages he donated contain photocopies and scanned copies of all of the original documents that remain in the possession of the Abilene and Manhattan, Kansas congregations.

This collection provides written documentation of the religious practices of both David and Ida Eisenhower. This particular aspect of David

18. Galambos, *Becoming the Leader*, 18.
19. Galambos, *Becoming the Leader*, 18.
20. Hatch, *General Ike*.
21. Kornitzer, *Great American Heritage*.
22. Lyon, *Portrait of the Hero*; Dodd, *Early Career of Abraham*.

and Ida Eisenhower's life has provoked considerable speculation, rumor, and conflicting accounts. The records support the conclusion that Ida Eisenhower was a regular and faithful participant in the activities of the Abilene Ecclesia of the International Bible Students Association (later Jehovah's Witnesses) from 1896 until 1946. Only one entry in the minutes of the Abilene congregation from 1920 to 1942 mentions David Eisenhower (dated December 1921), supporting the conclusion he was no longer an active Witness after about 1915. The Abilene congregation's minutes from 1920 to 1942 (no records exist before 1920) include:

1. 12–31–1920 – Ida Eisenhower elected as organist.

2. 6–29–1921—motion by Ida Eisenhower.

3. 12–22–1921—Ida Eisenhower elected as musician.

4. 12–29–21 – both David and Ida Eisenhower passed VDM questions and Ida Eisenhower was elected as musician. The VDM questions are a set of questions taken from an instructional booklet used to study Watchtower beliefs. This is the last known formal involvement of David Eisenhower in the Watchtower.

5. 9–29–1922 – Ida Eisenhower made two motions.

6. 12–20–22—Ida Eisenhower nominated as organist.

7. 12–27–1922 Ida Eisenhower elected as organist and made three motions; 35 noted that Ida Eisenhower was appointed to one of the committees existing then.

8. 12–27–1923 and 12–22–24—Ida Eisenhower selected as organist.

9. 9–30–1925—Ida Eisenhower chosen as leader for the children's class.

10. 12–31–1925—Ida Eisenhower elected as organist and children's class leader.

11. 12–22–1926, 12–28–1927, 12–26–1928, 12–29–1929, 10–8–1930, and 10–8-1931—Ida Eisenhower chosen as organist.

12. 7–11–1933—Ida Eisenhower elected as Assistant Treasurer.

13. 10–5-1933—Ida Eisenhower elected Assistant Service Treasurer.

24. 10–2–1935—Ida Eisenhower chosen as Treasurer.

25. 10–22-1937—Ida Eisenhower in charge of Abilene's Third Ward for season witnessing.

5

The River Brethren

IT WAS DAVID WHO introduced Ida to the River Brethren Church,[1] partly because many of his relatives were involved in this religious community. Ida easily adjusted to the Bible-centered Brethren community in which she was involved until she was introduced to the Watchtower.[2] D'Este describes the River Brethren as an "evangelical fundamentalist" sect whose "religious doctrine was more Methodist than Baptist."[3] They not only emphasized the literal interpretation of the Bible, but stressed practicing it.[4]

Although often incorrectly stated that "Ida and David Eisenhower were River Brethren," neither David nor Ida ever became actively involved in this sect after their marriage.[5] For example, in one of the most detailed histories of Eisenhower's early life, Davis opined only that Ida later "sought out an even more 'primitive' and rigid Christianity" than the River Brethren, leaving the reader totally up in the air as to what this group might

1. The River Brethren Church is an offshoot of the Mennonite Church. The term River Brethren is commonly used in the literature that discusses President Eisenhower, but the officially registered name during the Civil War and after was The Brethren in Christ Church. The term River Brethren caught on because the first church was located near a river, and the group baptized new members in the river (Witter, interview by Walter Barbash). This term is used here because most references to Eisenhower's religion use this term.

2. Smith, *Eisenhower in War*, 222.

3. D'Este, *Eisenhower: A Soldier's Life*, 15.

4. Smith, *Eisenhower in War*, 4.

5. D'Este, *Eisenhower: A Soldier's Life*. 17; Miller, *Ike the Soldier*, 77–78.

be.[6] Edmund Fuller and David Green, after claiming Eisenhower's parents were River Brethren, noted only that the president's grandfather was the Rev. Jacob Eisenhower, a Brethren minister, and that "the Eisenhower boys' religious training was strict, fundamentalist, and somewhat puritanical. They were well-schooled in Scripture."[7] Nothing was mentioned about the Eisenhower's Watchtower involvement. Another example is the following often-made claim, which ignores the facts:

> Ida and David Eisenhower, being very religious, insisted that their sons go to church and study the Bible. The whole family belonged to the River Brethren Church, which firmly believed in the pacifist philosophy of turning the other cheek. The church members did not believe in any type of fighting, and many members refused to go into the armed services. The Eisenhowers were very active in this church, and Dwight's grandfather was the minister of the local River Brethren.[8]

It is true Jacob, David's father, and his brothers, Ira and Abraham, were all River Brethren members, but Ike's cousin, the Rev. Ray L. Witter, son of A. L. Witter, claimed that although Ida and David sporadically attended Brethren services for several years, neither was ever an actual member.[9] A close family friend, R. C. Tonkin, even stated he "never knew any of the family to attend the River Brethren Church."[10]

Evidence Dwight attended Sunday school at Abilene's River Brethren church includes the claim by John Dayhoff (listed in the 1906 church records as a member of Dwight's class) that Dwight went to Sunday school with him. Both church records and oral history indicate Dwight attended the Brethren church for only about a year around 1906,[11] evidently just long enough to carve his initials on a Sunday school bench.[12] Dwight's first cousin, who also attended Sunday school with him, claimed Dwight never became a "member" of the River Brethren church and never attended

---

6. Davis, *Soldier of Democracy*, 111.

7. Fuller and Green, *God in the White House*, 213.

8. Cannon, *War Hero and President*, 18.

9. Miller, *Ike the Soldier*, 77–78; Dodd, "Religious Background," 221.

10. Tonkin, *I Grew Up with*, 48.

11. Morris E. Sider, archivist for the Brethren in Christ Church, Messiah College, Grantham, PA, from interviews of various dates and correspondence to the author dated October 24, 1994.

12. Jameson, *They Still Call Him Ike*, 14.

any other church "to any degree."[13] Nor was Dwight ever baptized "in any church" including the "Church of the Brethren in Christ in Abilene, Kansas" until he was baptized as a Presbyterian after he was elected President of the United States.[14]

According to the regular teacher, Ida Hoffman, when Dwight did attend Sunday school, he "never seemed to pay any attention or take any interest in the lesson."[15] Three of the Eisenhower children (including Dwight) were listed in the 1906 Souvenir Report of the Brethren Sunday School of Abilene, Kansas as involved in the church. Although no mention was made of any involvement by their parents, one reason could be the report focused on the activities of the church youth.

The brief attendance of the Eisenhower boys was likely partly due to the influence of Jacob, Dwight's grandfather, an active River Brethren minister until his death in May of 1906.[16] In Dwight's commencement speech given at Messiah College on May 29, 1965, he said he attended Sunday school at the River Brethren church in Abilene, Kansas. He added that the college president "showed me this morning that I had a very good average of attendance, at least in one year. As a matter of fact, all of my brothers went to the same Sunday school and the church is still standing."[17] The record the Messiah College president referred to was the 1906 Souvenir Report noted above, a copy of which is in the Messiah College archives.

Dwight's father, David, was still connected with the River Brethren through his employment at the church-owned Belle Springs Creamery. He worked at the creamery for twenty-four years, from the time he moved to Abilene in March 1892 until 1916.[18] The Belle Springs Creamery would grow to become "one of the largest and most successful independent creameries in the entire Midwest."[19]

Jacob, no doubt, also religiously influenced all the Eisenhower boys. For these reasons the influence of the Brethren church on the Eisenhowers up to this time was no doubt considerable, but in 1895 another religious tradition began to influence the Eisenhower family.

13. Witter, *Interview by Walter Barbash*, 22.

14. Moore, *Faith and the Presidency*, 333.

15. Davis, *Soldier of Democracy*, 49.

16. Dodd, "Religious Background."

17. Eisenhower, commencement address, Messiah College, May 29, 1965.

18. Ambrose and Immerman, *Milton S. Eisenhower*, 19–20.

19. D'Este, *Eisenhower: A Soldier's Life*, 26.

As noted, the River Brethren was a small denomination that had much in common with the Mennonites. Both were once called "the plain people" because of their simple lifestyles and dress. Although the River Brethren sect had modernized somewhat since the early 1900s, and no longer placed as much emphasis on clothing details as formerly, they were still comparatively strict in the 1800s. Marriage could be dissolved only by death, hard physical work was a prime virtue, and members could not use or grow tobacco, even after the turn of the century. Furthermore, the rituals the River Brethren practiced included strict Sabbath observance and

> until 1927 they were prohibited from taking out insurance. In these and other ways the River Brethren seek the "sanctification" of their company—an aim which their publications claim they stress even beyond other Mennonite branches . . . their clergy engage in secular occupations to support themselves. But their strict application of the rule that a tenth of all income must be given to the Lord makes it possible for this tiny denomination, with less than 8,000 members scattered on farms and in small towns in widely separated parts of the United States and Canada, to support five missions in Africa, four in India and thirty-five in under churched communities in this country.[20]

The early Watchtower teachings were in many ways similar to those of the River Brethren, both of which have changed in major ways since the Eisenhowers became involved in the Watchtower in 1896. The major differences that existed between the two sects were especially in doctrine.[21] Both groups were in many ways pietistic conservative Protestant sects, and both were opposed to war, although on different grounds. Both sects also stressed the importance of Bible study, condemned many of the same worldly habits (such as smoking), and were then very concerned about the last days, Bible prophecy, and eschatology.

BACKGROUND OF THE EISENHOWERS JOINING THE WATCHTOWER MOVEMENT

Many myths exist about Ida and her faith. For example, a Drew Pearson[22] column stated only that President Eisenhower's mother "once sold

20. Hutchinson, "President's Religious Faith," 363.
21. Dodd, "Religious Background."
22. Of interest is Eisenhower's statement to Swede in late February 1958 that he has

Bible tracts for the Jehovah's Witnesses," implying she only flirted with the Watchtower and was never deeply involved.[23] Ida did not flirt with her involvement in the Witnesses, as claimed by some, but was an active and "faithful member of Jehovah's Witnesses for 50 years."[24]

Pearson also adds the often-repeated but erroneous claim that "Ida was influenced in her old age by a nurse who belonged to the sect. Being Bible-minded, old Mrs. Eisenhower cheerfully agreed to help the Jehovah's Witnesses peddle Bible tracts. Actually, both of Dwight's parents were staunch members of a small sect called River Brethren."[25] The truth, plainly stated by Jack Anderson in another Drew Pearson column, was, "Ike is strangely sensitive about his parents' religion. They were Jehovah's Witnesses, though the authorized biographies call them 'River Brethren.'"

Described as a restless seeker of a true faith, which finally took her to the Bible Students, Ida spent the rest of her life in the Bible Students even though David left it after a few years.[26] A major catalyst precipitating Dwight's parents leaving the River Brethren fellowship for good and joining the Watchtower involved Ike's eight-month-old brother, Paul, who died of diphtheria in 1895.[27] This tragedy devastated the Eisenhowers, and the theological explanation provided by the River Brethren that Paul was in heaven did not satisfy them.[28] At this time, three neighborhood women— Mrs. Clara Witt, Mrs. Mary Thayer, and Mrs. Emma Holland—were able to comfort the Eisenhowers with the Watchtower hope that they would soon see their son in the resurrection taught to occur after Armageddon.[29]

The Watchtower believed death was like sleep, and many in the grave would be resurrected then. At the time, the Watchtower taught this resurrection would occur in the new world and was expected to arrive around 1914, then a mere nine years after Ida joined.[30] The three women also sold Ida a set of volumes titled *Millennial Dawn* (later renamed *Studies in the*

"not read a word" written by Drew Pearson in fifteen years (Eisenhower, *Ike's Letters*, 200).

23. Pearson, *Eisenhowers Seek to Clear*, 6.

24. Fleming, *Ike's Mom*, 1.

25. Pearson, *Eisenhowers Seek to Clear*, 6.

26. Galambos, *Becoming the Leader*, 19.

27. Dodd, "Religious Background"; Witter, 1964.

28. D'Este, *Eisenhower: A Soldier's Life*, 33.

29. Dodd, "Religious Background."

30. Gruss, *Prophetic Speculation*.

Scriptures) and a subscription to *Zion's Watch Tower and Herald of Christ's Presence*, since renamed *The Watchtower*.

Ida soon became deeply involved in the movement and influenced her husband to become involved a short time later.[31] In a collection of personal recollections, Edgar Eisenhower admitted their "parents' religious interests switched to a sect known as the *Bible Students*. The meetings were held at our house, and everyone made his own interpretation of the Scripture lessons. Mother played the piano, and they sang hymns before and after each meeting. It was a real old-time prayer meeting."[32]

Edgar added the members of the study group prayed and read Scriptures, and everyone had an opportunity to state his relationship with God:

> Their ideas of religion were straightforward and simple. I have never forgotten those Scripture lessons, nor the influence they have had on my life. Simple people taking a simple approach to God. We couldn't have forgotten because mother impressed those creeds deep in our memories. Even after I had grown up, every letter I received from her, until the day she died, ended with a passage from the Bible.[33]

Ida wrote that she first became acquainted with the Watchtower in 1895 when she was thirty-four and Dwight was only five years old.[34] Earl Eisenhower said of his parents' conversion: "They were deeply religious people . . . They also were rebels in religion . . . They had their own religion."[35] Their religious commitment was not nominal. In the words of one noted Eisenhower biographer, Ida's religion came "dangerously close to intolerant dogma."[36] Nor did she become involved in the Watchtower only in her later years, as was claimed by some, but rather when she was still a young woman in her thirties. [37]

31. Dodd, "Religious Background," 244.

32. Quoted in McCullun, *Six Roads from Abilene*, 21.

33. Quoted in McCullun, *Six Roads from Abilene*, 21.

34. Cole, *Jehovah's Witnesses*, 190.

35. Quoted in Johnson, *Life and Times*, 11.

36. Davis, *Soldier of Democracy*, 40.

37. For example, see Gullan, *Faith of Our*, 230.

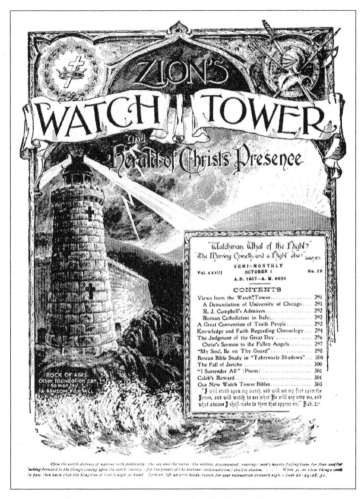

The Watchtower 1907 issue that Ida Would have read

Ida was baptized in the Watchtower faith in 1898, an act that later meant she was the equivalent of a Jehovah's Witnesses minister.[38] From her extensive study of the Eisenhower family's religious involvement, Dodd concluded Ida soon became a "faithful and dedicated Witness and actively engaged as colporteur [missionary] for the Watch Tower Society until her death" in 1946."[39] Not long after her conversion this religion dominated

38. Dodd, "Religious Background," 225.
39. Dodd, "Religious Background," 245.

the lives of everyone living in the Eisenhower household.[40] Ambrose and Immerman concluded the degree of religious involvement of Dwight Eisenhower's parents was so extensive that "next to their sons, the Bible and church activities were the center of David and Ida's life."[41] Some examples of the closeness of church and family include:

> David read from the Bible before meals, then asked a blessing. After dinner, he brought out the Bible again. When the boys grew old enough, they took turns reading. Ida organized meetings of the . . . Watchtower Society, which met on Sundays in her parlor. She played her piano and led the singing. Neither David nor Ida ever smoked or drank, or played cards, or swore, or gambled.[42]

This upbringing had a major influence on all of the Eisenhower boys: Dwight Eisenhower's faith was "rooted in his parents' Biblical heritage," and the Eisenhower boys' upbringing was "steeped" in religion.[43] In short, the Bible had a "lusty influence . . . in their lives."[44]

The Eisenhowers held weekly Watchtower meetings in their parlor where the boys took turns reading from and discussing the Scriptures and, evidently, also Watchtower publications. Dwight Eisenhower was also involved in these studies. He claimed he had read and studied carefully the entire Bible before he was eighteen.[45]

In answer to questions about the large amount of "writing and talking about Ida Eisenhower's connection with the Jehovah's Witnesses," Dwight's first cousin, the Rev. Ray Witter, answered, "I didn't know what [religion] was in the early years—they generally referred to that Sunday afternoon meeting as a Bible Class, but . . . I discovered it was Jehovah's Witness meetings that they, the [Eisenhower boys'] parents, attended."

He added it was once held at the Eisenhower home, and "later on it was held at other places, and while they didn't have ordained ministers— they had their form of doctrine and interpretation of the Bible that they followed."[46] Although the group preferred the label Bible Students until

---

40. Kornitzer, *Great American Heritage*, 134.

41. Ambrose and Immerman, *Milton S. Eisenhower*, 13.

42. Ambrose, and Immerman, *Milton S. Eisenhower*, 19–20. See also M. Eisenhower, *President Is Calling*, 13.

43. Fox, *Pro Ike*, 907; *Portrait of the Hero*, 38.

44. High, *What the President*, 2.

45. Jameson, *Ike Buried in Abilene*, 9.

46. Quoted in Witter, *Interview by Walter Barbash*, 28.

1931, when they met, they usually did not study the Bible directly but rather through Watchtower publications.

In the early 1900s the Bible Student study focus was a set of books titled *Studies in the Scriptures* as well as the current issues of the bimonthly magazine *The Watchtower*, both written by Pastor Russell and his wife. The Eisenhower boys usually skirted around the issue of their religious upbringing, but Dwight Eisenhower once openly acknowledged the group his parents were involved with was the Jehovah's Witnesses. In Dwight's words, his mother was "deeply religious," and his mother

> had gravitated toward a local group known as The Bible Class. In this group, which had no church minister, she was happy. Sunday meetings were always held in the homes of members, including ours. The usual program of worship included hymns, for which mother played the piano, and prayers, with the rest of the time devoted to group discussion of a selected chapter of the Bible.[47]

Mr. R. G. Tonkin estimated that when the Eisenhower boys were young, "about fifteen people" attended Watchtower meetings in Abilene.[48] The group met in Eisenhower's home until 1915, when their meeting attendance level forced them to rent a local hall. Later, a large Watchtower meeting house (now called a "kingdom hall") was built in Abilene.[49] The composition of the early Russellite group in Abilene included Henry N. Engle and his daughter Naomi, both school teachers and more educated than most of the agrarian Brethren. As a result they

> felt an intellectual and spiritual affinity toward David and Ida Eisenhower (both had been to college), and, a little later, for Dr. James L. Thayer, dental surgeon, whose mother Mrs. Mary Thayer first introduced the *Watch Tower* to the Eisenhowers. This company together with L. D. Toliver and the R. O. Southworths constituted the nucleus of the Abilene congregation of Russellites. From 1896 until 1915, the Bible Students . . . met on Sunday afternoons at the Eisenhower home for their meetings. During most of this twenty-year period, David Eisenhower (and occasionally L. D. Toliver) served the class as the Bible-study conductor, or "elder" as the group called its leader.[50]

47. Eisenhower, *At Ease*, 305.
48. Tonkin, *I Grew Up with*, 48.
49. Dodd, "Religious Background," 244.
50. Dodd, "Religious Background," 236.

Evidence Ida remained active in the Watchtower for her entire life includes a letter she wrote to a fellow Witness. The letter stated she had "been in the truth since ninety-six [1896 and] ... am still in ... it has been a comfort to me ... [that] Naomi Engle stay [sic] with me and she is a Witness too so my hope [sic] are good."[51] Ida died quietly in her sleep in 1946, still a Witness, "with almost a smile on her face."[52]

David and Ida's interest in the signs of the coming of Armageddon and the imminent return of Christ was highly influenced by the Watchtower preoccupation with end-time events, especially the date of Armageddon. Other persons, aside from Watchtower followers, likely also shared an interest in end-time date predicting, including David's uncle Abraham, who was evidently influenced by the end-time date speculation of the Tabor, Iowa evangelistic sect called the Hephzibah Faith Missionary Association.[53]

CONFLICTS BETWEEN THE RIVER BRETHREN AND WATCHTOWER

The Eisenhowers' Watchtower involvement created many family conflicts. The Bible Students were derisively called Russellites after their founder C. T. Russell. They taught that the Brethren and all other churches were very displeasing to God. Their second president, lawyer Joseph F. Rutherford (president from 1916 to 1942), went much further and viciously attacked all churches other than his own with slogans such as "Religion is a snare and a racket."[54] Under Rutherford, the Watchtower even taught all priests and ministers of other denominations are of Satan, leading their flocks to eternal damnation as a result of what he considered their false teachings, such as hellfire and the Trinity.[55]

As a result of this and other teachings, Dodd observed that the River Brethren and other denominations at the turn of the century "were rabidly opposed to Russellism." In 1913, the River Brethren *Evangelical Visitor* advertised a tract titled *The Blasphemous Religion which Teaches the Annihilation of Jesus Christ* as the "best yet publication against Russellism" and

---

51. Quoted in Fleming, *Ike's Mom*, 3; a photocopy in *Jehovah's Witnesses*, 192.

52. Eisenhower, *At Ease*, 306–7.

53. Dodd, letter to Jerry Bergman, 2.

54. Dodd, "Religious Background."

55. Bergman, *Jehovah's Witnesses: A Comprehensive*.

the editor felt every River Brethren minister should read it. In 1928 David's brother, Abraham Eisenhower, a Brethren minister,

> wrote to the *Evangelical Visitor* concerning Russellism: "Oh, fool-hearted nonsense. It is the devil's asbestos blanket to cover up the realities of a hellfire judgment. The word of God will tear off this infamous lie and expose the realities of an existence of life after death." This strong statement would reflect the general attitude of most of the Eisenhowers.[56]

Conversely, the many differences that did exist were seen to be of such central importance that when River Brethren church members became followers of Russell, the River Brethren and other churches became very concerned.[57] Dodd recalled the conversion of a number of Brethren to the Watchtower a "staggering blow to the Kansas Church" of the Brethren. Historian Climenhaga remarked the following about one incident after the conference of 1896: ". . . editor of the paper [then being printed in Abilene, Kansas] . . . Brother Engle's religious views changed during this period as editor. He contacted literature and persons of a cult whose beliefs were directly opposite that of the Brethren in Christ. His gradual acceptance of views of this cult made a change in editorship . . . necessary."[58] As a result, the 1899 conference "accepted Henry N. Engle's resignation, and appointed Samuel Zook as editor." Climenhaga did not name the literature, persons, or cult in question, but

> Bishop J. H. Wagaman and Professor Paul E. Engle, both of Upland, California, and a number of Brethren in California and Kansas identify the cult as "Russellism" and the heretical doctrine as the "soul-sleeping" doctrine. The writer learned from Miss Naomi Engle, herself a Witness and companion to Ida Eisenhower in her last years, that her father, Henry N. Engle, had read the *Watch Tower* from its very beginning. She said the Engles were introduced to Russell's literature by a Dickinson County farmer by the name of Reading.[59]

An editorial in the official River Brethren journal said the following about the Bible Students:

---

56. Dodd, "Religious Background," 246.
57. Dodd, "Religious Background," 234.
58. Climenhaga, *History of the Brethren*, 243–44.
59. Dodd, "Religious Background," 234–35.

> Bishop S. R. Smith was authorized to edit a pamphlet, in which
> Russellism would be explained and refuted. Pressure of work
> has prevented Bro. Smith from completing this work, and since
> there is a pressing need for a work of this kind (the Messiah Bible
> School to have reliable material in reference to this subject) ar-
> ranged . . . for the publication of five hundred copies of *Millennial
> Dawnism*, "The Blasphemous Religion which teaches the Anni-
> hilation of Jesus Christ," by I. M. Haldeman, D. D . . . We believe
> this pamphlet to be the best yet published against Russellism, and
> think that it should be in the hands of every minister, at least, of
> our church.[60]

The eighty-page Haldeman booklet claims virtually every major doctrine
held by orthodox Christianity was rejected by the Russellites, which Haldeman[61] calls a "wicked and blasphemous system." Among the Brethren
doctrines the Bible Students rejected were the hellfire (they believe hell is
the grave and simply non-existence), the immortality of the soul, the deity
of Christ (they believe he is not God but God's son), the hope of heaven for
all of the faithful (they teach the hope of most mankind is everlasting life
on earth), the basis of salvation, and the bodily resurrection of Christ (they
teach he was resurrected with a spirit body).

One of the best examples of misinformation was when Dwight's
"famous temper erupted after reading a newspaper article critical of his
mother's attendance at a Jehovah's Witness convention. Eisenhower's true
feelings about the Jehovah's Witnesses boiled over in a fiery letter to his
brother Arthur."[62] The letter suggested the Witnesses were "hypocrites" for
exploiting his mother's presence at a Watchtower convention in order to
jump on "the publicity bandwagon, even if that publicity is generated out
of a circumstance which they publicly deplore," adding that he doubted if

> any of these people, with their academic or dogmatic hatred of
> war, detest it as much as I do. They probably have not seen bodies
> rotting on the ground and smelled the stench of decaying human
> flesh. They have not visited a field hospital crowded with the des-
> perately wounded. But far above my hatred of war is the determi-
> nation to smash every enemy of my country, especially Hitler and
> the Japs . . . my hatred of war will never equal my conviction that

60. Haldeman, *Millennial Darwinism*, 2.

61. Haldeman, *Millennial Darwinism*, 78.

62. D'Este, *Eisenhower: A Soldier's Life*, 416.

it is the duty of every one of us, civilian and soldier alike, to carry out the orders of our government when a war emergency arises.[63]

According to popular columnist Drew Pearson, when confronted with his religious ancestry, Dwight Eisenhower looked for a "delicate way to clear the family name of this affiliation"[64] because Dwight is very

> sensitive about the fact that the Jehovah's Witnesses do not believe in saluting the flag or serving under arms. At the same time, he doesn't want to appear prejudiced against any religious sect. Both Ike and his brother, Milton, have discussed the problem with spiritual advisors. But they haven't quite figured out how to disclaim Ida Eisenhower's relations with the Jehovah's Witnesses without offending the sect and perhaps stirring up charges of religious prejudice.[65]

After both Dwight and his brother Milton checked the manuscript of Bela Kornitzer's book, *The Story of the Five Eisenhower Brothers*, "Milton privately asked Kornitzer to delete a reference to their parents' membership in the Witnesses sect."[66] In one of the last interviews given by the family, Milton said only "we were raised as a fundamentalist family. Mother and Father knew the Bible from one end to the other."[67] The Watchtower's response to this common omission was as follows:

> Though *Time* magazine claimed Ida Stover Eisenhower was a member of the River Brethren, a Mennonite sect, *Time* was merely continuing its consistent policy of slander in all that pertains to Jehovah's witnesses. She was never a River Brethren. She was one of Jehovah's witnesses. The first study in the *Watchtower* magazine in Abilene, Kans., started in her home in 1895. Her home was the meeting-place till 1915, when a hall was obtained. She continued a regular publisher with Jehovah's witnesses till 1942, when failing health rendered her inactive; but she remained a staunch believer.[68]

---

63. Eisenhower, *Papers of Dwight*, vol. 2, 1148–49.

64. Pearson, *Eisenhowers Seek to Clear*, 6.

65. Pearson, *Eisenhowers Seek to Clear*, 6.

66. Anderson, *His Vote Record*, 16b.

67. Quoted in Freese, "Man of the 20th Century," 25.

68. Knorr, *Religion Void of Principle*, 7.

Dwight's major concerns about the Watchtower were revealed when his mother died at the age of eighty-four in September of 1946. He wrote when his father died in 1942 that

> the Jehovah's Witnesses had taken over the arrangements, to the intense anger of Dwight and Milton, who felt they had really hijacked the occasion to generate publicity for their faith. During the war, there were newspaper stories from time to time that claimed the Supreme Allied Commander was—the irony of it!—the son of Jehovah's Witnesses. These stories infuriated Eisenhower, to whom they were an attempt to undermine the prosecution of the most righteous war in history. He made sure there was no repetition of what had happened with David. Ida's funeral service was held in the family home on South East Fourth Street, conducted by an Army chaplain from Fort Riley. All six brothers were there, as was Mamie.[69]

The emotion over Dwight's Witness background was indicated when *Time* magazine's Clare Booth Luce asked him about his religious background; Dwight "jumped to his feet, got red to the roots of his hair—he flushed . . . violently, under any emotion and he said, 'Now, I hope you're not going to bring that up. Everybody on my staff has been after me to say what my religion is and what my church is. I consider a man's faith is a matter between himself and God.'"

---

69. Perret, *Eisenhower*, 364–65.

6

Dwight's Father David Leaves the Watchtower

ALTHOUGH DAVID'S EARLY UPBRINGING was in the River Brethren, he very briefly attended Lutheran and Methodist churches before and during his college days and eventually converted to the Watchtower beliefs a short time after his wife did, and actively served in the Watchtower organization for about twenty years, from 1896 to about 1915 as an elder and Bible study conductor, a role he occasionally alternated with L. D. Toliver.[1]

However, unlike Ida, David's commitment to the Watchtower eventually changed, and he later became a Watchtower critic. Dwight's brother, Edgar Eisenhower, stated their father left the Watchtower partly because he "couldn't go along with the sheer dogma that was so much a part of their thinking."[2] Dodd concluded that by 1919, David Eisenhower's interest in the Bible Students had "definitely waned and before his death, in 1942, he renounced the doctrine of Russell."[3] One factor causing his disillusionment with the Watchtower was the failure of their end of the world prophecies, both in 1914 and 1915.[4]

1. Dodd, "Religious Background," 225.

2. Kornitzer, *Great American Heritage*, 261.

3. Dodd, "Religious Background," 224.

4. Lingerfeldt, interview. The Lingerfeldt family were also Witnesses and were personal friends of the Eisenhowers. Clyde's father used to stay at the Eisenhower home in Abilene during the summer and even taught one of the boys how to use a gun, which upset Ida. The Lingerfeldts were from North Carolina.

His sons later claimed David accompanied his wife in Watchtower activities primarily in an effort to appease her. Watchtower accounts usually referred only to Ida as a Witness, supporting the conclusion David had left the Watchtower after 1915. Ike's brother Arthur wrote that after his father left the Watchtower fellowship, he (David) remained an active student of the Scriptures and that his religious "reading habits were confined to the Bible, or anything related to the Bible," but not Watchtower literature. Nonetheless, when he left the Bible Students, David slowly relaxed his Bible reading and daily prayers tradition, later on even allowing card playing, cigarettes, and secular music in his home.[5]

Dwight observed that, although his family was somewhat independent, the whole family "was deeply religious. The Bible was the place they found [for] their source of inspiration, and during particular periods in the week my father would read to us and occasionally quarrel in his own mind; because the family always seemed to be dissenters, he would go back to his Greek Bible to determine whether he liked the translation in the version of the King James."[6]

THE PYRAMID OF GIZA EVENT

Although the Bible was central to David Eisenhower's thinking, Milton added that his father also read history, serious magazines, newspapers, and religious literature.[7] Historian Steve Neal even claimed that David Eisenhower's religious quest led him into "mysticism." As evidence, he cited David's use of "an enormous wall chart" of the Egyptian pyramids to predict the future.[8] Although the chart had "lines, angles, and captions," David did not assign them symbolic meaning the Watchtower did, nor was the chart "amazingly original" as claimed by D'Este.[9] Johnson wrote that, in their search for solace after several disappointments in Abilene, David and Ida "wandered into mysticism." He added that David

> drew an enormous chart of the Egyptian pyramids, and convinced himself that intersections of the pyramids' interior lines foretold

5. Gullan, *Faith of Our*, 227.

6. Eisenhower, commencement address, Messiah College, May 29, 1965.

7. Kornitzer, *Great American Heritage*, 261.

8. Neal, *Eisenhowers*, 13.

9. D'Este, *Eisenhower: A Soldier's Life*, 21.

events which occurred after the pyramids were built. Projecting this conviction, he reasoned that by extending the interior lines beyond the pyramids, and studying the intersections of the exterior lines, he could discover symbolic meanings. Believing or not, Ida went along.[10]

Actually, this enormous chart was a leftover idea from Watchtower teaching that David still accepted. The chart played a prominent role in Watchtower theology for more than thirty-five years, and was of such importance to David that his

> religious beliefs materialized in the form of an impressive (five or six feet high, ten feet long) wall chart of the Egyptian pyramids, by means of which he proved to his own satisfaction that the lines of the pyramids—outer dimensions, inner passageways, angles of chambers, and so on—prophesied later Biblical events and other events still in the future. As might be expected, this demonstration fascinated his children; the chart came to be one of the family's most prized possessions.[11]

Earl Eisenhower claimed his father used the chart when he was still involved with the Watchtower to prove Bible prophecy to his own satisfaction.[12] David also taught his boys the Watchtower teaching that we are now living in the last days from this chart when they were growing up.[13] The chart "according to David . . . contained prophecies for the future as well as confirmation of biblical events. Captivated by the bizarre drawing, the sons spent hours studying David's creation."[14] The claim this chart was David's creation is one of many still living myths about the Eisenhower family.

This chart has been used by many authors to demean David's intellect. For example, Angelo[15] said of Ida, "David was her dear husband, but she wanted their sons to do more than spend time mulling over mysterious connections between stars and pyramids." Actually, as a Watchtower follower, she too likely spent much time studying the "Bible in Stone," at least until this doctrine was repudiated by Russell's successor, J. F. Rutherford.

10. Johnson, *Life and Times*, 11.

11. Lyon, *Portrait of the Hero*, 38.

12. Kornitzer, *Great American Heritage*, 136.

13. Dodd, "Religious Background," 242–43; see also Davis, *Soldier of Democracy*, 41.

14. Neal, *Eisenhowers* (2nd ed.), 13.

15. Angelo, *First Mothers*, 93.

THE ORIGIN OF THE PYRAMID OF GIZA TEACHING

A particularly unique doctrine of Russell was the Pyramid of Giza, a central Bible Student teaching for decades that is still taught by several Watchtower offshoots.[16] The chart was first published by the Watchtower in *Millennial Dawn*, volume 1, in 1898, and a large wall-size version was made available later. It was based on the work of Piazzi Smith, Astronomer Royal of Scotland.[17]

Watchtower founder Pastor Russell used the pyramid, which he called the "Bible in Stone," as a basis for several of his prophecies, especially his belief that the return of Christ could occur as early as 1914.[18] The pyramid was also used to confirm Watchtower dispensational theology, the belief that history is divided up into dispensations made up of discrete eras.

The pyramid was of such major importance in early Watchtower theology that a huge ten-foot concrete pyramid was selected as a memorial to Watchtower founder Charles Taze Russell when he died. The markings on it made him appear more like an Egyptian Magus than a Christian, all of which are very embarrassing to Jehovah's Witnesses today—especially the cross-and-crown symbol, which was once commonly used by Witnesses on their literature. The pyramid still stands close to Russell's grave near Pittsburgh, Pennsylvania. Russell specifically condemned mysticism as demonism and taught that the pyramid had nothing to do with mysticism but was a second revelation, a "Bible in Stone" that both added to and confirmed the scriptural record.[19]

A few years after Russell died, the second president of the Watchtower, "Judge" Joseph F. Rutherford, made many doctrinal changes that initiated several Watchtower schisms. One of his changes was to condemn the pyramid teaching as demonism.[20]

Dodd noted the chart was still in the Eisenhower family home as late as 1944, but by 1957 she could no longer locate it in either the family home or the nearby Eisenhower museum. Dodd later learned the chart and other Watchtower effects were "disposed of."[21] Dodd concluded the Watchtower

16. Dodd, "Religious Background," 242.

17. Smyth, *Our Inheritance.*

18. Franz, *Proclaimers of God's Kingdom*, 20.

19. Russell, *Testimony of God's Stone Witness*, 313–76.

20. Rutherford, *Altar in Egypt*; Dodd, "Religious Background," 243.

21. Dodd, "Religious Background," 242–43.

items were probably destroyed by the family to reduce their embarrassment over their parents' involvement in the Jehovah's Witnesses.

Since then, another copy of the chart was located and now hangs in its rightful place in the Eisenhower library.[22] Interestingly, around the time Dwight Eisenhower became the Supreme Commander of the Allied forces in Europe, he made the trip to visit the pyramids in Giza. Historian Geoffrey Perret[23] mused that gazing upon the pyramids awoke in Dwight "strong memories of his father and the ten-foot chart" of the pyramids as well as David's belief that "within their geometry lay the answers to the eternal questions of human existence," such as why humans exist on earth.

DAVID'S DEATH

After a series of small strokes, David Eisenhower died on March 10, 1942, at the age of seventy-eight.[24] Before he died he was "quite ill" and was bed-ridden "most of the time."[25] Some historians claim (in contrast to much evidence) that when David Eisenhower died, he was a disappointed, bitter, and angry man.[26] If this is true, had he lived to see his son become a five-star general and commander in chief of the Allied Forces and, later, President of the United States, David no doubt would have felt very differently about his life.

It was Naomi Engle who "arranged a Jehovah's Witness funeral for David even though he had made it clear before his death that he was no longer a [Watchtower] believer."[27] The service was conducted by Witness James L. Thayer, assisted by Witness Fred K. Southworth.[28] On March 12, 1942, Dwight wrote the following in his diary:

> My father was buried today. I've shut off all business and visitors for thirty minutes, to have that much time, by myself, to think of him. He had a full life. He left six boys, and, most fortunately for him, mother survives him . . . He was a just man, well liked, well educated, a thinker. He was undemonstrative, quiet, modest, and

22. Nussel, *Truth Connection*, 7.

23. Perret, *Eisenhower*, 243.

24. Duncan, *Earning the Right*.

25. Irish, *Hometown Support*, 17.

26. Angelo, *First Mothers*.

27. Miller, *Ike the Soldier*, 80.

28. Cole, *Jehovah's Witnesses*, 192.

> of exemplary habits–he never used alcohol or tobacco. He was an uncomplaining person in the face of adversity, and such plaudits as were accorded him did not inflate his ego. His finest monument is his reputation in Abilene and Dickinson County, Kansas. His word has been his bond and accepted as such; his sterling honesty, his insistence upon the immediate payment of all debts, his pride in his independence earned for him a reputation that has profited all of us boys. Because of it, all central Kansas helped me to secure an appointment to West Point in 1911, and thirty years later it did the same for my son, John. I'm proud he was my father. My only regret is that it was always so difficult to let him know the great depth of my affection for him.[29]

Dwight's feelings in this note may not be entirely honest because he penned these words during his grieving almost immediately after his father died. Ike's brother, Milton remembered his father as the family anchor, the "one who kept everybody's feet on the ground. As I look back now, I realize Dad had a quiet influence on us that we didn't recognize until we got older and began to experience some of the responsibilities of life."[30] Neither of these assessments show any evidence of the claims of some that toward the end of his life David was a bitter, angry man.

In an interview with one of the Eisenhower boys, Hutchinson quoted him as saying, "Father was the disciplinarian . . . but otherwise he was a quiet, gentle man who avoided conflicts and would subordinate his views rather than become involved in argument. Mother was the determined one."[31] As a result of her "determination," Ida was still the focus of the family even at the death of her husband.

When his father died, Dwight also wrote he felt terrible because he very much wanted to be with his mother at this time, but that the country was at war, and this was therefore

> no time to indulge in even the deepest and most sacred emotions. I loved my Dad. I think my Mother the finest person I've ever known. She has been the inspiration for Dad's life a true helpmeet in every sense of the word. I am quitting work now, 7:30M. I haven't the heart to go on.[32]

29. Eisenhower, *Eisenhower Diaries*, 51. See also S. Eisenhower, *Mrs. Ike*, 179.

30. Kornitzer, *Great American Heritage*, 25.

31. Hutchinson, "President's Religious Faith," 364.

32. Irish, *Hometown Support*, 14.

Note how, even when talking about his Dad, Dwight's focus was on Ida—she was "the inspiration for Dad's life."

On August 27, 1942, Dwight also wrote to his good friend Charley Harger the following words, supporting Dwight's view that, if any credit for our success is due,

> it belongs to my Mother. We six boys have been, in the eyes of our parents, the investment that the two made during their lifetime. Any real or fancied success that accrues to any of us belongs to them, and my deepest regret, in connection with this particular occasion, was that my Father could not have lived a few more months so that the two of them, together, would have had that experience.[33]

Nonetheless, historian Professor Holl claimed his father's death "rekindled" Dwight's "traditional religious concerns."[34] As evidence, Holl notes this prayerful interlude was Dwight's first openly acknowledged religious activity since leaving West Point.[35] From this point on, his overt religious activity increased.

33. Irish, *Hometown Support*, 19.
34. Holl, *Religion, Politics, and the Evils of Communism*, 386.
35. Holl, *Religion, Politics, and the Evils of Communism*, 386–87.

7

Influences That Made Eisenhower

Religion nurtures men of faith, men of hope, men of love.[1]

THE STORY FOCUSED ON in this book includes Ike's family and especially on their religious influence on Ike's life and work. This set of factors produced "an almost unbelievable story—particularly so because the average American has been hardened against believing in the fairy tale success stories that come rolling off the Hollywood assembly line. It is a story that is amazing even to the reader of the Horatio Alger tale of success. It could have happened only in America, the fabled and fabulous land of opportunity."[2]

PARENTS' INFLUENCE

Both of Dwight's parents were actively involved in and highly committed to the Bible Students throughout most of their children's formative years. Evidence this faith had a major influence on the Eisenhower children while growing up comes from many sources, including both the Eisenhower family's published and unpublished writings.[3] Ida took the lead religiously, and

1. Dwight Eisenhower, Speech to Chaplains Association, Washington, DC, October 14, 1946.

2. Field, *Mister American*, 10.

3. Davis, *Soldier of Democracy*, 40.

her husband, David, although he later became disillusioned with certain Watchtower teachings, was active for over a decade.

This major religious influence of Dwight Eisenhower is commonly neglected and often totally ignored, even in authoritative works about him. That religion was critical in Ike's youth is clear. How critical it was is explained by Eisenhower biographer Rudolph Field, who concluded both "David and Ida were extremely religious folk. In fact, that description does not begin to suggest the intensity of their feeling. They were dedicated . . . to the ideal that this is God's world and that it behooves His children to live in it according to His precepts. To them religion was not a formal ceremonialism but the essence of life and that which gave it meaning. It was the dominant strain in the family picture."[4] A practical example is that neither parent cursed in front of their children, nor did they ever drink, smoke, or gamble.[5]

The exact influence of Ida's religion on the moral socialization and character development of her children was very "real but difficult to assess," partly because the many factors influencing the internalization of religious teachings are usually complex and interrelated. As is true in many families, some of Ida's religious beliefs were openly rejected by her children later in life, and others were completely embraced.[6] Kenneth Davis added that, until they died, each Eisenhower boy retained "a profound respect for the moral tenets that the parents derived, or thought they derived, from their religion."[7] In Milton Eisenhower's words, "Religion was as much a part of our home as eating or sleeping."[8] And in Dwight's words, Ida had "an inflexible loyalty to her religious convictions."[9] Fleming notes that "Ida Eisenhower was one of the most energetic [Watchtower] preachers in Abilene."[10] Finally, in the words of one of the Eisenhower boys, religiously, all of the Eisenhower children are "fundamentalists."[11]

Although the Eisenhower brothers at times have tried to conceal their Watchtower background, they did not hide the fact their home environment

---

4. Field, *Mister American*, 20.

5. Gullan, *Faith of Our*, 226.

6. Davis, *Soldier of Democracy*, 40.

7. Davis, *Soldier of Democracy*, 49.

8. Quoted in Ambrose and Immerman, *Milton S. Eisenhower*, 13.

9. Henschel, Obituary.

10. Fleming, *Ike's Mom*, 1.

11. Hutchinson, "President's Religious Faith," 364.

was dominated by "biblically literalistic" values, and that the Bible was their only

> authoritative guide, read every morning at family prayers, quoted again and again when family decisions were in the making. Both father and mother could quote the Bible for any occasion and almost from beginning to end . . . They owned a concordance, but the sons remember that on the rare occasion when reference to it became necessary both parents were almost furtive in seeking its aid.[12]

As Edgar stated, he and his brothers never forgot the scriptural lessons they learned while growing up and concluded the influence these lessons had on their lives was enormous. Edgar added that they never forgot these lessons because their mother impressed the Scriptures deep into their memories.[13] Furthermore, by their example, David and Ida taught "Christian openness and deep commitment to religious principles."[14]

Their religion was not just the "thou shall not's," such as no alcohol, gambling, or smoking, but, in Edgar's words, religion "to my father and mother was a way of life; they lived it. They believed in the brotherhood of man and, as a result, they were neighbors in the truest sense of the word. Mother was a slave to her friends and neighbors. We all learned a true sense of service from her."[15]

All the Eisenhower boys put an emphasis on a "personal God, with whom communion could be established by constant prayer. To inculcate this set of values, Bible reading was a very important activity of the Eisenhower household. In common with other pietist Protestant sects, they carried their religious ideals with them into other areas of life and stressed the virtues of brotherly love, simplicity, pacifism, hard work, [and] the pious life."[16]

In the end, although all of the Eisenhower boys left the Watchtower movement as adults and openly opposed certain Watchtower teachings, the values learned from their Bible studies with their parents openly influenced them throughout their lives. They were also openly reflected in the enormous success of all the children. As will be discussed, some Watchtower

---

12. Hutchinson, "President's Religious Faith," 364.

13. McCallum, *Six Roads from Abilene*, 21.

14. J. Eisenhower, *General Ike*, 27

15. S. Eisenhower, *Mrs. Ike*, 27.

16. Field, *Mister American*, 21.

values may even have been reflected in Dwight's statements against war he made later in his life. Some of the reasons why many persons, including the Eisenhower boys, were not more candid about their early Watchtower association are also discussed below.

Ida's influence on her sons was "incalculable," and more so on Dwight than his brothers, all who "venerated her."[17] Ida was quick to laugh and also quick to give sympathy. She demanded much, but she also gave much. Throughout World War II Eisenhower "thought often and fondly of Ida, wishing that somehow he could see her and be calmed and reassured by her presence and her wisdom."[18] He even once said being privileged to spend boyhood in her company produced indelible positive memories, and that she was, by far, the greatest influence on the lives of not only him, but all the Eisenhower boys.

EISENHOWER DEFENDS HIS PARENTS' RELIGIOUS BELIEFS

Even though Dwight Eisenhower disagreed with some of his parents' religious beliefs, he ardently defended their religious convictions. This is apparent in a letter Eisenhower mailed during the last week of one of his major World War II campaigns. Dictated to his brother, Arthur, on May 18, 1945, the letter was a response to a newspaper story about his mother's Jehovah's Witness faith, stressing her alleged "pacifism" and the irony that Mrs. Eisenhower's son was a high-level Army general.[19] Eisenhower wisely ignored the claim that Jehovah's Witnesses are pacifists and simply told Arthur his mother's happiness in her religion "means more to me than any damn wise crack that a newspaper man can get publicized."[20]

His respect for his mother was also vividly revealed in Dwight's words: "I think my Mother [is] the finest person I've ever known."[21] After Eisenhower became president, Dwight Pinkley asked him who he thought was the greatest man of our age. Without hesitation, Dwight replied "Winston Churchill," but then added the greatest person he ever knew was his mother, who

17. D'Este, *Eisenhower: A Soldier's Life,* 35.

18. D'Este, *Eisenhower: A Soldier's Life,* 35.

19. Ambrose, *Supreme Commander,* 187.

20. Eisenhower, *Papers of Dwight Eisenhower,* 1148.

21. Eisenhower, *Eisenhower Diaries.* 50–51.

taught me the principles of life that guided me. Had she lived while I was in the White House, she would have been invaluable to me and the nation . . . She could have advised me on appointees for the cabinet and other important positions. With her, I would never have gone wrong.[22]

Although Dwight rarely expressed his "inner thoughts" and "philosophical ponderings," enough of his writings exist on religion to form some basic conclusions about his religious beliefs.[23] Dwight repeatedly stated he accepted many of his parents' religious beliefs, adding they were "all religious but we don't go around saying 'I am a religious man' any more than we would say, 'I am an honest man,' or 'I am a clean man,' . . ."[24] John Bonnell put it this way: "To the very close of his life Dwight Eisenhower carried in his mind and heart the indelible imprint of his parents' religion."[25] This background is no doubt why Dwight's language was often lightly sprinkled with religious expressions, such as "praise be to the Lord" and "under God."[26]

EMBARRASSMENT ABOUT THEIR PARENTS' RELIGION

The Eisenhower sons' embarrassment about their parents' Watchtower involvement was vividly revealed whet it was noted both "Ida and David, but especially Ida, were avid readers of *The Watchtower*." At the time of Ida's death, a fifty-year collection of Watchtower publications was stored in their house on South East Fourth Street. The publication had arrived by mail from 1896 to 1946. It was Milton who bundled up the collection of the presumably embarrassing magazines and removed them from the Eisenhower house and away from the prying eyes of nosy reporters.[27, 28]

Milton gave them to a Witness neighbor, Mrs. James L. Thayer, one of the women that originally converted Mrs. Eisenhower. The disposal of Dwight's parents' Watchtower literature, charts, and other Watchtower

22. Pinkley, *Eisenhower Declassified*, 375.

23. Eisenhower, *Letters to Mamie*, 1978, 8.

24. Miller, *Ike the Soldier*, 77.

25. Bonnell, *Presidential Profiles*, 219.

26. Eisenhower, *At Ease*, 54, 55.

27. Miller, *Ike the Soldier*, 79.

28. The Eisenhower Library is now collecting older Watchtower literature to fill in the gap of this important part of Dwight's past.

items was only one indication of the many conflicts the Eisenhower boys likely experienced over their parents' religion. Another example (which I have been unable to verify) is the removal of an approximately eight-by-ten-inch picture of Ida and Dwight taken on the lawn of their Abilene home. In the picture Ida proudly displayed what looks like a Watchtower magazine, which was retouched so it was largely, but not totally, blocked out. These conflicts may be one reason why none of them ever became formally involved in the Watchtower movement or even another fundamentalist church.

SIBLING SUCCESS

The eldest Eisenhower boy, Arthur, once stated he could not accept the religious dogmas of the Witnesses although he had "his mother's religion" in his heart.[29] They also openly rejected certain Watchtower medical conclusions and theology, especially its eschatology and millennial teachings.

Although as adults none of Mrs. Ida Eisenhower's boys were what she and other Witnesses referred to as "in the truth," she was always hopeful they would someday again embrace the religion in which they were reared.[30] Leaving the religion in which they were reared was "a deep disappointment" to Ida, and possibly even to David.[31] Nonetheless, their Watchtower upbringing strongly influenced them in many ways throughout their lives.

Even in later life, Dwight preferred "the informal church service" with "vigorous singing and vigorous preaching" like that he grew up around.[32] Furthermore, Dwight's mother, Ida, was relatively supportive of her boys during most of their careers, occasionally stating that she was proud of them and their accomplishments, even those achievements which violated her Watchtower faith.

As is true of many Witness children, the Eisenhower boys also did not accept the Watchtower teaching that discouraged attending college and pursuing a career. The reasons for discouraging college attendance included the belief, supported by many examples, that this experience may adversely affect a Witnesses' faith. Nor could they accept the Watchtower teaching that it is futile to try to interfere with world events because these affairs

29. Kornitzer, *Great American Heritage*, 64.
30. Cole, *Jehovah's Witnesses*, 194–195.
31. Angelo, *First Mothers*, 83.
32. Dodd, *Early Career*, 233.

are strictly under God's control, like a movie script that had already been written and will be played out only according to the script.

Nonetheless, all of the Eisenhower children as adults did retain a strong love of the Bible and its basic teachings. For example, when Milton's wife, Helen, died when she was not yet age fifty, Milton said it was both his faith in the "basic Christian thesis" and his two children that sustained him through this very difficult period of his life.[33]

It is significant that all six of the Eisenhower boys did exceptionally well in their life and careers. All had relatively good, long-lasting marriages; none divorced, and all had stable families. They were successful in other areas as well. Edgar became a highly successful attorney in Seattle, Arthur a vice-president of a large Kansas City bank. Roy was a respected pharmacist, a pillar of his community, and the father of three children. He was one of the most popular of all the Eisenhower boys. One reason was his "ubiquitous good humor."[34]

Earl earned a degree in electrical engineering from Washington University in St. Louis and became a very successful businessman. Milton, the youngest, became the president of three major universities, including Pennsylvania State University and Johns Hopkins University.[35] Milton was also a voracious reader, a bookish intellectual, and an accomplished writer.[36] He eventually became the Assistant to the Secretary of Agriculture, Dr. Jardine, and a regular White House guest of President Calvin Coolidge.[37]

All six Eisenhower boys were also very involved in their occupations—so involved that they rarely assembled together as a family unit after each had left Abilene to begin their careers. The first full family reunion was not held until June of 1926.[38] The success of the Eisenhower boys, Field concluded, was due to their home life, their parents, and their community values.[39] The single blight on the family was, as Assistant Director of the Office of War Information, Milton was involved in the internment of Japanese Americans during World War II—a position from which he soon resigned due to his concern about how internment was being handled.

33. Ambrose and Immerman, *Milton S. Eisenhower*, 164.

34. Field, *Mister American*, 24.

35. Angelo, *First Mothers*, 107.

36. Field, *Mister American*, 26.

37. D'Este, *Eisenhower: A Soldier's Life*, 187.

38. D'Este, *Eisenhower: A Soldier's Life*, 184.

39. Field, *Mister American* , 27.

Ida and David Eisenhower's religious beliefs clearly had a major influence on their children, but their "unorthodox if not eccentric" religious views were not overtly forced on them. Neal claims that, in violation of modern-day Watchtower policy, the Eisenhower boys were "encouraged to reach their own conclusions" regarding religion, and this may have influenced them to have "later joined more conventional Protestant denominations."[40]

THE ULTIMATE SUCCESS

Dwight's story takes on special meaning because he was reared in a poor family that literally lived on the "wrong side of the railroad tracks." Although his parents were (by middle-class American standards of the time) poor, they were hard-working, honest citizens. His "father and mother fostered in Ike, together with his four brothers, the simple values that Americans have always regarded as fundamental: honesty, love and fear of God, self-reliance, love of hard work, and individualism. The children responded to their rearing, and in the course of time, all of them became remarkably successful."[41]

Exactly what about his upbringing, however, produced Dwight's greatness? D'Este's statement that "the path from the poverty of turn-of-the-century Abilene, Kansas, to supreme Allied commander was as improbable as it was spectacular" only describes, and does not explain, Dwight's achievements.[42] The question is important because the fate of the world's way of life probably was on the shoulders of Dwight Eisenhower more than almost any other man in the twentieth century. D'Este declared "the war against Germany fell on his [Dwight's] shoulders in June 1944, a responsibility of awesome and terrifying potential for failure—one faced by very few, if any, military commander in history."[43]

40. Neal, *Eisenhowers* (2nd ed.), 13.

41. Field, *Mister American*, 10.

42. D'Este, *Eisenhower: A Soldier's Life*, 5.

43. D'Este, *Eisenhower: A Soldier's Life*, 4.

8

Marriage and Children

DWIGHT MARRIED A YOUNG woman he met soon after graduating West
Point in 1915. She was Mamie (Mary) Geneva Doud (born November 14,
1886, in Boone, Iowa). Mamie was the daughter of a stable and financially
prosperous Christian family. The Doud family attended Corona Street
Presbyterian Church in Denver, where the Doud girls regularly attended
Sunday school.[1]

John Doud, Mamie's father, was described as a man of "deep religious
convictions."[2] Like David Eisenhower, he preferred "when in need of
spiritual counsel, to read his Bible in solitude rather than worship in public.
First, last and always, he lived to love and protect his family."[3] A graduate
of the University of Chicago, he strongly valued education and learning, a
value he instilled in his daughter.[4] The Doud home was filled with books,
and John was a voracious reader, a trait Mamie learned while growing up
that she never lost. Mamie's mother, Elivera Carlson, was also deeply religious and "the spirit of Christ found its way into the hearts and minds of
the children, the grandchildren, and great-grandchildren."[5]

Mamie and Dwight met while visiting friends at Fort Sam Houston, in
San Antonio, Texas in October 1915. Dwight "was sure he wanted to marry

1. Dewhirst, *Dutiful Service*, 5.
2. Brandon, *Mamie Doud Eisenhower*, 44.
3. Brandon, *Mamie Doud Eisenhower*, 45.
4. Kimball, *I Remember Mamie*, 13.
5. Kimball, *I Remember Mamie*, 15.

her" on the first day they met—and later said she was "the prettiest girl he had ever seen."[6] Although popular with the young men, Mamie also took an instant liking to Dwight, who she described as just about the most handsome man she had ever met.[7] She added he was a "far cry from the society boys at home."[8] Even though Mamie had a booked social calendar, it soon became clear Dwight was a persistent suitor, and within a year they were engaged.[9]

They became engaged soon after Christmas and were married in Doud's Denver home on July 1, 1916. Mamie had just turned nineteen and Dwight, a recent West Point graduate, was twenty-five.[10] Their marriage forced Mamie to change her life in many major ways, some of which she found very difficult. The young girl from a well-to-do family had no exposure to the difficult military life a soldier's wife was forced to endure in the early 1900s.[11] Although in many ways opposites, they would merge to produce a remarkably successful partnership.

It soon became clear, as is often true in the case of most men who make it to the White House—or anywhere else of importance—that Mamie's role was critical in Dwight's success.[12] During their many long separations, Dwight relied on her for both emotional and moral support.[13] As will be discussed, her religious beliefs helped greatly in adjusting to her new role and especially to the fact that Dwight was gone for months at a time for most of their marriage. During their long separations—often for many months—Dwight greatly missed his family, and the separations were very hard on both of them, but his service to his country was always put first.[14]

Mamie Eisenhower also felt much the same way as Dwight did about God's role in not only Dwight's life, but also in her life. After almost sixty years of marriage, she said she told God every day, "I'm so thankful . . . I don't know exactly how to explain it, but everything [in my life] was a pattern, like it had been planned. But it wasn't planned by us. God planned

6. Johnson, *Life and Times of a Great General*, 29.

7. Dewhirst, *Dutiful Service*, 6.

8. S. Eisenhower, *Mrs. Ike*, 34.

9. S. Eisenhower, *Mrs. Ike*, 35.

10. Dewhirst, *Dutiful Service*, 8.

11. S. Eisenhower, *Mrs. Ike*, 33–34, 43.

12. Dewhirst, *Dutiful Service*, 5.

13. Wickman, *Ike and 'The Great Truck Train'*.

14. S. Eisenhower, *Mrs. Ike*, 229.

it."[15] She also once said, "Ike had a great responsibility, and it had come so unexpectedly in lots of ways. [God] must have chosen this man."[16]

Her faith was also obvious when she related her belief that her fears for Ike's safety were calmed by the same beliefs that reassured Patton, namely "nothing was going to happen to [Ike] until God was through with what he had put him on this earth to do . . . He must have chosen this man . . . [especially given the] many times [Ike] came near death."[17]

THEIR CHILDREN

Their first child, Doud Dwight, was born on September 24, 1917. Because he looked so much like Ike, Mamie began calling him Little Ike, soon shortened to Ikey, then to Ikky. The cute blond child, the delight of both Mamie and Ike, cemented their marriage and changed their world. Tragically, Ikky died on January 2, 1921, at age three from meningitis, an infection of the brain membranes that is commonly fatal in small children.

The death devastated Mamie and Ike (especially because Ikky died in Dwight's arms), and this event touched them deeply for the rest of their lives.[18] They both relied heavily on their religious faith to deal with Ikky's tragic death. Their second son, John Sheldon David, was born on August 22, 1922. When rearing John, Mamie was especially overprotective in response to Ikky's death.

Dwight's appointment as Supreme Commander in Europe radically changed the lives of both Mamie and the Eisenhower's son, John, forever.

---

15. D'Este, *Eisenhower: A Soldier's Life*, 110.

16. Quoted in D'Este, *Eisenhower: A Soldier's Life*, 314.

17. S. Eisenhower, *Mrs. Ike*, 227–28.

18. Dewhirst, *Dutiful Service*, 14.

9

World War II

IN TIMES OF ADVERSITY, Dwight often stated he vividly felt the need for divine assistance and that his instinct for prayer was deeply ingrained in him.[1] No better example existed than World War II. In Dwight's words, during WWII he "turned to God when there was no one else to help." An example was one night when an armada of American aircraft was blown off course due to unexpectedly high winds, causing imminent danger to thousands of sky troops. Eisenhower recalled

> praying, "O God, they are in thy Almighty Hand." Incredibly enough, the lead plane later regained its bearings and the drop was at least partly successful. On the eve of the massive D-day assault on Europe, the soul-racking problem arose as to whether to send two American airborne divisions against the Nazi-fortified Cherbourg peninsula. British Air Chief Leigh-Mallory advised against what he termed "this futile slaughter," and yet it seemed that to cancel the airborne attack would endanger the whole critical invasion of Utah Beach. I could only go to my tent to review every step of our elaborate planning and to ask God's guidance in making the right decision. I finally decided that the aerial attack would go as planned, and the paratroopers accomplished their dangerous mission with casualties far below those predicted by the experts.[2]

1. Morin, *Dwight D. Eisenhower*, 13.
2. Quoted in Gammon, *All Believers Are Brothers*, 2–3.

Another experience eloquently illustrates this side of Dwight Eisenhower. D'Este records that shortly after midnight at Sidi Bou Zid, Tunisia (North Africa), on February of 1943, "Eisenhower's spirits rose momentarily as he silently observed an infantry company commander address his men." The prayer by a man with no outward stamp of piety moved Eisenhower "as deeply as any [prayer] I have ever heard." The man's prayer was as follows:

> Almighty God, as we prepare [for] . . . action from which some of us may not return, we humbly place our faith and trust in Thee. We do not pray for victory, nor even for our individual safety. But we pray for help that none of us may let a comrade down—that each of us may do his duty to himself, his comrades and his country, and so be worthy of our American heritage.[3]

Eisenhower commented that, after hearing this prayer, he had walked away teary eyed. Eisenhower used this occasion to engage in his habit of seeking solitude. For a few brief moments he found "peaceful contemplation in the ominously quiet moonlit desert."[4] During these difficult times he often "offered up a silent prayer for the safety and success of all the troops under his command."[5] He later wrote there were times during the war when "There was nothing we could do but pray," and pray they did, often "desperately."[6]

In the past at least, the military is one area of secular life in America in which religion is often not only allowed, but actually encouraged. Prayer and religious observances were one of the few activities the Japanese allowed prisoners under their watch. Furthermore, ministers, priests, and rabbis played a critical role in sustaining the men in prison, both spiritually and emotionally.[7] These religious activities were considered critical in helping many men to endure the horrors of war.[8]

Before he moved to Normandy in France, Eisenhower stayed at Telegraph Cottage and slept on a cot crammed into a nearby bomb shelter. Eisenhower was forced to make many trips to the shelter, where "he cursed

---

3. Quoted in D'Este, *Eisenhower: A Soldier's Life*, 393.

4. D'Este, *Eisenhower: A Soldier's Life*, 393.

5. D'Este, *Eisenhower: A Soldier's Life*, 432.

6. D'Este, *Eisenhower: A Soldier's Life*, 432.

7. Moore, *Faith and the Presidency*, 312; Froom, 1954.

8. Moore, *Faith and the Presidency*, 312–13.

the Germans with colorful profanity and admitted that whenever he heard a rocket nearby he would pray, "Oh Lord, keep that engine going."[9]

General's Eisenhower's prayers during World War II became legendary. An example is on July 9, 1943, when he was commander of the Allied Expeditionary Forces on a mountaintop overlooking Malta, Dwight knelt in prayer to ask for God's help just as the Allies began their all-out assault on Sicily. As the weather was rapidly deteriorating, Ike had to decide if he should proceed

> with the carefully planned invasion. After praying fervently, he ordered the attack to go forward, and it succeeded beyond all expectations. In June 1944, Eisenhower had to make an even more momentous decision—whether to proceed with the D-Day invasion of France. Weather conditions again caused problems, and Eisenhower seized a small window of opportunity to send the Allied troops on shore. "If there were nothing else in my life to prove the existence of an almighty and merciful God," he later reflected, those events did it." [10]

D-DAY

Shortly before D-Day—the most important battle of World War II—Eisenhower recorded a proclamation to be "broadcast to the world on the day of the invasion" which closed with the words, "let us all beseech the blessing of Almighty God upon this great and noble undertaking."[11] Ike interpreted the war at its core was "a battle between contending spiritual forces" and a war that was in fact a "spiritual battle." He even wrote the war against Nazism was "a holy war . . . an array of the forces of evil against those of righteousness."[12]

In response to questions of his faith, Dwight told Clare Boothe Luce in 1952, "Do you think I could have fought my way through this war, ordered thousands of fellows to their deaths, if I couldn't have got down on my knees and talked to God and begged him to support me and make me feel that what I was doing was right for myself and the world. . . I couldn't live a day of my life without God."[13]

9. D'Este, *Eisenhower: A Soldier's Life.* 541.

10. Smith, *Faith and the Presidency*, 227.

11. D'Este, *Eisenhower: A Soldier's Life*, 526.

12. Chernus, *General Eisenhower*, 59.

13. Quoted in Smith, *Faith and the Presidency*, 227.

Cover of the 19 June 1944 issue of Life magazine with Gen. Dwight D. Eisenhower.

Dwight also stressed that religion is critical to confront "militant atheism and brazen materialism" and that "religion and atheism were locked in a global struggle."[14] Ike worked tirelessly for world peace, even appealing to the "Universal Fatherhood of God and the Brotherhood of all men" as an argument for world peace.[15]

Eisenhower also stated he believed it was "faith in God and the Judeo-Christian ethic" that "inspired the Founding Fathers of the United States." Dwight then cited the many times he personally turned to God for guidance, concluding the events that occurred after he prayed provided positive

14. Smith, *Faith and the Presidency*, 230.
15. Quoted in Smith, *Faith and the Presidency*, 246.

evidence to him, supporting his conclusion that God *had* intervened in response to his prayers.

Dwight especially believed God was with him in his battle against "Hitler and all that he stood for."[16] He stressed his religion gave him the "courage to make the decisions you must make in a crisis and then the confidence to leave the result to [the] higher power. Only by trust in oneself and trust in God can a man carrying responsibility find repose."[17]

A close associate once wrote that wherever General Eisenhower was quartered he

> never saw Ike Eisenhower without a Bible somewhere in sight—on his desk, in a bookcase nearby, or on a table in his office. It was a Bible for use, as the well-worn pages showed. He once said, "Like stored wisdom, the lessons of the Bible are useless unless they are lifted out and employed. A faithful reading of the Scripture provides the courage and strength required for the living of our time."

FIDELITY

Another area where Dwight's religion likely had an effect on his morality was in the sexual area. Although he was separated from his wife for many months at a time due to his military career, there lacks any evidence that he was unfaithful to her. Of those who worked with Ike, some who even "traveled with him almost everywhere," all testified he never behaved improperly toward women.[18] The claim of an affair with his driver, former model Kay Summersby, has little support and has much evidence against it.[19] Smith concluded Summersby's claim of an affair with Ike was fabricated, full of holes, and that Summersby "offered no material evidence to substantiate her claims."[20]

The Eisenhower Library has the original Summersby diaries on which the book *Past Forgetting: My Love Affair with Dwight D. Eisenhower* was based. In spite of the potentially misleading title, the Summersby diaries

---

16. Eisenhower, *At Ease*, 52.

17. Hutchinson, "President's Religious Faith," 362.

18. Pinkley, *Eisenhower Declassified*, 363.

19. Smith, *Faith and the Presidency*, 257; Pinkley, *Eisenhower Declassified*, 361–68; J. Eisenhower, *Letters to Mamie*, 11–12.

20. Smith, *Faith and the Presidency*, 257.

revealed no clear evidence of an improper relationship between the two.[21] A search of the Eisenhower Library archives found no evidence that a non-professional relationship ever existed.[22]

Pinkley concluded the Ms. Summersby affair claim was pure fiction designed solely to help her sell her book about her relationship with Eisenhower. The account of the putative affair by John Eisenhower's daughter, Susan, also supports this conclusion and adds several important details.[23] Evidence of the claim of Ike's faithfulness to his wife include the fact Dwight wrote an average of two letters a week (a total of 319 letters) to his wife from 1942 to 1945 during the height of World War II.[24] In these letters, he repeatedly wrote he loved only her, and that he was looking forward to returning home to her and resuming their life together.[25]

21. Summersby and Wyden, *Past Forgetting.*
22. Burnes, *Ike Files,* 74.
23. Eisenhower, *General Ike,* 240–42.
24. Eisenhower, *Letters to Mamie,* 7.
25. Eisenhower, *Letters to Mamie,* 99.

IO

God and War

Without God, there could be no American form of Government, nor an American way of life. Recognition of the Supreme Being is the first—the most basic—expression of Americanism. Thus the Founding Fathers saw it, and thus, with God's help, it will continue to be.[1]

DWIGHT EISENHOWER ONCE SAID of his parents they were "true conscientious objectors to war. Though none of her sons could accept her conviction in this matter, she refused to try to push her beliefs on us just as she refused to modify her own."[2] As noted, Dwight's mother was very distraught about her son's violation of certain Watchtower beliefs, especially his choice of a military career. According to Dwight's first cousin, Ida "committed herself even to the pointed question 'why he ever took up such a vocation' and her belief it was not of God and that it was [of] Satan, she was much opposed to [the] military and wasn't too happy, naturally."[3]

Eisenhower believed (or hoped) his mother's views would not affect his career. He even once said, "I know full well that the government is not going to measure my services as a soldier by the religious beliefs of my

1. Dwight D Eisenhower remarks recorded for the "Back to God" program of the American Legion, February 20, 1955.

2. Eisenhower, *At Ease*, 305.

3. Witter, Interview by Walter Barbash, 32.

mother."[4] He added, "Moreover, at heart, the country has never had a more loyal citizen than she."[5]

IDA NOT A PACIFIST

Many reporters termed Dwight's mother "a religious pacifist."[6] In Dwight's words, his mother "was opposed to militarism because of her religious beliefs."[7] In fact, the Watchtower has established in the courts they are *not* pacifists but rather are conscientious objectors, opposed *only* to wars initiated and carried out by humans. The Watchtower teaches involvement in war, *except* those that God demands that we fight, is not only a violation of God's law ("thou shalt not murder" and "thou shall love thy neighbor") but is wrong because Watchtower doctrine considers it an improper use of time during what they believe are the last few remaining years before Armageddon.

They teach that in these last days, their followers are to be dedicated to converting others to become Witnesses before the end of this present system of things, which has been proclaimed by the Watchtower since the late 1800s to be "just around the corner." They are, in their words, "conditional pacifists," even though the Watchtower often argues against all war on pacifist grounds.

In the early and middle 1900s, Jehovah's Witnesses also eschewed all political involvement because they felt—and still believe today—the soon-to-be-established kingdom of God on Earth, called the Millennium, was the only solution to all of humanity's problems.[8] In Milton Eisenhower's words, as good Jehovah's Witnesses his parents were "more concerned with the millennium that, unfortunately, hadn't come in their day, than they were with contemporary social institutions."[9]

Milton added his parents were aloof from politics, but "as I became older, I used to hold many conversations with them in a futile attempt to show them that they were wrong."[10] Evidently, all of the Eisenhower boys

---

4. Eisenhower, *Selected Speeches*, vol. 2, 1148.

5. Eisenhower, *Selected Speeches*, vol. 2, 1148.

6. For example, see *Life Magazine*, 1969.

7. Kornitzer, *Great American Heritage*, 87.

8. Kornitzer, *Great American Heritage*, 276.

9. Kornitzer, *Great American Heritage*, 278.

10. Kornitzer, *Great American Heritage*, 277.

disagreed with Watchtower teachings in this area. Of course, as Watchtower followers, Ida and David (at least until he left the sect) were discouraged from all involvement in politics—even voting became a disfellowshipping offense after the 1940s. The reason is because politics was viewed as a very corrupt enterprise, and any involvement in such would corrupt the person who was involved, thus causing sin. This conclusion many in America may be inclined to agree with in view of the corruption engendered in the aftermath of the election of President Triumph and the Russian collusion claims. Ultimately, however, Ida accepted Dwight's decision and knew the importance of prayer for her son in spite of his decision—in 1944 she said, "All Dwight wants is my prayer for his success."[11]

DWIGHT'S OPPOSITION TO WAR

The value Dwight most strongly developed after his experience in WWII which may have had its roots in his mother's religion was his strong opposition to war as a solution to human conflicts. Dwight even stated he doubted if people who hated war because of academic or dogmatic reasons detested it as much as he did, for the reason he hated war as only "a soldier who has lived it can, as only one who has seen its brutality, its futility, its stupidity." Dwight added that, although he hated war, he hated the Nazis and what they stood for even more.[12]

Dwight's open opposition to war was also shared by several of his brothers, including Edgar. Edgar once wrote to Ike about his aversion to war, and in his response Ike chastised Edgar for misunderstanding the cause of war and, reiterating his own long-standing disgust with war, he wrote that unquestionably any

> soldier would agree with almost any cynical philosophy you might care to develop respecting the progress of a civilization that allows itself to get plunged into a world war every quarter of a century. The mistake that people like yourself make is in assuming that the soldier—and I mean the professional—likes it . . . The average soldier hates it, probably a lot more than you do.[13]

---

11. Quoted in Duncan, *Christmas Prayers*, 14.

12. Quoted in Taylor, Speech at Poughkeepsie, 9.

13. Quoted in *Eisenhower: A Soldier's Life*. 633.

Another reason he hated war was because he was "truly trying to follow in the footsteps of the Prince of Peace, and to establish a just peace for the world."[14] Eisenhower concluded to achieve peace America must understand

> "Bullets and guns and planes and ships" could "produce no real or lasting peace." Neither could "edicts and treaties, no matter how solemnly signed," nor could economic arrangements, no matter how favorable they were. "Only a great moral crusade" carrying out God's will would be successful. Because the United States was "the greatest force that God" had "ever allowed to exist on His footstool," it must help the world attain a secure and lasting peace. The Christmas message of "Peace on Earth, Good Will Toward Men," he proclaimed, was a basic aspiration of "Christian, Jew, Moslem, . . . [and] of every other person in the world who has faith in an Almighty God."

He concluded war is the least acceptable solution to our problems because, in the end, it settles nothing. Dwight expressed this same conviction in an address given in Pittsburgh in October 1950, when he said, "Possibly my hatred of war blinds me so that I cannot comprehend the arguments that its advocates adduce. But, in my opinion, there is no such thing as a preventive war . . . the fact [is] that war begets conditions that beget further war."[15]

Dwight's hatred of war was also manifested in his opposition to the atomic bomb. Almost alone among leading American military leaders, he did not believe the atomic bomb was the only way to defeat the Japanese.[16] Mostly, he correctly feared that once the atomic bomb was introduced into the world, other nations would also build powerful atomic bombs and nuclear escalation could result. In this opinion he proved very correct, and as of 2018 the atomic bomb threat produced by Iran and North Korea are a major concerns. Furthermore, as Eisenhower feared, the Cold War between USA and Russia developed partly due to the atomic bomb issue.[17]

More evidence exists that Dwight retained many of Ida's humanitarian values and truly hated war. For example, when it came to respect for others, Dwight's code of honor was "extraordinarily rigorous." Just before the end of World War II, a train full of German prisoners of war were being

---

14. Smith, *Faith and the Presidency*, 245.

15. Quoted in Taylor, *Speech at Poughkeepsie*, 91.

16. Holl, *Civil Religion*, 130.

17. Holl, *Civil Religion*, 130.

shipped across Germany, and after it arrived and the doors were opened, it was discovered that 130 of the prisoners had suffocated

> in the jam-packed boxcars through inadequate ventilation. Eisenhower ordered a complete investigation by the Inspector General. Four days later he asked the American legation in Berne, Switzerland, to forward his apology—of all unheard-of things—to the German high command. "If it is found that United States personnel were guilty of negligence," said his message, "appropriate action will be taken with respect to them. The Supreme Commander profoundly regrets this incident and has taken steps to prevent its recurrence."[18]

This event occurred at a time when German soldiers were murdering, in cold blood, many thousands of prisoners of war—especially in Poland and Russia.

DWIGHT'S APOCALYPTICAL BELIEFS

Another important Watchtower influence on Ike was their central teaching that all history is a struggle between good and evil—from Adam's sin due to Satan's influence, to the final conflict between good and evil to be fought at the battle of Armageddon. Chernus observed Dwight's references to "deliverance in a holy war" reflected this apocalyptic teaching with its dualism between good and evil, adding Dwight was reared

> in a religious community that used such language. Thirty years as a soldier, and three and a half years pursuing unconditional surrender on the battlefield, made him even more comfortable employing its powerful rhetorical effects. In assessing the postwar situation, he often divided humanity into two mutually exclusive groups: the selfless or self-disciplined (his ancestors would have called them the saved) and the selfish (whom his ancestors would have called the damned). In traditional Christian terms these were the forces of God and the Devil.[19]

He added "since God was the absolute, one had to be either absolutely for or absolutely against him," and most

---

18. Irving, *War Between*, 12.

19. Chernus, *General Eisenhower*, 59–60.

versions of Christian theology allowed for no middle ground. At the same time, though, he was equally faithful to his Christian heritage when he reminded his audiences that no one could claim to be free of the taint of selfishness (his ancestors would have called it sin) . . . Within Eisenhower's discourse, then, there was a clear temptation to project all evil onto the other and an equally clear hesitation to yield to that temptation.[20]

When the Soviet leader Joseph Stalin died in March of 1953, "Eisenhower believed the United States stood at a turning point in history, a time of unique danger and opportunity. His father [David Eisenhower] had predicted such moments of judgment." Furthermore, Eisenhower's "religious worldview was informed by dialectical struggle between divine and demonic forces in history, an understanding not dissimilar to that of his father."[21]

A central Watchtower teaching from their beginning in 1879 was their preoccupation with the end times ending in the battle of Armageddon, and the clear-cut separation of humans into the good and evil, of God and of Satan.[22] The evil persons will be destroyed at Armageddon, and the righteous will gain everlasting life in paradise on Earth. An example, Chernus notes, is Dwight's statement that the only factor which can stop the youth of today from "living in the Golden Age of history" is a "failure to teach the values of English-speaking civilization," such as Christian morality, the sanctity of marriage, and the love of God and neighbor. Further, this concern

> established the same kind of dualism that was so basic to the worldview of Eisenhower's sectarian Christian ancestors. The difference between right and wrong, between good and evil, was not only clear-cut but unbridgeable, allowing no middle ground. It was as vast as the distance separating the two roads of the Last Judgment, one leading to heaven and the other to hell.[23]

He added that, although Ike "rarely spoke of those roads in specifically sectarian Christian terms, the hope for a heavenly Golden Age and the fear of dismal gray hell were always present, by implication, in his [Dwight's] speeches."[24]

20. Chernus, *General Eisenhower*, 59–60.

21. Holl, *Civil Religion*, 131.

22. Stevens, *Salute!*; Stevenson, *Year of Doom: 1975*; Stroup, *Jehovah's Witnesses*.

23. Chernus, *General Eisenhower*, 88–89.

24. Chernus, *General Eisenhower*, 89.

Another message that could be read between the lines of this complex model is the conclusion the "United States now carried the banner of civilization against the forces of communism that threatened to undo civilization." In Eisenhower's view, "Communism's collectivism . . . and its atheism all stemmed from the same root . . . denying the individual the right to practice the spiritual virtue of voluntary self-restraint." Eisenhower "skillfully played his many variations on that single theme, implying that from every angle the U.S. system stood immutably opposed to the communist system."[25]

Chernus concluded this dichotomy was rooted in Dwight's "religiously based worldview and, more specifically, in the apocalyptic tradition on which generations of Christians had been raised—including Eisenhower himself. The choice was between the Millennium and damnation. No middle ground was possible. Occasionally Ike used overtly religious language to make the point."[26]

Unfortunately, Ike may at times have carried this dichotomy too far—a sin the Watchtower has also committed throughout its history. An example is that he viewed the German Nazi culture and war as a whole as the "embodiment of spiritual evil." As a result, Ike ordered his troops to not fraternize with any German children,

> whom he feared had absorbed the evil of their elders; some individuals were incurably evil, and personal contact with them could be dangerous. This order stirred considerable opposition, and the general soon found himself telling reporters that U.S. troops could have dealings with German children, if they judged it safe. He justified this new approach to the journalists by reverting to Augustinian terms: "The fine line sometimes between wickedness and good is not too clearly drawn."[27]

The Watchtower's dichotomy was between Witnesses, who were in the "truth," and therefore must be careful when associating with "worldly" people, who were part of Satan's system. This is a prime example of this good-versus-evil division. Chernus noted Eisenhower occasionally spoke as if

> the apocalyptic battle had been fought and won. But since this kind of language might encourage apathy in the fight against the

25. Chernus, *General Eisenhower*, 89.

26. Chernus, *General Eisenhower*, 89–90.

27. Chernus, *General Eisenhower*, 60.

new forms of impending chaos, he used it sparingly. When he did speak of the peace that had been won, it was almost always a prelude to a call to defend that peace against continuing threats. This naturally led to a view of peace as something still to be attained in the future.[28]

Conversely, at one level he rejected the apocalyptic beliefs of his parents. Holl wrote, "Eisenhower had pounded [in him a] fiery Armageddon as a child and had rejected his father's apocalyptic religion. While the prospects of nuclear holocaust were depressing, Eisenhower was an incurable optimist." [29] Such mixed reactions to one's rearing are not unusual, as any ex-Witness can attest.

Nonetheless, although he hated war, Eisenhower said "more than any other war in history" World War II was "an array of the forces of evil against those of righteousness . . . no matter what the cost, the war had to be won."[30]

These apocalyptical sentiments were also expressed by others. A *Life* magazine editorial, in response to Eisenhower's statement made on June 6, 1944, just before D-Day, noted America was "about to embark upon a great crusade," and this crusade was for religion and freedom, just as were previous crusades. After noting for nearly two thousand years Western Christendom has "made slow, painful but steady headway toward" human rights, the editiorial stated:

> All our religious doctrine and most of our rational reflection have taught us that all men are brothers, equal in the sight of God and entitled to an equal chance to prove themselves in life. Said Hitler, "We are not out against the hundred and one different sects of Christianity, but against Christianity itself." And he has proved it! The Nazi state can and does sterilize whomever it sees fit to sterilize.[31]

Furthermore, in addition to the Nuremberg anti-Semitic laws, Nazi Germany

> forbid any marriage which its minions think may contaminate the purity of the so-called Aryan Volk. This master race, when purified, is to be a race of Nietzschean heroes, to which all other races

28. Chernus, *General Eisenhower*, 60.

29. Holl, *Civil Religion*, 130.

30. Quoted in LaFay, *Eisenhower Story*, 21.

31. *Life Magazine*, June 12, 1944, 284.

are inferior. A permanent caste system in continental Europe is a professed part of Hitler's New Order, as it would eventually be a part of his plan for the world. Frenchmen, Poles, Norwegians, Belgians, imported by the millions to work in the Reich, already knew what this slavery means.[32]

EFFECTS OF DWIGHT'S RELIGIOUS BELIEFS ON HIS ATTITUDE TOWARD WAR

Dwight's interest in Christianity became more open as he was given greater and greater responsibilities during World War II.[33] Smith concluded the war prompted Eisenhower to "reexamine his purpose in life and deepen his relationship with God."[34] His religious inclination at this time was mainline Protestantism, and he was later influenced by the Rev. Billy Graham. Graham, in turn, was very impressed with Eisenhower's sincerity, humility, his dependence on God, and his realization of the need for a spiritual renewal, plus his ability to take advice from born-again Christians.[35]

During the heat of war, Dwight was also reassured by thinking of his mother and "her faith in God."[36] Dwight often talked about how God was with him during the war. Both during battle and while waiting to go into battle, he prayed all would go well for his men and their cause to destroy the evil of Nazism.[37] During the many trying times during the war he prayed "harder than he had ever prayed in his whole life."[38] Dwight, in an outburst of joy, once exclaimed, "Praise God from whom all blessings flow!"[39]

When Mamie wrote to Ike requesting he use his influence to have their son, John, reassigned to a less dangerous role in the military, Ike wrote back explaining doing this would be unethical, could hurt John's career, and "so far as John is concerned, we can do nothing but pray[for him]."[40]

---

32. *Life Magazine*, June 12, 1944, 284.

33. Quoted in Gustafson, *Religion of a President*, 611.

34. Smith, *Faith and the Presidency*, 223.

35. Pierard, *Billy Graham and the U.S. Presidency*, 116.

36. D'Este, *Eisenhower: A Soldier's Life*. 353.

37. D'Este, *Eisenhower: A Soldier's Life*, 349.

38. D'Este, *Eisenhower: A Soldier's Life*, 359.

39. D'Este, *Eisenhower: A Soldier's Life*, 654.

40. D'Este, *Eisenhower: A Soldier's Life*, 632.

DWIGHT AND DIVINE DESTINY

Patton referred to Dwight Eisenhower as "Mr. Divine Destiny." Blumenson added that if "Patton's destiny lay in the hands of God . . . Eisenhower was clearly the executive instrument."[41]

Dwight did not blindly rely on God to insure that all would go well. In fighting the war, he used his best judgment based on his extensive knowledge of military history. In dealing with the dilemma of being besieged by "insistent advice," Eisenhower recalled Lincoln's response during the Civil War to those persons who claimed their advice to Lincoln was "God's will." Ike wrote, "Lincoln's reply—which was one of wonder as to the confidence in which others quoted God's will while he, who so earnestly sought it, was left in the dark—has always been to me a classic expression of common sense. He had to follow his own convictions. I was in the same fix."[42]

Hatch claimed Dwight's religious upbringing is what motivated him to develop his "considerate conqueror" policy in Europe, requiring victors in war to treat the defeated people with respect as fellow humans.[43] Eisenhower strongly believed World War II was fought to protect "freedom of speech and worship which rested on a religious foundation."[44] He also stressed that America's greatness depended on its acknowledgement of God.[45] These views were critical, too, in guiding Eisenhower's policy during the Cold War.

For example, Dwight condemned the Soviet Union because of its atheism, writing hundreds of million's people "behind the Iron Curtain are daily drilled in the slogan: 'There is no God, and religion is an opiate.' But not all the people within the Soviet accept this fallacy; and some day they will educate their rulers—or change them."[46] This comment turned out to be prophetic when the old Soviet empire fell apart and was replaced by modern Russia. Dwight's strong "faith in the Almighty" openly influenced all of his governmental and presidential policies.[47] For example, Dwight wrote, ". . . in time of test or trial we instinctively turn to God for new

41. Blumenson, *Patton*, 182.

42. D'Este, *Eisenhower: A Soldier's Life*, 791.

43. Hatch, *General Ike*, 11.

44. Smith, *Faith and the Presidency*, 229.

45. Smith, *Faith and the Presidency*, 230.

46. Eisenhower, *Papers of Dwight Eisenhower*, 24.

47. Angelo, *First Mothers*, 105.

courage and peace of mind. All the history of America bears witness to this truth. Out of faith in God, and through faith in themselves as his children, our forefathers designed and built this republic."[48]

Eisenhower at times expressed his religious feelings more openly in his letters sent to those friends he knew as a youth. For example, in a personal letter to Charley Harger dated April 18, 1943, he wrote,

> since I heard, some days ago, of Mrs. Harger's death, I've been wanting to write you a letter expressing my deep and sincere sympathy. To me, Abilene is not just a little town of neat stores and homes and shaded streets, it is an entire community of the oldest, best and truest friends I have in the world. The loss of any of them, or any loss suffered by any of them, is a tragedy for me. So in your grief I hope you will understand that an old Abilene boy, here in Africa, is earnestly praying to God that he will out of his great kindness and mercy, help you bear this burden.[49]

On March 22, 1943, since he had learned in the previous week another friend, Georgia, had died, Eisenhower also wrote,

> a letter from Art says that your father also passed away. I am sure you must know how earnestly my sympathies go out to you. My oldest and warmest friends still live in Abilene and among them I counted with complete confidence both Georgia and your Father. Last year I lost my Father and a brother, and my own terrible sense of loss tells me how deeply you are suffering. I hope that providence will give you the strength to help and that time will serve to dull the keenness of your distress.[50]

Dwight also enthusiastically celebrated Christian holidays such as Christmas—which during the war helped him to bounce back from fatigue and to temporarily shut out the war (when he was growing up, Watchtower followers celebrated Christmas). He also enjoyed singing religious songs such as "God Rest Ye Merry, Gentlemen."[51]

48. Quoted in Hutchinson, "President's Religious Faith," 364.

49. Irish, *Hometown Support*, 25.

50. Irish, *Hometown Support*, 25.

51. D'Este, *Eisenhower: A Soldier's Life*, 372.

General Dwight D. Eisenhower addresses American paratroopers prior to D-Day.

I I

Hitler's Plan for WWII:
Eradicate the Jews, Eradicate the Church

THE BASIS OF THE *Life* magazine editorial cited above that supported the conclusion Hitler was against "Christianity itself" is simple. Hitler *claimed* the war was about concerns such as purity of the Aryan race or the need for lebensraum (living space) for future population expansions of the superior Aryan race. He made it clear he hated Christianity and was going to eliminate it after the war ended because he believed, by protecting the weak, Christianity "had crippled everything noble about humanity."[1] Consequently, Christianity was the main source of opposition to Hitler's policies, especially his racist policies.

In Hitler's words, "the heaviest blow that [has] ever struck humanity was the coming of Christianity," which was the "invention of the Jew Saul."[2] The Jesuits were "swine," and all of Christianity was "Jewish Christianity" that was comparable to "Jewish Bolshevism." His reasoning was based on his belief that Christianity was an "illegitimate" Jewish child and was, as a Jewish child, swine like its parent that must be eradicated. Hitler concluded both were evil and both had to be destroyed, and he made it very clear this was a major goal of the Nazi movement.[3]

---

1. Kershaw, *Hitler. 1936–45*, 936.

2. Hitler, *Hitler's Secret Conversations*, 6; Azar, *Twentieth Century*, 154.

3. Kershaw, *Hitler. 1936–45*, 330, 488; Cochrane, 1976.

In short, Hitler opposed Christianity because he saw Christianity and science as diametrically opposed to each other.[4] He concluded science must win in the end, and the Christian church would eventually be eradicated. Hitler even believed the science of Darwinism explained the creation of the superior German race.[5] He attempted to use science—especially Darwinism—to create the thousand-year Reich utopia on Earth, and made it absolutely clear there would be "no place in this utopia for the Christian Churches" in his plans for Germany's future.[6]

The long-term goal of producing a superior race, the putative Aryan race, was what drove Hitler's regime. Eradicating "'Jewish-Bolshevism' was central, not peripheral, to what had been deliberately designated by him as a 'war of annihilation.'"[7] To the Nazis, the Jews were like tuberculosis germs which could infect a healthy body. Therefore, the germ must be destroyed lest it infect others.[8] In the end, the Nazi regime's leaders had sealed their fate as a result of the "regime's genocide and other untold acts of inhumanity . . . the regime had only its own collective suicide in an inexorably lost war to contemplate. But like a mortally wounded wild beast . . . it fought with the ferocity and ruthlessness that came from desperation."[9]

As Hitler rapidly lost touch with reality, he hoped for miracles that would favor his military position. He kept tilting at windmills, ready "in the event of ultimate apocalyptic catastrophe, and in line with his undiluted social-Darwinist beliefs, to take his people down in flames with him if it proved incapable of producing the victory he had demanded."[10]

Hitler realized eradication of Christianity was a long-term goal and he "was prepared to put off long-term ideological goals in favor of short-term advantage."[11] Hitler had to fight one major battle at a time—and elected to fight Christianity in due time, but it was needed for now to help Hitler win the war against the Soviet Union.[12] Only after the war was won would Germany be able to fully implement the "final solution" to the so-called

4. Azar, *Twentieth Century*, 154.

5. Bergman, *Hitler and the Nazis*.

6. Kershaw, *Hitler, 1936–45*, 330, 488.

7. Kershaw, *Hitler, 1936–45*, 461.

8. Kershaw, *Hitler, 1936–45*, 582–83.

9. Kershaw, *Hitler, 1936–45*, 582–83.

10. Kershaw, *Hitler, 1936–45*, 615.

11. Kershaw, *Hitler, 1936–45*, 238.

12. Bergman, *Hitler and the Nazis*.

"Christian problem."[13] In the meantime, "calm should be restored . . . in relations with the Churches."[14] But it was "clear," wrote Geobbels, one of the most aggressive anti-church radicals, that "after the war" Germany would be forced to find a "solution" to the fact there exists an "insoluble opposition between the Christian and a Germanic-heroic worldview."[15]

Although this was the long-term plan, evidence of the early stages of Christianity's destruction could be seen during war. Dachau concentration camp held the largest number of Catholic laypersons and priests—over 2,400—in the Nazi camp system. These inmates came from about twenty-four nations and included parish priests and prelates, monks, friars, teachers, and missionaries. Over one third of the priests in Dachau alone were killed.[16] One Dachau survivor, Father Johannes Lenz, claimed the Catholic Church was the only steadfast fighter against the Nazis. Lenz tells the agony and martyrdom of the physical and mental tortures Dachau inmates experienced. Men and women were murdered by the thousands in Dachau, and those who survived were considered "missionaries in hell."

Official Nazi publications taught both anti-Semitic and anti-Christian doctrines, and those who believe the anti-Semitic goals of Nazism should also acknowledge the anti-Christian goals of Nazism, "for both had a single purpose. Hitler's aim was to eradicate all religious organizations within the state and to foster a return to paganism."[17]

Many of the documents proving the Nazi's plans to "eliminate Christianity and convert its followers to an Aryan philosophy" are in the online version of *Rutgers Journal of Law and Religion*.[18] These facts all support Dwight's perception of World War II as a war of good against evil, and that religion was central to the struggle. When Eisenhower saw what Nazism did to their own people in the concentration camps, he ordered extensive documentation (including photographs) because he feared—correctly as it turned out—that future Holocaust-denier movements would exist.

Eisenhower also required the German people in the surrounding villages tour the camps to see the many piles of emaciated corpses for themselves. Some were even forced to bury the dead. Eisenhower wanted

13. Kershaw, *Hitler, 1936–45*, 516.

14. Kershaw, *Hitler, 1936–45*, 39.

15. Kershaw, *Hitler, 1936–45*, 449.

16. Lenz, *Untersuchungen über die Künstliche*.

17. Dimont, *God and History*, 397.

18. https://lawandreligion.com.

unassailable proof so that if someone in the future claimed the Holocaust never happened, historians could produce hard evidence of this evil.

THE CHURCH'S RESPONSE TO
THE NAZI MOVEMENT AND WWII

Ironically, most of the German churches "turned the other cheek to Hitler's evil. The state's conflict with the Churches was a source of great bitterness by church members, but, amazingly, Hitler was largely exempted from blame."[19] As a result of Hitler's success blaming someone else,

> the head of the Protestant Church in Bavaria, Bishop Meiser, publicly offered prayers for Hitler, thanking God "for every success which, through your grace, you have so far granted him for the good of our people." The negative features of daily life, most [people] imagined, were not of the Führer's making. They were the fault of his underlings, who frequently kept him in the dark about what was happening.[20]

Many churchmen wanted to believe Hitler was on their side, and were convinced by Hitler's deception. To those groups within Germany critical of the Nazi regime

> Hitler could in a face-to-face meeting create a positive impression. He was good at attuning to the sensitivities of his conversation-partner, could be charming, and often appeared reasonable and accommodating. As always, he was a skilled dissembler. On a one-to-one basis, he could pull the wool over the eyes of hardened critics. After a three-hour meeting with him at the Berghof in early November 1936, the influential Catholic Archbishop of Munich-Freising, Cardinal Faulhaber—a man of sharp acumen, who had often courageously criticized the Nazi attacks on the Catholic Church—went away convinced that Hitler was deeply religious.[21]

The fact that many Christians in Germany then were nominal cultural Christians indoctrinated into the Nazi worldview helps to "explain how the SS troops could perform monstrous acts of cruelty and yet return home for Christmas and attend church and still think of themselves as good

19. Kershaw, *Hitler, 1936–45*, 28.
20. Kershaw, *Hitler, 1936–45*, 28.
21. Kershaw, *Hitler, 1936–45*, 29.

Christians. They were not murderers, they were men who were building a race of supermen and helping the inferior people get on with their evolutionary journey."[22]

Although Hitler fooled many parishioners and priests in the church, he did not completely hide his strong contempt for Christianity from everybody.[23] For example, when Germany invaded Poland, around two hundred executions a day occurred for weeks—all without trials—including the Polish nobility, clerics, and Jews, all which were eventually to be exterminated.[24] Furthermore, since the inception of Nazism, "Nazi fanatics" had openly conducted a "campaign against the church."[25] The infamous concordant the Vatican was forced to sign with Hitler in 1933 to guarantee the freedom of the Catholic Church was, in fact, a ruse. The persecution of the church continued without letup even after this concordant was signed.

An example is not long after the ink on the 1933 agreement was dry, the head of the German Catholic Action organization, Dr. Erich Klausner, was murdered by Hitler's storm troopers. In an attempt to discredit the church, monks were brought to trial on immorality charges. In 1935, the Protestant churches were placed under state control. Ministers and priests protesting Nazi policies were sent to concentration camps with Jews and communists.

Pope Pius XI, realizing the anti-Christian nature of Nazism, charged Hitler with "the threatening storm clouds of destructive religious wars . . . which have no other aim than . . . that of extermination." But the Nazi shouts of "Kill the Jews" drowned out the warning voice of the pope and the agonized cries of the tortured confined in Germany's concentration camps.[26]

Institutional religion was declining in Germany at this time, and Nazism was seen by the party as its replacement.[27] In the end, to their detriment the church and most church members largely stayed out of politics—the same path many think the church should also follow in the United States today. As a result of the people's passiveness in Germany, never before "in history has such ruination—physical and moral—been associated

22. Lutzer, *Hitler's Cross*, 95.
23. Bergman, *Hitler and the Nazis*.
24. Kershaw, *Hitler, 1936–45*, 243.
25. Kershaw, *Hitler, 1936–45*, 702.
26. Dimont, *God and History*, 397.
27. Kershaw, *Hitler, 1936–45*, 840.

with the name of one man," Adolph Hitler.[28] The ruination of Germany, though, "had far deeper roots and far more profound causes than the aims and actions of this one man."[29] Rather, "the previously unprobed depths of inhumanity plumbed by the Nazi regime could draw" on the fact that

> wide-ranging complicity at all levels of society has been equally apparent. But Hitler's name justifiably stands for all the time as that of the chief instigator of the most profound collapse of civilization in modern times. The extreme form of personal rule which an ill-educated beerhall demagogue and racist bigot, a narcissistic, megalomaniac, self-styled national savior was allowed to acquire and exercise in a modern, economically advanced, and cultured land known for its philosophers and poets, was absolutely decisive in the terrible unfolding of events in those fateful twelve years.[30]

The fact is, Hitler was "the main author" of a war that cost over fifty-five million lives and left millions more grieving over their lost loved ones and were eventually forced to rebuild shattered lives. He

> was the chief inspiration of a genocide the likes of which the world had never known, rightly to be viewed in coming times as a defining episode of the twentieth century. The Reich whose glory he had sought lay at the end wrecked . . . The arch-enemy, Bolshevism, stood in the Reich capital itself and presided over half of Europe . . . in its maelstrom of destruction Hitler's rule had also conclusively demonstrated the utter bankruptcy of the hyper-nationalistic and racist world-power ambitions (and the social and political structures that upheld them) that had prevailed in Germany over the previous half a century and twice taken Europe and the wider world into calamitous war.[31]

The church's main sin was not of commission but omission, not in inspiring the Nazis to commit their many crimes, but in not doing much to stop them. Although the major institution in Germany and Europe that fought against the Nazi crimes was the church, it did far too little too late. Hitler saw Christians and the church as weak and, as Lutzer noted, had contempt for both Protestants and Catholics and was fully

---

28. Kershaw, *Hitler, 1936–45*, 841.
29. Kershaw, *Hitler, 1936–45*, 841.
30. Kershaw, *Hitler, 1936–45*, 841–82.
31. Kershaw, *Hitler, 1936–45*, 841.

convinced that all Christians would betray their God when they were forced to choose between the swastika and the Cross: "Do you really believe the masses will be Christian again? Nonsense! Never again. That tale is finished. No one will listen to it again. But we can hasten matters. The parsons will dig their own graves. They will betray their God to us. They will betray anything for the sake of their miserable jobs and incomes."[32]

Hitler was largely proved correct here. The failure of Christianity was not that it produced the Nazi monster, but that it did far too little to stop it. However, there were a few Christians who did stand up to the Nazis. That the church was not *totally* silent was testified to by the great physicist Albert Einstein, who said that when the Nazi revolution came, he

> looked to the universities to defend it, knowing that they had always boasted of their devotion to the cause of truth; but no, the universities were immediately silenced. Then I looked to the great editors of the newspapers, whose flaming editorials in days gone by had proclaimed their love of freedom; but they, like the universities, were silenced in a few short weeks . . . Only the Church stood squarely across the path of Hitler's campaign for suppressing truth. I never had any special interest in the Church before, but now I feel a great affection and admiration for it because the Church alone has had the courage and persistence to stand for intellectual and moral freedom. I am forced to confess that what I once despised I now praise unreservedly.[33]

Nonetheless, most all other institutions did far *less* to oppose Hitler than the churches.[34] Nor did Hitler wait until the war ended to begin his goal of destroying Christianity. After the first few years of Hitler's rule, the Gestapo and the Nazi Party singled out the clergy for heavy doses of repression to guarantee their silence and their parishioners' obedience. Thousands of clergymen, both Catholic and Protestant, endured house searches, surveillance, Gestapo interrogations, jail and prison terms, fines, and worse.[35]

Altogether, Hitler's killing machine murdered about six million Jews and about as many Christians—a little-published fact that caused Jewish historian Max Dimont to declare "the world blinded itself to the murder

32. Lutzer, *Hitler's Cross*, 104.

33. Cited by Wilhelm Niemoller in *Kampi und Zeugnis der bekennenden Kirche* (*Struggle and Testimony of the Confessing Church*), 526.

34. Gerstenmaier, *Church Conspiratorial*.

35. Johnson, *Nazi Terror*, 224.

of Christians" by Nazi Germany.[36] In Poland alone, 881 Catholic priests were annihilated.[37] In addition, many more priests would end up dying in concentration camps. General Eisenhower was aware of much of this, and it is no surprise that a man who hated war saw *this* war as a conflict between good and evil that must be fought.

THE NAZI CONCENTRATION CAMPS

The Nazi concentration camps have been studied extensively largely relative to the Jewish experience. The largest subgroup of jailed conscientious objectors, both in the United States and Germany, were Jehovah's Witnesses, yet they have been largely ignored by historians.[38] Kogon notes it "would be fascinating . . . to write a psychology of Jehovah's Witnesses" experience in the concentration camps. Most were middle-class people that worked in the trades. Kogan writes inmates in the concentration camps displayed a "veritable spectrum of mental reactions and outward behavior patterns, ranging from the extreme of lofty anticipation of the hereafter down to thoroughly earthly appetites."[39]

In the last decade, much has been written about the German Jehovah Witnesses' experiences, which is unique in many ways because the primary reason they were imprisoned was due to their refusal to fight in the German army.[40] Actually, of the many religions existing in Nazi Germany, the Witnesses, Gypsies, and the Jews were the *only* groups to be uniformly persecuted in Germany: "The Third Reich was not willing . . . to tolerate [any] minority Christian sects who might prove a challenge . . . [but] only one group, the Jehovah's Witnesses, were the victims of total persecution."[41] Professor Beckford concluded the level that Hitler persecuted Witnesses far surpassed that which even the Witnesses had previously experienced, or ever expected, and that the

> brutality and ruthlessness of persecution in Germany must have
> shocked even the most hardened veterans of Watchtower clashes

36. Dimont, *God and History*, 391–92.

37. Azar, *Twentieth Century*, 154.

38. Bettelheim, *Informed Heart*, 280; Reynaud and Graffard, *Witnesses and the Nazis*.

39. Kogon, *Theory and Practice*, 302.

40. Bergman, *Nazi Concentration Camps*.

41. King, *Strategies for Survival*, 213; Kaplan, *State and Salvation*.

with civil, military, and religious authorities. German Bible Students had been subject to periodic harassment since the First World War and were inured to being charged with alleged subversion or financial chicanery . . . In February 1933, however, Hitler formally prescribed all Watchtower activities and stipulated penalties for infraction of his edict ranging from fifteen months to five years in prison. Nazi ideologists accused them of sympathizing with the Jews, being implicated in international communism and showing disrespect for the Führer. [42]

Rutherford at first tried to placate the Nazis; possibly this accounts for his anti-Semitic banter in a document titled "Declaration."[43] Professor Slupina claimed the Nazis

> cruelly persecuted Jehovah's Witnesses without mercy. Using an extremely sophisticated killing machine, they attempted to consign the Witnesses to oblivion by systematically exterminating them. Despite their political neutrality, Jehovah's Witnesses were among the first to be banned and persecuted by the Nazis, who came to power in 1933 . . . Of all the Christian associations the Nazis targeted, they were by far the most severely and mercilessly persecuted.[44]

The Witnesses in the concentration camps were forced out of their social element, yet stuck to their values in the face of extreme hardship. Often, Bettelheim claims, Witnesses as persons appeared to be "hardly touched by the camp experience" and they "not only showed unusual heights of human dignity and moral behavior, but seem protected against the same camp experience that soon destroyed persons considered very well integrated by my psychoanalytic friends and myself."[45]

Bettelheim stresses the behavior of the Jehovah Witnesses did not correspond to what would be expected according to psychoanalytic theory. They expected those who had well-integrated personalities would survive better under the brutality in the concentration camps than those with less-well integrated personalities. The Jehovah's Witnesses, Bettelheim notes, were set apart from the social life of the camp. Although not highly

---

42. Beckford, *Trumpet of Prophecy*, 33–34.

43. See the 1934 *Yearbook of Jehovah Witnesses* and Penton, *Jehovah's Witnesses and the Third Reich*, 148–49.

44. Slupina, *Persecuted and Almost Forgotten*, 266.

45. Bettelheim, *Informed Heart*, 20–21.

integrated with those around them, they *were* highly integrated within their *own* small social group (i.e., other Jehovah's Witnesses in the camps).

Thus, the Witnesses would not necessarily contradict Bettelheim's conclusions relative to the importance of social integration in surviving the concentration camp experience. The Jehovah's Witnesses formed supportive, even intimate relationships, with others of their faith, but their other close social connections tended to be limited to relatives and select group members. Of note is when the Nazis were defeated, the Communists in the German Democratic Republic repeated the same behavior of the Nazis and imprisoned many Witnesses in their new concentration camps—about sixty were murdered or died in the concentration camps in the new "democratic" government.[46]

Eisenhower was no doubt aware of this whole problem involving Witnesses, but I have not been able to find any written records of his reactions. It even may have been on his mind when he spoke of the need to defeat Nazi Germany.

---

46. Slupina, *Persecuted and Almost Forgotten*, 266.

12

Persecution in America amidst WWII

From this day forward, the millions of our school children will daily proclaim in every city and town, every village and rural school house, the dedication of our nation and our people to the Almighty. To anyone who truly loves America, nothing could be more inspiring than to contemplate this rededication of our youth, on each school morning, to our country's true meaning.[1]

ACCORDING TO THE EMINENT jurist Archibald Cox, in the United States—a country that claims to champion religious freedom above all others—the Witnesses were "the principal victims of religious persecution . . . in the twentieth-century . . . Although founded earlier, they began to attract attention and provoke repression in the 1930s, when their proselytizing and numbers rapidly increased."[2]

Their teachings, such as those opposing war, have "led the sect into bitter conflict with civil authorities" in democratic, as well as, in totalitarian states. The major reasons for the conflicts include their refusal to be part of the army or to undertake war-related work, but they are not pacifists; rather they

1. Dwight D Eisenhower, Statement by the President Upon Signing Bill to Include the Words "Under God" in the Pledge to the Flag, June 14, 1954.

2. Cox, *Court*, 189.

believe that they are already enlisted in the army of Jehovah and cannot give allegiance to another power, that of the civil state. Thus, whilst they are exemplary citizens in matters of tax payment and obedience to moral and criminal laws, they will not undertake civil duties which they see as conflicting with their duty to Jehovah—God. Witnesses will not vote . . . , salute a national flag or recognize a national anthem, and they refuse to enlist. In peacetime they are normally tolerated in democratic countries, but in wartime and in totalitarian regimes they frequently face imprisonment.[3]

One major conflict for Dwight existing *prior* to Rutherford's Watchtower presidency was the teaching against all involvement, including non-combat service, in all secular wars. One result of the ban was, in World War I, out of 2,810,296 men inducted, 3,989 persons claimed conscientious objector (C.O.) status, and 450 were sentenced to long prison terms.[4] Of these, 138 were Mennonites, and the next largest number were Jehovah's Witnesses, 27, followed by Dunkard Church members, 24.

As a result of the Watchtower's stand on war, in 1918 Rutherford and six members of his high-level staff were sentenced to twenty years each in the federal penitentiary in Atlanta.[5] The trial was widely publicized and the verdict generally approved by the media. Ray Abrams added that when the editors of the religious press learned about the Watchtower leaders' twenty-year sentences, practically every religious publication

> great and small, rejoiced over the event. I have been unable to discover any words of sympathy in any of the orthodox religious journals. "There can be no question," concluded Upton Sinclair, the "the persecution . . . sprang in part from the fact that they had won the hatred of 'orthodox' religious bodies." What the combined efforts of the churches had failed to do the government now seemed to have succeeded in accomplishing for them—the crushing of these "prophets of Baal" forever.[6]

This fact indicates the widespread dislike for the Witnesses then, and is no doubt one reason why Dwight distanced himself from them later in life.

---

3. King, *Strategies for Survival*, 248.

4. Abrams, *Preachers Present Arms*, 135.

5. Abrams, *Preachers Present Arms*, 183.

6. Abrams, *Preachers Present Arms*, 183–84.

Compared to other modern religions, members of the Jehovah's Witnesses have experienced the most conflicts from citizens in their own country.[7] As one scholar concluded in a work sympathetic to the Witnesses, "no chapter in human history has been so largely written in terms of persecution and intolerance as the one dealing with religious freedom . . . and the Jehovah's Witnesses are living proof of the fact that even in this nation, conceived as it was in the ideals of freedom, the right to practice religion in unconventional ways is still far from secure."[8]

A summary by the American Civil Liberties Union,[9] which often argued cases before the courts in favor of the Watchtower, concluded "the record of violence against [the Jehovah's Witnesses] has been unparalleled in America since the attacks on the Mormons." They added, "not since the persecution of the Mormons years ago has any religious minority been so bitterly and generally attacked as members of the Jehovah's Witnesses . . . Documents filed with the department of justice by attorneys . . . showed over 3,035 instances of mob violence in forty-five states during 1940, involving 1,488 men, women and children."

The conflicts were of such intensity that the then Attorney General Francis Biddle made a nationwide radio appeal to the American people to stop the violence, stressing that "Jehovah's Witnesses have been repeatedly set upon and beaten. They had committed no crime; but the mob adjudged they had, and meted out mob punishment."[10]

LEGAL SUCCESS

One long-term, positive result of these events is the Witnesses prevailing in many important court cases relating to freedom of religion, the press, and speech. A study of the factors that led to this mayhem concluded Witnesses, who were often willing to confront the state, were

> impressively organized, pridefully evangelistic, and often scornful of the leaders of traditional religions, the members of the sect repeatedly collided with the law. Their willingness to do battle in the courts has been crowned with remarkable success. Their record in the United States Supreme Court shows they have won more than

7. Bergman, *Modern Religious Objection.*

8. Sorauf, "Jehovah's Witnesses," 336.

9. American Civil Liberties Union, *Persecution of Jehovah's Witnesses*, 1.

10. Whalen, *Armageddon*, 183.

ninety percent of the fifty or so cases brought before that tribunal. The story of this success begins with *Cantwell vs. Connecticut* in 1940.[11]

One reason the Watchtower often prevailed in court was a result of the secularization of American society. For the first two hundred years of America, the Protestant, Catholic, and Jewish faiths dominated, and the courts and secular institutions often deferred to them. A Catholic passing out tracts on the street corner rarely faced problems; a Jehovah's Witness often faced arrest. Secularization changed this, and all religions, even what many regarded as bizarre sects and cults, were now legally on equal footing. In a society less oriented toward defending only the traditional religions, it became less and less popular to favor mainline faiths.

The problems resulting from the Watchtower's "hatred of things government, church and business" was well put by Archibald Cox, who wrote they were persecuted "partly because of the vehemence of their religious attacks on the established order and partly because of the militancy of their proselytizing . . . they stood on street corners and canvassed from house to house, offering" Watchtower Bible and Tract Society tracts.[12] In other words, when they condemned corrupt governments, politicians, and even churches and others who did not live up to their moral code, they were condemned.[13]

Another reason for the vehemence of the Witnesses in defending their position was because they were fully convinced after the second coming of Christ, the forces of godlessness will be defeated at the battle of Armageddon. Since these events are believed to be imminent, all Witnesses are required to preach to the unconverted and "rally the forces of good that will inherit the earth. This they do by public evangelism—selling their books from door-to-door and to street corners. In the 1930s and 1940s, moreover, their evangelism was more aggressive, even strident, than it has been in recent decades, and many non-Witnesses, especially Roman Catholics, found it offensive."[14]

The Watchtower interpreted what they viewed as persecution as both fully expected and actually necessary, because the

11. Semonche, *Religion and Constitutional*, 44.

12. Cox, *Court*, 189–90.

13. *Cantwell v. Conn.*, 310 US 296 (1940), 48.

14. Sorauf, "Jehovah's Witnesses," 336.

Witness work for THE THEOCRACY appears to be about done in most of the countries of "Christendom." Now the totalitarian rule has suppressed the Theocratic message, and it should be expected that when they quit fighting amongst themselves all the totalitarian rulers will turn their attention to [the complete suppression of everything pertaining to] the THEOCRATIC GOVERNMENT. What then does it mean that the THEOCRATIC GOVERNMENT is now suppressed in many nations? It means that the hour is rapidly approaching when the 'sign' of Armageddon will be clearly revealed and all who are on the side of Jehovah will see and appreciate it.[15]

In contrast to the typical assumption that religious conflicts were far more common in the earlier, more intolerant periods of history, intolerance has been a major problem in the twentieth century, possibly surpassing most other periods in history. And the Jehovah's Witnesses have been among the most embattled of all twentieth-century religious sects. As noted, Watchtower leaders have brought on much of the persecution against their followers by, for example, rigidly requiring their members to follow policies many governments deem hostile to the secular state and its authority.[16]

The history of many conflicts between the Watchtower and the secular state often involved two unyielding and rather rigid power structures, with millions of Jehovah's Witnesses caught in the middle. The Watchtower's intransigence, though, is no excuse for the inhumane, often brutal manner in which the secular state has frequently responded to the Witnesses. The blame for the enormous suffering resulting from this conflict falls on *both* the Watchtower leaders and the secular state.

This persecution illustrates how completely committed Witnesses were, and still are today, to the Watchtower. Moreover, it also illustrates the imperfections of the courts and especially the importance of the judges' own personal biases and beliefs in deciding cases. Many, especially Southern judges, were blatantly biased against those who were different, including blacks, northerners, and those who did not conform to "polite society" then—a society we today see as neither very polite nor just. The major questions this history covers are still very much with us today: How does the government deal with issues related to free speech and religion, and to what extent can the government regulate religion in areas such as the public

15. *Watchtower*, September 1, 1940, 265.
16. Bergman, *Adventists and Jehovah's Witnesses*.

schools? Should we allow unpopular religious ideas in the public arena, our schools, and in the streets of our nation?

As a result of their human rights struggles, Starr[17] concluded that the Watchtower has achieved greater success in arguing for basic religious freedom rights before the American Supreme Court than all other religious groups combined. Professor Cushman estimated that between 1938 and 1946 alone, the Witnesses brought twenty major religious freedom cases before the court and were victorious in a total of fourteen.

By this means they have not only forced the clarification of many human rights issues but, in at least two instances, have forced the Supreme Court to reverse itself. Although the Watchtower stand has produced a certain vindication, the conflicts continue today, only in different forms, in spite of occasional Supreme Court victories on basic freedom issues. This problem has been both consistent and pervasive since the Watchtower's founding in 1879.[18] This subject is covered in more detail in Appendix I.

17. Starr, *Human Rights.*
18. Penton, *Jehovah's Witnesses in Canada.*

13

Explosions and Exploitation

MANY, IF NOT MOST, accounts of President Eisenhower have largely or totally ignored the full extent of his mother's and the family's Watchtower involvement, even though the Eisenhower boys did, in times of lowered vigilance, admit their affiliation with the Watchtower. So why did Eisenhower distance himself from the Watchtower in his adult life? Chapter 7 discusses the widespread dislike for Witnesses as one reason, but there was another reason for his distance as well (and maybe his brothers' distance as well).

CLAIMS OF EXPLOITING IDA

Ida was a frequent focus of the media. Ida's interviews "made great copy" but she was "uncomfortable granting interviews about Ike and their private life."[1] This fact, however, did not seem to stop Jehovah's Witnesses from using Ida to propagate their views. This is supported by the problem that ensued when the family concluded the Watchtower Society attempted to exploit Ida Eisenhower's name and reputation.

Early in 1942 Roy, who lived in Junction City, died only two months shy of his fiftieth birthday. Since he was the son living closest to Ida—only about twenty-five miles away—he looked after her. His death, and Ida's age and poor health, made it necessary for the family to hire help to care for

---

1. D'Este, *Eisenhower: A Soldier's Life*, 312.

Ida.[2] They hired a lifelong friend and Jehovah's Witness, Naomi Engle. This set of events caused problems in connection with the Watchtower.

In the 1940s, according to Edgar Eisenhower, Ida's "deep, sincere and even evangelical religious fervor" was used by the Watchtower "to exploit her in her old age."[3] In 1944, this concern prompted Edgar to write a letter to Naomi, who at the time was the live-in companion/caregiver for Dwight's then eigthy-two-year-old mother. As was the practice for all Witnesses, young and old—and as Jehovah's Witnesses today are well known for—all able-bodied Witnesses are expected to actively proselytize and "witness" to others.

They are required to do this primarily by distributing Watchtower literature from door to door and talking about Witness beliefs to all who will listen.[4] The Watchtower teaches, as taught in Matthew 28:19–20, that aggressive proselytizing activity, including witnessing on the street corners and elsewhere, is required of all Christians.

Conversely, Edgar felt the Eisenhower name was being exploited in this Witness work and objected to his mother "being taken out of the home and used for the purpose of distributing [Watchtower] religious literature."[5] Edgar added that he was "willing to fight" for his mother's "right to continue to believe as she saw fit, but . . . she could be easily and mistakenly influenced in performing any service which would be represented to her as helpful to the advancement of [the Watchtower] religious beliefs."[6]

He then requested his mother no longer "be taken from place to place and exhibited as the mother of General Eisenhower—solely for the purpose of attempting to influence anyone [to accept the Watchtower beliefs] . . . I want mother shielded and protected and not exposed or exhibited . . . mother's home should be maintained solely for her intimate friends and relatives and . . . no stranger should be permitted to live in the house regardless of who he may be . . ."[7]

Would Edgar have objected if Ida used the Eisenhower name for a cause such as education, health, or even to advance a church such as the Lutherans or Methodists? Most likely he objected only to what he felt was

2. Irish, *Hometown Support*, 18.

3. Kornitzer, *Great American Heritage*, 139.

4. Rogerson, *Millions Now Living*.

5. Lingerfeldt, interview; Kornitzer, *Great American Heritage*, 139.

6. Kornitzer, *Great American Heritage*, 139.

7. Kornitzer, *Great American Heritage*, 140.

the Watchtower exploiting his mother to spread a set of beliefs he and his brothers by that time openly opposed. D'Este notes this incident revealed the Eisenhower children's "true feelings about the Jehovah's Witnesses."[8]

This account was also distorted by the press. Historian Kerry Irish wrote that when Ike found the time to write to Joe Curry, he had learned through Frances and other persons "newsmen continued to hound his mother and that Naomi Engle seemed to encourage such activity." Ike felt Mrs. Engle was "too unsophisticated to deal with these people, and he hoped that his brother Milton might be able to provide his mother some peace." Ike then asked Curry to write again because he felt his mother could no longer appropriately respond to the situation, and because "Naomi does send me a note about every month or so, but she does not give me as vivid a picture of mother's health and condition as you do. I always feel grateful to you."[9]

Although Naomi Engle no doubt did encourage the publicity, it had nothing to do with being unsophisticated, but rather, as an active Witness, she was only carrying out her religious obligation to warn others before the impending battle of Armageddon. Furthermore, the evidence is clear: Ida herself welcomed the attention in order to spread her faith; it allowed her to fulfill her obligation to witness to others.

This problem was eventually solved by removing the Jehovah's Witness, the life-long friend of the family who was then caring for Ida Eisenhower, from Ida's home and replacing her with a Mrs. Robinson, a "respectable Presbyterian."[10] Also, about this time, Milton returned to the area as president of Kansas State University, allowing him to render some personal care to Ida.[11]

THE BOECKEL INCIDENT

Dr. Holt, the former director of the Dwight D. Eisenhower Library in Abilene, Kansas, indicated the Watchtower Society may have been involved in passing off documents as authentic that were evidently forgeries.[12] This charge stems from interviews with family members by J. Earl Endacott, a

8. D'Este, *Eisenhower: A Soldier's Life*, 416.

9. Irish, *Hometown Support*, 3435.

10. Faber, *Mothers of American Presidents*, 45.

11. Irish, *Hometown Support*, 18.

12. Holt, *Unlikely Partnership*.

former Eisenhower Library curator, regarding the 1944 incident leading to the dismissal of Ida's nurse, Mrs. Engle, who was then an active Jehovah's Witness.

Endacott's source for this information was Mrs. Robinson, who, as noted, became Ida's nurse after Engle's dismissal. Robinson claimed Engle and another Witness had Ida write her name several times on a blank sheet of paper under the pretense of giving her "practice." According to Mrs. Robinson, the most legible signature was then physically cut from the sheet and pasted on the bottom of a letter and sent to a Mr. Boeckel. Robinson claimed the letter was, in fact, *not* written by Ida Eisenhower, but rather by Engle.

Endacott concluded Engle had "more loyalty to the Witnesses" than to the Eisenhowers to whom she was distantly related. Later, "in one of her lucid moments Ida told Mrs. Robinson what had happened and gave the sheet with the cut-out name to her." Then, when the Eisenhower Foundation took over the home, "Mrs. Robinson told me the story and gave me the sheet which I still have."[13]

The letter Ida allegedly wrote was to Richard Boeckel, a young man who had become a Jehovah's Witness while still in the army.[14] In August of 1944, Boeckel attended a Watchtower assembly in Denver, where he met Lotta Thayer, Ida's Abilene neighbor. Boeckel explained in his conversations with Mrs. Thayer about the difficulty of being a Witness in a military environment.

Thayer then reportedly told him her neighbor was General Eisenhower's mother and added "she's one of Jehovah's Witnesses," and asked Boeckel if he would like her to write to him.[15] As a result, Boeckel wrote to Ida, and part of the letter Ida allegedly wrote back to him stated a friend of hers, returning from the United Announcers Convention of Jehovah's Witnesses,

> informs me of meeting you there. I rejoice with you in your privilege of attending such convention. It has been my good fortune in the years gone by to attend these meetings of those faithfully proclaiming the name of Jehovah and his glorious kingdom which shortly now will pour out its rich blessings all over the earth. My friend informs me of your desire to have a word from General

13. Endacott, Records, Documentary Historical Series, box 4, Eisenhower Presidential Library.

14. Boeckel, "Soldier Who Became a Preacher."

15. Boeckel, "Soldier Who Became a Preacher."

Eisenhower's mother whom you have been told is one of the witnesses of Jehovah. I am indeed such and what a glorious privilege it has been in associating with [other Witnesses] . . . Generally, I have refused such requests because of my desire to avoid all publicity. However, because you are a person of good will towards Jehovah God and His glorious Theocracy I am very happy to write you . . . It was always my desire and my effort to raise my boys in the knowledge of and to reverence [sic] their Creator.

She closed by stating,

My prayer is that they all may anchor their hope in the New World, the central feature of which is the Kingdom for which all good people have been praying the past two thousand years. I feel that Dwight my third son will always strive to do his duty with integrity as he sees such duty. I mention him in particular because of your expressed interest in him. And so as the mother of General Eisenhower and as a Witness of and for the Great Jehovah of Hosts (I have been such for the past 49 years) I am pleased to write you and to urge you to faithfulness, as a companion of and servant with those who "keep the commands of God and have the testimony of Jesus."[16]

To encourage Boeckel to accept Watchtower doctrines, the letter mentioned several events current in 1944 when the letter was written, which the Watchtower taught then were evidence Armageddon would occur very soon. The letter concluded, "Surely this portends that very soon the glorious Theocracy, the long-promised kingdom of Jehovah . . . will rule the entire earth and pour out manifold blessings upon all peoples who are of good will towards Him. All others will be removed [killed at Armageddon]. Again, may I urge your ever faithfulness to these 'Higher Powers' and to the New World now so very near."

Merle Miller related an experience involving Boeckel and this letter that reveals the irony of Eisenhower's mother's faith:

one time when Boeckel refused, as a good Witness must, to salute his superior officers at Fort Warren, he said that he was a Witness and that his refusal to salute was "based on my understanding of the Bible." One officer reportedly said, "General Eisenhower ought to line you Jehovah's Witnesses up and shoot you all!" Boeckel then, again according to *The Watchtower*, said, "Do you think he would shoot his own mother, sir?" 'What do you mean by that?'

16. Quoted in Cole, *Jehovah's Witnesses*, 194–95.

"Reaching in my pocket and taking out Sister Eisenhower's letter, I handed it to him . . . He read the letter . . . [and] handed it back to me. 'Get back to ranks,' he said, 'I don't want to get mixed up with the General's mother.'"[17]

According to Endacott, it was this letter, dated August 20, 1944, that contained the taped-on signature of Ida Eisenhower affixed to it and closed with "Respectfully yours in hope of and as a fighter for the New World."[18]

This putative Ida Eisenhower letter, Endacott concluded, was "not in the words of Ida, who at the time could hardly write her own name." Furthermore, in 1944, she was evidently not always mentally alert although her *physical* health was generally fairly good for a woman of her age. Her memory started to fail soon after her husband died and occasionally was so poor she could not even remember her own sons' names.[19] Furthermore, in stark contrast to the letter she wrote in her own hand dated 1943 (only one year earlier), this letter was very well written.[20]

When the Eisenhower sons found out about this event (evidently from a reporter who published the letter putatively written by Ida Eisenhower to Mr. Boeckel) and other similar incidents, they wrote to Mrs. Engle claiming she was exploiting Ida.[21] This letter from the Eisenhower boys was evidently ignored by Engle and, consequently, Milton was given the task of dismissing her. It was at this time Milton hired the non-Witness, Mrs. Robinson, to replace Mrs. Engle to help care for Ida.

In favor of the letter's authenticity, Richard Boeckel would immediately have been suspicious when he received a letter with Mrs. Eisenhower's signature obviously taped on it. He would have tried to confirm the letter was genuine by calling her or by another means, before he made claims about receiving a letter from Ida Eisenhower. His story (and a photo reproduction of the letter which shows no evidence of a taped-on signature) was published in Marley Cole's book *Jehovah's Witnesses* and other sources, and Boeckel repeated the claims about the letter in his life story published in the October 15, 1980, volume of *Watchtower*. An inquiry to the Watchtower

---

17. Miller, *Ike the Soldier*, 79; see also Boeckel, "Soldier Who Became a Preacher."

18. See Cole, *Jehovah's Witnesses*, 191, for a photocopy of the original.

19. M. Eisenhower, *President Is Calling*, 188; Faber, *Mothers of American Presidents*, 46; Gullan *Faith of Our*, 231.

20. See photocopy in Cole, *Jehovah's Witnesses*, 191.

21. Kornitzer, *Great American Heritage*.

Society World Headquarters about this matter produced the following reply:

> You inquire about allegations made by the director of the Eisenhower Library in Abilene, Kansas, that a letter published as being from Ida Eisenhower may be a forgery. We have no reason to believe that Sister Eisenhower was coerced into signing her name, or that she signed her name to something that she did not agree with.[22]

They then speculate that possibly

> Sgt. Boeckel's letter was read to Sister Eisenhower, and she may have asked for assistance in drafting a reply. Mrs. Engle or someone else may have drafted the letter and read it to Mrs. Eisenhower for approval, much as a manager may ask a secretary to draft a letter that conveys certain thoughts. The content of the letter is certainly not out of character for her. Therefore, even if it were true (which we do not know) that Sister Eisenhower did not directly dictate all of the words of the letter, that would not be evidence that the letter lacked authenticity. If the director of the Eisenhower Library is concerned about the matter, he can no doubt contact the Watchtower Bible and Tract Society directly.[23]

The Eisenhower Library elected not to pursue the forgery claim. Suspicion the letter was a forgery is also supported by a Watchtower teaching first introduced in 1936 called the Theocratic Warfare Doctrine.[24] The Theocratic Warfare Doctrine essentially teaches that in order to further the Watchtower's interests, it is appropriate to withhold the truth from "people who are not entitled to it."[25] Reed defined Theocratic Warfare Strategy as the approval to lie "to outsiders when deemed necessary" and also to deceive outsiders in order to advance the Watchtower's goals.[26] In the words of Kotwall, the Watchtower teaches that "to lie and deceive in the interest of their religion is Scripturally approved."[27]

---

22. *Watchtower*, April 15, 1999, 1.

23. *Watchtower*, April 15, 1999, 1.

24. Rutherford, *Riches*.

25. Bergman, *Lying in Court*; Reed, "Court Rules"; Reed, *Dictionary of "J.W.ese"*; Franz, *Aid to Bible*, 1060–61.

26. Reed, *Dictionary of "J.W.ese"*, 40; Reed, *Jehovah-Talk*, 129; Reed, *Court Rules*.

27. Kotwall, *Encourages Lying*, 1.

Jehovah's Witnesses do not always lie outright, but many lie according to the court's definition—not telling "the whole truth and nothing but the truth," which means the court requires the *whole* story, not half-truths or deception.[28] In the words of Raines, theocratic warfare *in practice* means "deceiving" to protect and advance the interests of "God's people" and God's "organization the Watchtower."[29]

When researching the Eisenhowers' religion, historians have been forced to rely on interviews with those who knew David and Ida because, it is often claimed, "so little original documentation exists" about the details of their personal beliefs.[30] Dodd's thesis on the Eisenhowers' religion is one of the most reliable sources on this issue because she used scores of personal interviews with the family, many of whom she was personally acquainted with, to study the religious background of the Eisenhower family in the late 1950s. Unfortunately, many other sources discussing the Watchtower Society are not as reliable. After considering all of the evidence, I have concluded that the letter was very likely both written, possibly by dictation, and signed by Ida, who agreed to the letter.

THE FINAL EXPLOIT

After a four-year long illness, Ida Eisenhower died on September 11, 1946, in Abilene, Kansas. The Watchtower considered the pallbearers to be "of Satan's world" and noted they even wore "the uniform caps of the American Legion and the Veterans of Foreign Wars"—two groups openly at war against the Witnesses in the 1940s.[31]

An article published in the official Watchtower magazine, *Awake!*, noted that when Ida died, private funeral services for her were conducted in her home, and public services were handled by a Fort Riley Army chaplain. The Watchtower concluded this arrangement was inappropriate, writing the

> pallbearers were three American Legionnaires and three Veterans of Foreign Wars. Was that appropriate? . . . In 1942 her husband, also one of Jehovah's witnesses, died. One of Jehovah's witnesses preached the funeral service. Mrs. I. S. Eisenhower, like

28. Bergman, *Lying in Court*.

29. Raines, "Deception by J.W's", 20; Bergman, *Lying in Court*.

30. Branigar, *No Villains*, 1.

31. Hutchinson, "President's Religious Faith," 365.

all Jehovah's witnesses, believed religion a racket and the clergy in general, including army chaplains, to be hypocrites. She harbored no special pride for "General Ike"; she was opposed to his West Point appointment. It was gross disrespect to the deceased for an army chaplain to officiate at the funeral.

The American Legion particularly, and also the Veterans of Foreign Wars, are repeatedly ringleaders in mob violence against Jehovah's witnesses. Hundreds of instances could be cited, but illustrative is the one occurring the Sunday before Mrs. Eisenhower's death, in nearby Iowa. There war veterans broke up a public Bible meeting of Jehovah's witnesses, doing much physical violence. Hardly appropriate, then, was it, for such to act as pallbearers? Only death could keep the body of Mrs. Eisenhower from walking away from a funeral so disrespectful of all that she stood for.[32]

Her funeral was considered a problem by the Watchtower because, in the 1940s, all involvement with the military, even in military funerals, had been forbidden by the Watchtower for decades. Even though violation of this rule was grounds for expulsion, Ida was still highly spoken of by the Witnesses even after she died.

Dwight's religious orientation as an adult in the 1990s was described as "moderate and tolerant, simple and firm," quite in contrast to the confrontational Watchtower sect of the first half of this century.[33] Although he stated his mother was highly "individualistic" and "not able to accept the dogma of any specific sect or denomination," Miller notes "that is what Eisenhower wanted to believe and perhaps on occasion actually did, but Ida herself contradicted it."[34]

After C. T. Russell died, Witnesses were normally required to rigidly conform to Watchtower beliefs, and little deviance was allowed. This was true even in areas most people regard as very minor, such as the celebration of birthdays. Violation of Watchtower requirements can result in total isolation, and not even Witnesses relatives can normally associate with disfellowshipped Witnesses. Another factor likely influencing Ida's acceptance by Witnesses may have been her easy-going personality. Ida, in the words of her grandson, John, was "a very good-humored person."[35] Nonetheless, violation of Watchtower norms no doubt created some conflicts.

32. Knorr, *Religion Void of Principle*, 7.
33. Fox, *Pro Ike*, 907.
34. Miller, *Ike the Soldier*, 78.
35. J. Eisenhower, letter to Jerry Bergman.

DID IDA EISENHOWER LEAVE
THE JEHOVAH'S WITNESSES?

No evidence exists that either parent was not a devoted Watchtower adherent when the Eisenhower boys were growing up or that Ida no longer saw herself as a Witness later in life. Ida's son John Eisenhower recalls attending Watchtower services with her in Abilene as late as 1938 when he was only sixteen.[36] Other letters Ida Eisenhower mailed at about the same time she allegedly wrote about her Witness commitment to Boeckel include a handwritten letter to fellow Witness Mrs. H. I. Lawson of Long Island, New York, mailed in 1943.[37] The authenticity of this letter has never been disputed. No evidence exists that only a year later she rejected Watchtower teachings or had resigned from the sect as some infer.

In addition, a front-page *Wichita Beacon* article (dated April 1943) about Ida's Watchtower assembly attendance gave no indication she was disenchanted with the Jehovah's Witnesses at this time.[38] The article stated "the 82-year-old mother of America's famous military leader . . . was the center of attraction at the meeting Sunday, and her name was heard in just about every conversation, speech and discussion. The program's subject was 'how to become a good Jehovah's Witness.'"

These facts do not prove the controversial 1943 letter is authentic, nor do they demonstrate the view that Ida became a Witness only when she was older and senile, as implied by some authors. Miller concluded Ida *never* left the Watchtower.[39] Evidence exists that as late as autumn of 1944 she was still actively involved in the Watchtower. Duncan noted in 1944 she had what the Watchtower terms a "Bible study" with a "Negro family."[40] A "Bible study" is the study of a Watchtower book, often with a person interested in becoming a Witness, such as someone the Witness met in their door-to-door ministry. This "Bible study" was usually the first step in becoming a Witness.

Conversely, some vague hints do exist that Ida's loyalty to the Watchtower may have waned as she grew older. All of her sons left the Watchtower, as did her husband, because they were opposed to some of their basic

36. J. Eisenhower, letter to Jerry Bergman.

37. Cole, *Jehovah's Witnesses.*

38. Fleming, *Ike's Mom,* 1.

39. Miller, *Ike the Soldier,* 79.

40. Duncan, *Christmas Prayers,* 28.

teachings. Furthermore, when Judge Rutherford became the Watchtower president in 1916, he introduced many—if not most—of their more objectionable teachings, such as their opposition to orthodox medicine, flag saluting, vaccines, blood transfusions, and the teaching of all other religions, all of which the Judge regarded as "a snare and a racket."

If Rutherford had not introduced these new ideas and had retained the teachings of the first president, C. T. Russell, in these areas, the Eisenhower family concerns about the Watchtower would likely not have been nearly as great. Russell's focus was on the return of Christ and the thousand-year reign of Christ, called the Millennium, was also a concern of many other Christians both in the 1800s and today—as illustrated by the explosive sale of the Left Behind series by Tim Lahaye, first published in the 1990s.

Importantly, when Rutherford took over the Watchtower as president and chief theologian, many (if not most) of the original Bible Students left the Watchtower due to the many doctrinal changes made by the new administration, and for Ida to leave then would not be unusual or unexpected. Furthermore, Ida may have been much more at home with the Bible Students that split off from the Watchtower after Rutherford began to introduce his more controversial teachings.

Although these events no doubt affected Ida Eisenhower's beliefs, no *direct* evidence exists that her allegiance to the Watchtower wavered, and all of the evidence, including interviews with individuals who knew her, indicate she died a faithful Watchtower believer. Even if Ida's allegiance to the Watchtower diminished as she got older, this would not affect the fact that all her boys were reared according to Watchtower principles, but it would help us to better understand Ida Eisenhower.

14

Pre-Presidency Life and Work

Religion has always been the most effective process of developing human character strong enough to forget the motivation of selfishness and to act on the larger concept of duty to God, to humanity, and to Country.[1]

IN JUNE 1942, WHEN Dwight was selected over 366 senior officers to command the American forces in Europe, the Dwight Eisenhower name soon "became a household word" in all of America.[2] After World War II ended, both the Democrats and Republicans explored the popular and highly respected general, then [president of Columbia University, as a possible presidential candidate. Some even called him "the new Lincoln."[3] Senator Henry Cabot Lodge and others pressured him to place his name on the GOP convention ballot.

After much deep soul searching and clear evidence of widespread support, Dwight decided to run as a Republican. He was the unanimous choice at the 1952 Republican Convention in Chicago, with Richard Nixon as his running mate.[4] His "magnificent warm smile" and persona of humility

1. Dwight Eisenhower, Speech to Chaplains Association Washington, DC, October 14, 1946.

2. Field, *Mister American*, 11.

3. Field, *Mister American*, 12.

4. Cohen, *Eisenhowers*, 20.

also helped to boost his popularity.[5] In short, Eisenhower was the perfect candidate at this time in our history because the "Cold War" problem then required a man of his skills and proven success in war.

Dwight D. Eisenhower (born October 14, 1890, died March 28, 1969) became the thirty-fourth President of the United States and served for two terms (from 1953 to 1961). In 1952 he received the largest number of votes ever recorded up to that time for a presidential candidate.[6] In 1956 he topped his own record prevailing by an even greater margin than in 1952.[7] An August 1955 Gallup Poll recorded a 79 percent approval rating for Eisenhower, an almost unheard-of level for a sitting president.[8] He also was the only modern president whose popularity never dropped below 50 percent.[9] In 1955, Dwight was widely recognized as the number one statesman in the world.[10]

The "caustic conclusions" about Eisenhower's presidency commonly voiced by some scholars in the 1950s had begun to radically change by the 1970s, partly as a result of a careful study of his administration. One major reason for this re-evaluation was the recent opening of several major collections of official records and Eisenhower's personal papers to scholars.[11]

A 1960s Gallup poll voted Eisenhower the most popular and admired living American.[12] In the year 2010, preparations began for a seventh presidential monument, this one dedicated to Eisenhower.[13] The first six are to Washington, Jefferson, Lincoln, both Teddy and Franklin Roosevelt, and Kennedy. This movement is not difficult to understand. Surveys now place Eisenhower in the list of the top ten best presidents in our history.[14] Larson noted that the lessons of several presidents after Eisenhower have allowed us to reflect on the Eisenhower era and, as a result, with the benefit of hindsight and a recent in-depth study, "we are now witnessing a flood of

5. Field, *Mister American*, 12.

6. Miller, *Piety along the Potomac*, 3.

7. Wicker, *Dwight D. Eisenhower*, 2.

8. Pusey, *Eisenhower: The President*, 289.

9. Hayward, *Politically Incorrect Guide*, 135.

10. Pusey *Eisenhower: The President*, 289.

11. Smith, *Faith and the Presidency*, 253; Pach, 1991, xii.

12. Jameson, *Heroes by the Dozen*, 183.

13. Shribman, *America Still Likes Ike*, A5.

14. Larson, *Eisenhower's World View*, 41.

books" on Eisenhower and, since then, "every book that has come out on Eisenhower has been favorable."[15]

He was so extraordinarily popular with the American people in the 1950s in part because of his personal appeal to the common people and their perception of his deeply ingrained and mature "spiritual values."[16] One representative survey of ministers from every part of the United States found they favored Eisenhower at a level of eight to one over Stevenson, a Unitarian.[17] His administration's' "significant interest in religion seemed to increase the public's esteem and admiration for the man from Abilene."[18]

One example is the *Episcopal Church News* editors asked both candidates in what way their religious convictions would affect their work as America's chief executive. Stevenson answered, "A man's personal religious beliefs had no proper place in our political life, except as they may influence his public acts and thus affect the public welfare." Eisenhower, by contrast, "insisted that only by trusting in God could he effectively carry out the responsibilities of the office and help the United States solve its problems."[19]

HIS WORLD VIEW: CREATIONISM

Eisenhower's family background and his life experiences shaped Dwight's faith more than sterile theological arguments or philosophical reasoning. A major Bible Student doctrine was belief in creationism. The importance of this doctrine is illustrated by the fact that acceptance of Darwinism is a disfellowshipping offense. The first book they published against evolution was an 1898 work titled *The Bible versus the Evolution Theory,* and the most recent book they published on this topic was the 1985 work called *Life— How Did It Get Here? By Evolution or By Creation?* The latter book was published in twenty-seven languages and, as of 2017, had a total printing of over thirty million copies. The Watchtower Society has also published hundreds of articles supporting creationism and has been critical of Darwinism since 1900.

This teaching took hold on Dwight: "the design of the universe, the reality of the conscience, the respect people felt for moral law, and the human

15. Larson, *Eisenhower's World View.*

16. Miller, *Piety along the Potomac,* 10; Grinder and Shaw, 2011.

17. Smith, *Faith and the Presidency,* 238.

18. Smith, *Faith and the Presidency,* 222.

19. Smith, *Faith and the Presidency,* 235.

craving for affection all persuaded him that God existed."[20] One of Eisenhower's favorite sayings was, "It takes no brains to be an atheist."[21] Dwight had an unshakable belief in the Bible teaching that God is the creator and sustainer of all life.[22]

Eisenhower's worldview may have influenced certain statements he made, such as his conclusion, based on his reading of our founders' writings, that America is a religious nation today because the country's fathers expressed their

> full reliance on 'the laws of nature and nature's God' and because they published before the world these self-evident truths: 'that all men are created equal, that they are endowed by their Creator with certain unalienable rights . . .' In contrast with this concept of the sacredness of life, modern atheistic dictatorships treat men as nothing more than animals . . . How many materialistic psychologists and smart-alec professors sneer that men invented God in a childish search for security; yet, I have noticed that men in the foxholes or at the moment of death turn to some higher Power for comfort and courage . . . although I have seldom displayed or discussed my religious philosophy with anyone, a deep Bible-centered faith has colored my life since childhood.[23]

Another example is Ike's statement that at the "core of our nation is belief in a Creator who has endowed all men with inalienable rights, including life, liberty and the pursuit of happiness. In that belief is our country's true hallmark, a faith that permeates every aspect of our political, social and family life."[24] Yet another example is a commencement speech that Dwight gave at Messiah College on May 29, 1965, when he said Messiah College's president "emphasized that man is not just an educated mule. He is a spiritual being at the same time. Therefore, you people educated in this kind of college and believing so definitely in the precepts of your church will be interested in the important part of man just as well as his physical being."[25]

He then suggested that the audience read the opening passages of the Declaration of Independence, where they would "find that our founding

20. Smith, *Faith and the Presidency*, 227.

21. Smith, *Faith and the Presidency*, 227.

22. Hutchinson, "President's Religious Faith," 369.

23. Quoted in Gammon, *All Believers Are Brothers*, 3–4.

24. Speech over radio and television, Washington, DC, December 3, 1959. From Eisenhower, *Quotable Eisenhower*, 85–86.

25. Copy in Messiah College archives, Eisenhower box.

fathers, in trying to explain the kind of government that they envisioned, laid out that, first of all, *we are created by some Supreme Being—a Creator—* and we are endowed with certain unalienable rights and among these are life, liberty, and the pursuit of happiness."[26]

In a talk he gave at Poughkeepsie, New York, on June 26, 1948, Eisenhower elaborated on this belief that the political freedoms we enjoy in America

> include a faith, related to some religion, that man is more than an animal, that he possesses a soul. If we have not that faith, then why should any of us admit that any other is born with equal rights to himself? Each of us instinctively recognizes, and our forefathers so stated, that an individual, because he was born, possesses certain rights. And to prove that we must go back and depend upon faith, and faith alone; and I say it is a faith, akin to religion, to most of us.[27]

Yet another example is a 1947 talk to the Daughters of the American Revolution, in which Eisenhower said insistence on "individual freedom springs from unshakable conviction in the dignity of man, a belief—a religious belief—that through the possession of a soul he is endowed with certain rights that are his not by the sufferance of others, but by reason of his very existence."[28] Five years later, at the dedication of the Eisenhower Presidential Museum in Abilene, Eisenhower said he believed in

> a Provident God whose hand supported and guided them; faith in themselves as the children of God, endowed with purposes beyond the mere struggle for survival; faith in their country and its principles that proclaimed man's right to freedom and justice, rights derived from his divine origin. Today, the nation they built stands as the world's mightiest temporal power, with its position still rooted in faith and in spiritual values.[29]

Morin concluded Dwight's belief about "religious faith and man's instinct to be free" were not only directly related, but that "faith in God is the necessary base for a free nation."[30] Morin gave an example that Dwight cited "the early Christians and the Jews" and that Dwight "often mused over the phrase in

26. Copy in Messiah College archives, Eisenhower box, page 3, emphasis mine.

27. Quoted in Taylor, *Speech at Poughkeepsie*, 50.

28. Quoted in Holl, *Religion, Politics, and the Evils of Communism*, 384.

29. Quoted in Holl, *Religion, Politics, and the Evils of Communism*, 384.

30. Morin, *Dwight D. Eisenhower*, 133.

the Declaration of Independence which says that all men 'are endowed by their Creator with certain inalienable rights . . .' The significant word . . . is 'Creator.' It signified to him that the American nation was founded on a basis of religious faith."[31] Dwight concluded, "A free government without a foundation of faith makes no sense," and this fact was a major strength of democracies in their conflicts with Communists.[32]

The importance of religion and creationism is clear in Dwight's conclusion that one "cannot explain free government in any other terms than religious. The founding fathers had to refer to the Creator to make their revolutionary experiment make sense; it was because "all men are endowed by their Creator with certain inalienable rights" that men could dare to be free."[33] He also wrote that the "central facts of human life are human freedom, human rights, human obligations—all expressing that human dignity which is a reflection of man's divine origin and destiny."[34]

Eisenhower concluded not only that "religion and democracy were closely linked" but that "free government . . . had a spiritual basis."[35] In a letter to his lifelong friend Swede Hazlett, he wrote, "I believe fanatically in . . . the rights of the individual . . . because of his being created in the image of a supreme being . . ."[36] In a speech given to Congress in Washington, DC, on January 5, 1957, President Eisenhower said the

> Middle East is the birthplace of three great religions—Moslem, Christian and Hebrew. Mecca and Jerusalem are more than places on the map. They symbolize religions which teach that the spirit has supremacy over matter and that the individual has a dignity and rights of which no despotic government can rightfully deprive him. It would be intolerable if the holy places of the Middle East should be subjected to a rule that glorifies atheistic materialism.[37]

A critical factor influencing Eisenhower's administration was his conclusion, as "'eloquently stated' in the Declaration of Independence. Those who settled America . . . had 'faith in a Provident God whose hand supported and guided them; faith in themselves as the children of God, endowed with

31. Morin, *Dwight D. Eisenhower*, 9, 133–34.

32. Morin, *Dwight D. Eisenhower*, 134.

33. Quoted in Hutchinson, "President's Religious Faith," 363.

34. Quoted in Hutchinson, "President's Religious Faith," 367.

35. Smith, *Faith and the Presidency*, 230.

36. Quoted in Chernus, *General Eisenhower*, 91.

37. Eisenhower, *At Ease*, 128.

purposes beyond mere struggle for survival'; and faith in the principles of freedom and justice that were of 'divine origin.'"[38] This translated into all men being created equal, all descendants of Adam and Eve, all brothers and sisters. This view was in great contrast to the Nazi worldview belief that all men were not created equal, and the key to a great and prosperous society is the application of Darwinian eugenics. The government must, for the good of society, encourage the best and brightest race to have large families and prevent inferior humans from causing race degeneration by interbreeding with the superior Aryan race. This issue was a main motivator of Eisenhower to prevail in a war he saw as good against absolute evil.

38. Quoted in Smith, *Faith and the Presidency*, 229–30.

15

Questions about Eisenhower's Piety

EXACTLY HOW SINCERE DWIGHT'S outward display of piety was is difficult for outsiders to judge. Some claim his religious utterances were made primarily to enhance his popularity and win votes.[1]

A confounding factor is the fact that America was more receptive to theism (and Christianity) when Eisenhower was a general and president than today. It was also the time of the worst war the world has ever seen, and during war and national disasters religion is more openly expressed, and its expression is more accepted. D'Este notes that in the United States June 6 was the national day of prayer, one of the most extraordinary days in American history. When the American troops landed on the beach of Normandy in France on D-Day, news of the

> landings spread like wildfire through the night and early morning. Church bells tolled, stores closed, Broadway shows and sporting events were called off as Americans in record numbers flocked to churches. Roosevelt called the invasion of Normandy on June 6, 1944, "a mighty endeavor to preserve . . . our civilization and to set free a suffering humanity." That night FDR went on national radio to deliver a prayer for "our sons, pride of our Nation," asking God to "[g]ive strength to their arms, stoutness to their hearts, steadfastness in their faith . . . in our united crusade."[2]

1. Smith, *Faith and the Presidency*, 233.
2. D'Este, *Eisenhower: A Soldier's Life*, 532.

Another factor is that both the media and the intelligentsia, as well as many Eisenhower biographers, were liberals who "had rarely seriously explored the religious culture of the American heartland which Dwight was reared in."[3] For this reason, many pundits erroneously concluded Dwight's religious views were too political, too secular, and he only expressed religiousness to respond to what he felt was the need, as a politician, to appear religious.

ARGUMENTS AGAINST DWIGHT'S PIETY CLAIMS

One argument against Eisenhower's inner piety is the well-known fact he could (and at times did) use very strong off-color language, including taking God's name in vain.[4] An example was:

> Eisenhower was brought up in an atmosphere of intense piety and professed to be the most religious man he knew. Yet when chided by General MacArthur for never attending a place of worship Ike replied that he had "gone to the West Point Chapel so g.d. often," he was never going inside a church again. As president, of course, he formally joined the Presbyterians and behaved in public as if God were honorary chairman of the Republican Party. His private exclamations, however, remained a curious combination of the sacred and the profane—in the Cabinet, for example, he was liable to blurt out, "Goddamnit, we forgot the silent prayer."[5]

Ida herself described Dwight as her "most troublesome boy," who possessed a temper that would "flash quicker than lightning in August."[6] He was not alone in this family trait. Dwight's father also at times "completely lost control of himself."[7] Dwight most always expressed his temper in words, not in physical violence. It is often assumed strong language is inconsistent with being religious, a stereotype based on the popular view of conservative Christianity.

Actually, Witnesses, especially during Rutherford's thirty-year presidency (1916–1946), commonly used very strong, even obscene,

---

3. Holl, *Civil Religion*, 122; see also Cosmin and Lachman, *One Nation*.

4. Smith, *Faith and the Presidency*, 257.

5. Brendon, *Ike; His Life and Times*, 9–10.

6. Angelo, *First Mothers*, 74.

7. Angelo, *First Mothers*, 82, 102, 103.

language—even in their religious journals, which were considered quasi-inspired.[8] The issue of using strong language by Witnesses even ended up as part of several court cases.[9]

It must be remembered that as Commander in Chief of the largest war effort in history, Dwight was under enormous pressure—especially after repeated defeats by the better trained and, at first, better equipped German military machine. In the African theater, after the move to Algiers, Eisenhower's frayed nerves was obvious.

> German air raids, some of them heavy, robbed him of sleep. Inconsequential things tended to bother him, such as a letter from a woman in Texas who wrote to chastise Eisenhower for his use of profanity and suggest that his energies would be put to better use in prayer. "The General was sort of annoyed by that, and hurt too. He said: 'Damn it, I don't curse. I just use some words as adjectives.'"[10]

Others argue his piety was hypocritical done for political gain. Professor Holl notes Eisenhower declared July 4, 1953, a day of prayer and penance—then hypocritically spent the day fishing, playing golf, and bridge.[11] In one study of Eisenhower's faith, Smith concluded Dwight did not have a well-developed biblical worldview grounded in extensive study of the Scriptures and Christian literature. Of note is the fact that his large Gettysburg home library contained relatively few religious books, but a large number of American history books.

The charge that his piety was for show is likely invalid for several other reasons. The reality is few of us fully live up to the ideals we espouse. Conversely, most Eisenhower scholars who have studied Dwight's religious behavior have concluded his "faith was sincere and more experientially than intellectually grounded" and "few doubted the sincerity of Eisenhower's faith."[12] The fact is Eisenhower found much comfort in his experientially grounded faith, a conclusion grounded in interviews with those who spent

---

8. The vice-president of the Watchtower Society then, attorney Hayden Covington, was also known to use strong profanities.

9. *Moyle v. Rutherford.* 261 App. Div. 9698, 26 N.Y.S. 2nd 860 (1940), 568–74; and the "fighting words case," *Chaplinsky v. New Hampshire,* 315 U.S. 568 (1942).

10. D'Este, *Eisenhower: A Soldier's Life,* 377–78.

11. Holl, *Civil Religion,* 120.

12. Smith, *Faith and the Presidency,* 254.

much of their life with him, such as Andrew Goodpaster. Many of his top officials who were close to him were convinced of his sincerity.[13]

Secondly, many of Dwight's major religious claims were made *after* he left office. Miller claimed Eisenhower went "well beyond the standard obeisance to God of a public figure" and did not use God terminology simply to win political favor with voters, but as a result of his "deeply felt religious faith," a phrase he "constantly used."[14] That his religious claims were sincere is also supported by Eisenhower's account of the accident he experienced when he was still a teenager:

> Of the many instances when religious faith has sustained me in life, the first came when I was a teen-ager, and [this event] marked a turning point in my life. I had fallen, skinned my left knee and, when a painful infection later became so bad that I fell ill with a high fever, my parents discovered my swollen and discolored leg. Old Dr. Conklin, the family physician, eventually advised amputation to save my life. When the horror of this prospect swept over me, I raised from the bed to shout, "Not me! I won't allow it! I'd rather die!" Later I made my older brother Edgar promise not to let the doctor cut off my leg no matter what happened, and he literally stood guard duty outside my bedroom during every call of the doctor at our home. Though I was desperately ill for two weeks, my parents respected my own decision. At the same time they, both deeply religious, included in their daily prayers petitions for my recovery, never doubting that the Almighty would hear them. In two weeks I was out of bed and able to walk. To me, this demonstration of their faith was a lesson I never forgot.[15]

Dwight also believed the dictum "God helps those who help themselves." The illness that struck him in 1949 was a turning point for Eisenhower. He finally fully recognized he had been careless in taking care of his health and accepted the fact his health was ultimately his personal responsibility. He also

> believed strongly in the power of his own volition, and he was always leery of the phrase "With the help of God." As he once explained, . . . "I believe that the Lord deals us a hand, that's right, but he expects *us* to play it." He was especially confident of playing

13. Smith, *Faith and the Presidency*, 234.

14. Miller, *Piety Along the Potomac*, 34.

15. Quoted in Gammon, *All Believers Are Brothers*, 2.

his hand at this moment in time because he was coming off a great victory of willpower. He had stopped smoking.[16]

Remember, by the time he was eighteen, Dwight had personally read the entire Bible twice and continued this habit as an adult.[17] Dwight was also active in "witnessing for Christ." For example, when he was still president of Columbia University,

> he agreed to be a "witness for Christ" at Riverside Church on Laymen's Sunday, October 16, 1949. "I don't feel qualified to preach a sermon," he commented, "but I would like to read one chapter from the Bible that has helped me more than anything else I have ever read." That chapter was Romans 12, which are emphasized the "simple virtues" that marked his own life.[18]

When asked what was his favorite book, the first book on Dwight's list was the Bible, the second was *Connecticut Yankee in King Arthur's Court*, and the third was *The Works of Shakespeare*. When asked for his favorite Bible verse, he could not give a *single* favorite, but used Psalm 127:1 and 2 Chronicles 7:14 for his 1953 inauguration and Psalm 33:12 for his 1957 inauguration. And Ike later stated he believed "the American people will have to get back to biblical Christianity" in order to prosper.[19]

16. Lasby, *Eisenhower's Heart Attack*, 50.
17. Morin, *Dwight D. Eisenhower*, 13.
18. American Bible Society, *Dwight Eisenhower's Bible-Based*.
19. Quoted in Hopper, *Eisenhower Project*, 141–42.

16

Religion a Handicap
When Running for Office

SOME OF HIS CRITICS openly argued Eisenhower's religious background made him unfit to become president: "Both Eisenhower and Stevenson were vigorously challenged by some Protestant[s] . . . for their religious ties. The association of Eisenhower's mother with the Jehovah's Witnesses was exploited to make the GOP candidate appear as an 'anti-Christian cultist' and a 'foe of patriotism.'" [1] Furthermore, some argued President Eisenhower's devout religious beliefs and the claim he was guided by biblical principles in some ways hurt him and his policies.[2] Some critics even claimed that, due to his religiousness, Eisenhower was ill-informed, naive, and lacked intelligence.

The usual political mudslinging—such as Truman claiming Dwight was "communistically inclined" —probably did less to hurt him than many candidates because most of the charges were so obviously false. John Birch Society founder Robert Welch even called Dwight a communist agent.[3] In fact, most mudslinging was so inappropriate—such as Judge Armstrong's calling him the "incompetent and self-glorifying Jewish Ike Eisenhower"[4] —that it probably did Ike more good than harm. Nonetheless, in contrast

1. Roy, *Apostles of Discord*, 20.
2. Smith, *Faith and the Presidency*, 248.
3. Seldes, *Never Tire of Protesting*, 219.
4. Quoted in Seldes, *Never Tire of Protesting*, 215–16.

to these irresponsible charges, Dwight's religious background (especially his personal religious beliefs) was a significant issue in his presidential campaign.[5]

REASONS FOR RELIGIOUS DISTANCE

Some reasons for the press's and Ike's lack of openness about his Watchtower background include embarrassment over the Watchtower's staunch opposition to saluting the flag and other patriotic activities because Witnesses endeavor to be neutral in all political conflicts. Jehovah's Witnesses were generally scorned then, not only by the media, but also by most churches and by society in general, especially during the first half of the 1900s. Eisenhower's one-time speech writer, Stanley High, once wrote, "Jehovah's Witnesses make hate a religion," and "on the rest of U.S . . . they look down their spiritual noses."[6]

Although saluting the flag was a major issue, as discussed earlier in this book, other reasons existed for Eisenhower to distance himself from the Watchtower. One is they were not "anti-Christian" or "communistic," but just . . . different.

Other concerns included the Watchtower's post-C. T. Russell opposition to the use of aluminum cooking utensils, fluoridation of drinking water, vaccinations, the germ theory, medicine in general, and their advocating many ineffectual medical "cures" including radio solar pads, radiesthesia, radionics (quack treatment of disease by use of magnetism, vibration analysis, and electronics), iridiagnosis (diagnosis by evaluating the iris of the eye), the grape cancer cure, phrenology (reading bumps on the head to determine personality), and others. Most all of these concerns were dropped after Rutherford died on January 8, 1942.[7] Of note is the fact, except for their remaining rules about blood transfusions, advocation for all of these other medical treatments and "cures" have now been abandoned. As for blood transfusions, only transfusions of *whole* blood and its four main parts are still not allowed.[8]

---

5. Keller, "Intellectuals and Eisenhower," 229; Schaaf, *Mamie Doud Eisenhower*, 35; Gowran, *Ike Sheds All Aloofness*.

6. High, *Armageddon Inc*, 18.

7. Bergman, *Jehovah's Witnesses*.

8. Muramoto, *Recent Developments*.

In view of this history of supporting various medical nostrums, it is clear Dwight Eisenhower had reasons to hide his Watchtower background when he ran for president.

SOME INFLUENTIAL PEOPLE OPPOSE IKE

In addition, some influential persons were opposed to Eisenhower expressing *any* form of theism. For example, the well-known journalist H. L. Mencken's feelings about religion (and Jews) are clear in the following account about his publisher, Alfred Knopf. Mencken condemned Knopf for publishing a book of prayers written for soldiers and tried to convince him to not publish such "disgraceful" works but "got nowhere." He concluded a book of prayers disgraced Knopf and its trademark because "such trash undid the work of years, and left the house imprint ridiculous."[9] Mencken added that Alfred's wife, Blanche,

> undertook to defend them, on the ground that they sold well. Yes, I said, they sold the firm down the river. She said that there would be fewer of them hereafter, and that she was making hard efforts to unearth better books. I doubt it. She and Alfred have both lost most of their old skill and intelligence in that direction. They actually admire some of the worst books they are printing. The idea for the book of prayers, she said, came from Bernard Smith, the sales manager. What his name was before he changed it I do not know. *He, too, is a Jew and moreover, a jackass.*[10]

In the book were prayers by Generals Eisenhower and George Patton. Dwight said his prayer was based on one he once heard a company commander reciting "to his men, on a wet, cold night, just before starting a march to the front line," and that it struck him

> more forcibly than almost any other I have heard. Possibly the drama of the occasion had something to do with my reactions, but in any event, it was a better prayer than I could compose. While I cannot repeat it verbatim, I am sending it to you in words that approximate the original.[11]

The prayer by Eisenhower included in the book (which the editor claimed was revised especially for the Knopf volume) was as follows:

9. Fecher, *Diary of H. L. Mencken*, 316–17.

10. Fecher, *Diary of H. L. Mencken*, 316–17, italics added.

11. Mygatt, *Soldiers' and Sailors*, 13.

The Eisenhower presidential campaign in Baltimore, Maryland, on of September 1952

ALMIGHTY God, we are about to be committed to a task from which some of us will not return. We go willingly to this hazardous adventure because we believe that those concepts of human dignity, rights and justice that Your Son expounded to the world, and which are respected in the government of our beloved country, are in peril of extinction from the earth. We are ready to sacrifice ourselves for our country and our God. We do not ask, individually, for our safe return. But we earnestly pray that You will help each of us to do his full duty. Permit none of us to fail a comrade in the fight. Above all, sustain us in our conviction in the justice and righteousness of our cause so that we may rise above all terror of the enemy and come to You, if called, in the humble pride of the good soldier and in the certainty of Your infinite mercy. *Amen.*

General Dwight D. Eisenhower

United States Army

Supreme Commander of American-British Forces in Europe[12]

12. Quoted in Mygatt, *Soldiers' and Sailors*, 13.

Mencken's anti-religious sentiments were common among media persons and professors alike, although their conclusions were usually not voiced as openly or blatantly as Mencken did.

ATTEMPTS TO AVOID DISCUSSING
HIS WATCHTOWER BACKGROUND

Dwight, or at least his supporters, attempted to avoid some of the problems of associating with the Witnesses by trying to ignore his Watchtower background. Dwight's 1952 Republican national sheets listed his religion as "River Brethren" and the White House press office also records Ike's parents as River Brethren.[13] When pressured to reveal his religion, Dwight stated "Protestant," adding he was not a member of any particular church.[14]

When President, Dwight's personal assistant, Albert Washburn, wrote to a woman in answer to a question about Dwight's religion that he was a "Protestant." Specifically, his religious heritage was given as "River Brethren," and Washburn claimed Dwight's mother had "become interested" in the Witness work only in "her later years,"[15] implying the Witness faith had no impact on Dwight's religious life.

The Eisenhower boys' Watchtower background is not widely known or acknowledged, due in part to the antagonism many people had (and still have today) against the Watchtower followers.[16] This antagonism is illustrated in the wording of a quote that claimed "late in life" Ida became "of all things, a member of the sect known as Jehovah's Witnesses . . ."[17] The problem is also illustrated in the difficulty Dwight Eisenhower had in responding to inquiries about his religious past:

> Even years later, after Dwight was in the White House, letters would arrive from many parts of the country demanding to know: was it really true that Ike's mother had been a Jehovah's Witness? And if so, how was it possible that he had never admitted it publicly? Composing diplomatic answers to such mail was one of the least pleasant tasks facing his Presidential secretariat.[18]

13. Freudenheim, *Religion of Ike's Parents.*

14. *Evening News,* Harrisburg, Pennsylvania, March 26, 1952, 18.

15. Quoted in Keller, "Intellectuals and Eisenhower," 236.

16. Sellers, *How Americans View.*

17. Gunther, *Eisenhower, The Man,* 52.

18. Faber, *Mothers of American Presidents,* 47.

Eisenhower took a strong stand against certain forms of religious intolerance, which may have stemmed from his knowledge of the severe persecution that Jehovah's Witnesses faced, especially during World War II.[19] Others claimed Eisenhower identified with Protestantism and was not always sensitive to the concerns of Catholics. This factor could relate to the Watchtower's strong anti-Catholic stand, especially during Rutherford's presidency.

Conversely, Dwight's religious activities produced much support from many Protestant ministers—one poll found the public generally preferred him over his opponent, Adlai Stevenson, by a whopping margin of eight to one.[20] Ike's popularity with the common people was often attributed to his overt religiousness. During the Cold War, Ike played "what amounted to a pastoral role" in comforting the American people with his "wise leadership" and "spiritual example."[21]

Eisenhower even "promoted religious values" in a way that "linked personal and religious faith."[22] This factor proved to be a major attraction for many, if not most, Americans. The closest parallels to Dwight Eisenhower were the presidencies of Ronald Reagan, George H. W. Bush, and George Bush, in which moral and religious values also played a key role in their elections and, in the case of Reagan and George H. W. Bush, their reelections. This was all helped by the post-war "religious resurgence that some supporters called a 'revival.'"[23]

Keller claimed a "central organizing theme of Eisenhower's first presidential campaign was religious in character, Ike even called it a 'crusade.'"[24] Dwight's published war memoirs even used the semi-religious term "crusade" in the title—*Crusade in Europe*.[25] He decided to run as a Republican even though he had earlier declared he was a Democrat.[26] One speculation as to why is because the Republican Party was then, as it is now, more conservative religiously.

19. Keller, "Intellectuals and Eisenhower," 281–83.

20. Gustafson, *Religion of a President*, 612.

21. Pierard and Linder, *Civil Religion*, 184–85.

22. Pierard and Linder, *Civil Religion*, 185.

23. Pierard and Linder, *Civil Religion*, 189; Linder, *Eisenhower, Dwight David*.

24. Keller, "Intellectuals and Eisenhower," 229.

25. Eisenhower, *Crusade in Europe*.

26. Ferrell, Eisenhower Was a Democrat, 134

After noting Dwight "grew up with faith in the power of prayer," Morin related that in 1952,

> shortly before Eisenhower was to appear before his first press conference as a candidate for the Republican nomination for president, he was in Suite 600 in the Sunflower Hotel in Abilene. Two of his Kansas backers came to the hotel to escort him to the conference. At the door they were asked to wait. Eisenhower was praying.[27]

Dwight allocated about 10 percent of his presidential campaign speeches to "religious appearances," and the major issues he covered in his speeches at non-religious events often had a "religious dimension."[28] While campaigning, Eisenhower "often spoke about religion and the value of prayer and singing of religious songs."[29] His speeches were so packed with spiritual messages that some of his advisors urged him to tone down the religious content—something he refused to do, arguing, "America must lead a crusade to defeat the enemies of Christianity and Godless atheism."[30]

As Holl documented, every major Eisenhower biographer now "acknowledges the importance of religion in Eisenhower's upbringings."[31] To fully understand his presidency, it is also necessary to understand the many efforts he made to advance Christianity during his administration. Some argue he did more than almost any other president to encourage the development of religious values, specifically Christian values, in America. He was also regarded as one of the most religious presidents in American history.[32]

While Eisenhower seemed spiritually transformed when he took office, the "rest of the government had been undergoing its own profound reaffirmation, publicly acknowledging American ideas and the country's belief in God."[33] Some examples of this profound reaffirmation will now be discussed.

27. Morin, *Dwight D. Eisenhower*, 13.
28. Keller, "Intellectuals and Eisenhower," 230–31.
29. Keller, "Intellectuals and Eisenhower," 233.
30. Smith, *Faith and the Presidency*, 234–35.
31. Holl, *Civil Religion*, 119–20.
32. Holl, *Civil Religion*.
33. Moore, *Faith and the Presidency*, 334.

INAUGURATION BEGINS WITH PRAYER

On Inauguration Day, Eisenhower joined Richard Nixon and about 140 members of his administration for a preinaugural church service. Elson claimed this was the first time a president had attended such a service and invited his major administrative staff.[34] Eisenhower's first formal religious act as president was to preface his inaugural address with a prayer he wrote hours before he was sworn in as president. This was not the norm before him; he violated the tradition from the start of the ceremony with his prayer, and knew he would be creating a precedent.[35] At the inauguration, Dwight firmly grasped his wife by each shoulder, and

> bent and kissed her cheek. She gasped with surprise, flashed him the briefest of smiles, and regained her composure. The tens of thousands of spectators who saw this unprecedented action buzzed excitedly; no president had ever publicly kissed his wife after taking the oath of office. In a flash of movement, President Eisenhower was back at the raised desk, ready to break another precedent. Instead of beginning his inaugural address, his first words as Chief Executive were a prayer to Almighty God.[36]

When Eisenhower was sworn in as president before Chief Justice Vinson on January 20, 1953, Dodd recorded he said the following during the ceremony:

> "My friends, before I begin the expression of those thoughts that I deem appropriate . . . [to] ask that you bow your heads." Low exclamations of surprise rippled along the press tables, for this prayer was not a scheduled part of the program. Turning the "inaugural platform into an altar of worship," the president, the first ever to open his inaugural address with a plea for divine guidance, addressed his first words, not to the nation, but to God . . . the prayer, which he had composed himself.[37]

The prayer he then said, which Dwight had written shortly before he was driven to the capitol to take the oath of office,[38] was as follows:

---

34. Keller, "Intellectuals and Eisenhower," 251–52.

35. Pierard, *Civil Religion*, 116.

36. Brandon, *Mamie Doud Eisenhower*, 307.

37. Dodd, "Religious Background," 1–2.

38. Moore, *One Nation under God*, 333; Morin, *Dwight D. Eisenhower*.

> Almighty God, as we stand here at this moment, my future associates in the executive branch of government join me in beseeching that Thou will make full and complete our dedication to the service of the people in this throng and their fellow citizens everywhere. Give us, we pray, the power to discern clearly right from wrong, and allow all our words and actions to be governed thereby, and by the laws of this land. Especially we pray that our concern shall be for all the people regardless of station, race or calling. May cooperation be permitted and be the mutual aim of those who under the concepts of our Constitution, hold to differing political faiths, so that all may work for the good of our beloved country and for Thy glory. Amen.[39]

Dwight ended his address with the following admonition: "This is the work that awaits us all, to be done with bravery, with charity, and with prayer to Almighty God."[40] Observers noted that after the prayer a "rustle of surprise swept the great audience gathered in Washington for his first inauguration when he prefaced his speech with a prayer."[41] Eisenhower's Abilene friend, Henry Jameson, noted the "world was impressed by the immortal Inaugural Prayer he scribbled on the back of an envelope en route to the Capitol, but Eisenhower didn't see anything particularly unusual about it. It came natural to him."[42]

The Results of the 1952 Presidential Election.
Note even a few Southern States Supported Eisenhower

39. Quoted in Keller, "Intellectuals and Eisenhower," 254; and Schaaf, *Mamie Doud Eisenhower*, 32.

40. Moore, *One Nation under God*, 334.

41. Morin, *Dwight D. Eisenhower*, 13.

42. Jameson, *They Still Call Him Ike*, 41.

THE PUBLIC'S REACTION TO HIS PIETY

The public reaction to Eisenhower's prayer was so positive that "Thousands of letters poured into the White House from Republicans and Democrats alike applauding his act" and the administration received a large number of requests for copies of the text.[43] Dwight, in turn, was "surprised at the widespread comment on what seemed wholly natural to him."[44] In response to the demand, the Republican Party printed a large number of copies of the prayer with a beatific image of Eisenhower on the cover.

Dwight's prayer was even set to music by M. Robert Rogers, the chairman for the President's Committee for Arts and Sciences.[45] On January 8, 1957, Eisenhower sat with his wife in Constitution Hall to listen to the Howard University Choir sing his prayer while the National Symphony Orchestra provided musical background. Perret added the prayer would be used by the new administration in a private meeting

> at the Commodore Hotel in New York on January 12, 1953. Eisenhower had called his cabinet members, and Nixon, to meet with him there for two days to discuss various aspects of the transition, to finalize inaugural arrangements and to hear the draft of his inaugural address. As the waiters cleared the table after lunch, he asked Ezra Taft Benson to open what amounted to his first cabinet meeting with a prayer. A surprised and delighted Benson did so.[46]

President Eisenhower's proposal to open his cabinet meetings with prayer also garnered a fair amount of attention and support. Before he agreed to implement this new policy, Eisenhower decided support for it "would have to be almost unanimous."[47] After determining he had the support needed, President Eisenhower initiated the practice of opening cabinet meetings with prayer, both silent and, occasionally, spoken prayer.

Not all Americans supported Eisenhower's overtly religious stand. The Freethinkers of America denounced his inaugural prayer as "wholly uncalled for . . . display" of religion,[48] but otherwise very few persons

43. Smith, *Faith and the Presidency*, 228.

44. Morin, *Dwight D. Eisenhower*, 13.

45. Keller, "Intellectuals and Eisenhower," 254.

46. Perret, *Eisenhower*, 429.

47. Keller, "Intellectuals and Eisenhower," 257.

48. Quoted in Smith, *Faith and the Presidency*, 228.

complained his policies violated the separation of church and state.[49] One example is secular humanist Paul Blanshard, who argued the inauguration prayer was a symbol of what he believed was diluting the division between religion and government in Washington, namely, an unacceptable fusion of the concepts of God and government.[50]

IKE JOINED THE PRESBYTERIAN CHURCH

The question of why Dwight was not a church member until late in life has repeatedly surfaced.[51] Long-time family friend Henry Jameson claimed Dwight's career in the military "made it difficult to be a regular church-goer until he was out of uniform. But few who knew him ever questioned that he was a devout man."[52]

When Dwight ran for president, the wife of *Time* magazine founder, journalist Clare Booth Luce, wrote that Eisenhower told her his family did not believe one had to join a church to be a faithful Christian.[53] Eisenhower added, "I would have nothing but contempt for myself if I were to join a church in order to be nominated President of the United States. I think that would be an unbearable piece of hypocrisy."[54]

This position is also supported by Dwight's attempt to keep his religion private. When he joined the Presbyterian Church, he told the minister he did not want his joining reported to the press. When it was leaked to the press, his reaction was to threaten to leave the church.[55]

Luce convinced Dwight to join a church only by explaining to him he was a role model for the nation's youth and asked, "What would happen on Sunday mornings when the young were told that they have to go to church and they responded with 'Why do I have to go to church? The President of the United States has never gone to church and refuses to go to church.'" To this Eisenhower reportedly responded, "Oh, boy, I never thought of that." Luce added that instead of thinking the decision was hypocritical, Eisenhower realized it was "a constructive and necessary thing you have to do for

49. Smith, *Faith and the Presidency*, 231.
50. Blanshard, *God and Man*, 13.
51. Moore, *One Nation under God*, 333.
52. Jameson, *They Still Call Him Ike*, 41
53. Smith, *Faith and the Presidency*, 223.
54. Quoted in Keller, "Intellectuals and Eisenhower," 238.
55. Keller, "Intellectuals and Eisenhower," 252.

the morals and religion of the rising generation, not to mention your own contemporaries."

Mrs. Luce then suggested Eisenhower embrace the Presbyterian Church, the church that Mamie was a long-time member of, and the church in which they were married.[56] Also, many of the Eisenhower's political associates—including John Foster Dulles and Douglass McKay—were already members of the Presbyterian Church.[57] Dwight attended church the week after he had this discussion with Mrs. Luce and faithfully attended after that date. On February 1, 1953, the second Sunday after Dwight's inauguration, he was baptized in the National Presbyterian Church in Washington, DC.[58] Dwight even often attended church by himself if Mamie was unable to attend with him.[59]

Moore concluded Dwight's decision to "join a church was no half-hearted conversion, rather Eisenhower firmly believed he had been elected president of a country founded on basic religious principles and he needed to show his spiritual fidelity."[60] Milton Eisenhower believed that Dwight joined a church to provide "spiritual stimulation . . . to protect American democracy and freedom in the world."[61]

RELIGIOUS TOLERANCE OF A CHURCH MEMBER

Many of those who attacked Eisenhower's religion did so on the grounds that he "never joined a church until after he became president," implying that his Sunday worship as president "smacked of hypocrisy."[62] Although most of Eisenhower's adult years "were spent outside organized religion," and he was sixty-three before he formally joined a church, his lifelong behavior, personal statements, and beliefs on religion must be evaluated when judging his religious life.[63]

56. Keller, "Intellectuals and Eisenhower," 238.

57. Gustafson, *Religion of a President*, 612.

58. Smith, *Faith and the Presidency*, 224.

59. Slater, *Ike I Knew*, 188–89.

60. Moore, *One Nation under God*, 333.

61. Quoted in Smith, *Faith and the Presidency*, 224.

62. Fuller and Green, *God in the White House*, 218.

63. Dodd, *Early Career*, 233.

When he did attend church, Ike told his son, John, "I enjoy going to church. You always get an idea or two."[64] He must have enjoyed going: he regularly attended as president and even circulated some of the sermons he heard among members of his staff and cabinet.[65]

Others even accused Eisenhower of being religiously intolerant.[66] This charge had more to do with perceptions of favoritism, or his efforts to get the administration's attention on some issue, than with intolerance. This accusation could also relate to Eisenhower's strong religious beliefs and opinions. At times, he was caught in the middle of the liberal-conservative religious war, with each side trying to claim he sided with the other side.

Yet others have accused Eisenhower of the opposite—holding to a permissive, simple religion largely for appearances instead of adhering to well-founded, firmly held theological views.[67] Some complained Dwight watered down specifics and became a "very fervent believer in a very vague religion," a religion "designed to appeal to the 'widest possible public.'"[68] Some also felt he failed to recognize "false and bad religion" and the need to evaluate the claims made by various churches.[69] This allegation is openly false, as is obvious from his rejection of some Witness ideas and the acceptance of others.

As president, it is well-documented Dwight promoted both religious tolerance and the furtherance of the "spiritual basis for the nation's government."[70] The Eisenhower administration tried to be "neutral" and not favor one religious group over another, but did make exceptions. Keller noted one exception was the Presbyterians, in which he concluded Eisenhower was "exceptionally active," especially in many of their endless fundraising projects. Eisenhower also tried to provide "a higher profile for Protestantism in the nation's capital."[71]

He "maintained very cordial relations with most of the nation's religious communities," however, and frequently met with religious delegations, and "sent hundreds of messages to religious gatherings and groups,

64. J. Eisenhower, letter to Jerry Bergman.
65. Gustafson, *Religion of a President*, 612.
66. Keller, "Intellectuals and Eisenhower," 271.
67. Holl, *Civil Religion*, 122, 124.
68. Smith, *Faith and the Presidency*, 232–33.
69. Smith, *Faith and the Presidency*, 233.
70. Keller, "Intellectuals and Eisenhower," 266.
71. Keller, "Intellectuals and Eisenhower," 266.

and spoke to numerous religious assemblies."[72] His own mixed religious background led him "to minimize theological differences and stress the importance of religious toleration."[73] In many ways, Eisenhower became an ecumenical religious leader, which explains why "hundreds of ordinary citizens wrote to the president each week to ask him to help them solve their personal problems or to answer their religious questions."[74]

In short, Eisenhower did attempt to show sensitivity to all religions, such as when he appointed a Catholic to the Supreme Court "because so many issues were coming before the Court involving the Catholic Church."[75] Catholic William Brennan was selected by President Eisenhower and sworn in as a Supreme Court judge on October 16, 1956. Dwight stressed that regardless of our religious or other differences, prayer has "bound all Americans together in their efforts to reach out toward the Infinite."[76]

72. Smith, *Faith and the Presidency*, 222.

73. Smith, *Faith and the Presidency*, 231.

74. Smith, *Faith and the Presidency*, 253.

75. Keller, "Intellectuals and Eisenhower," 283.

76. Holl, *Civil Religion*, 128

17

Prayer in Ike's World and the Nation

MANY EXAMPLES EXIST TO illustrate the fact that prayer was central in Ike's life and presidency. This fact, as we will show, influenced almost every aspect of his two terms in office. It also influenced the nation in more ways than one.

THE PRAYER BREAKFAST

Eisenhower also began the Christian prayer breakfast tradition in the White House. As Milton claimed, since childhood he and his family had always prayed before each meal.[1] Thus, it is no surprise the regular prayer breakfast was another religious practice first instigated by the Eisenhower administration.[2] This practice, influenced by Billy Graham and U.S. Senator Frank Carlson, was originally called the Presidential Prayer Breakfast. The event name was soon changed to the National Prayer Breakfast to include all Americans.

The first Presidential Prayer Breakfast, held in February, 1953, was attended by over five hundred congressmen, cabinet members, Supreme Court justices, and others.[3] As a result of its popularity, the breakfasts were moved to the Hilton Mayflower Hotel, where an average of four hundred usually attended. Mormon Conrad Hilton, a strong supporter of the prayer

1. Antrim, *Why the President*.
2. Keller, "Intellectuals and Eisenhower," 259.
3. Smith, *Faith and the Presidency*, 232.

breakfast, underwrote the event for several years.[4] The event proved so popular—several thousand eventually attended—certain logistical problems, including high costs and security, were soon raised by the staff. The prayer breakfast proved especially popular with foreign ambassadors. The practice soon spread, and prayer breakfasts were set up in cities throughout the United States.[5]

Both houses of Congress sponsored prayer breakfasts, and when Ike was asked if he wanted to participate, Carlson claimed Eisenhower "without a second's hesitation" said he would be delighted to.[6] At the first prayer breakfast, Eisenhower opined, "prayer today is a necessity," and our prayers, although imperfect, can nonetheless help to tie us together as a nation.[7]

Billy Graham usually delivered the lead address during the first fifteen years of the prayer breakfast, evidently each time also offering listeners an invitation to follow Christ.[8] The prayer breakfast was successful partly because "many members of Eisenhower's staff and cabinet were thoroughly religious individuals."[9] Eisenhower "especially admired" the religious devotion of Mormon Ezra Taft Benson.[10] The religious values of these people no doubt influenced Eisenhower to appoint them to government positions.

Dwight's remarks presented on February 2, 1956, at the Annual Breakfast of the International Council for Christian Leadership illustrated the high level of support he had for the prayer breakfasts:

> It is a touching thing that Mr. Hilton has done in presenting to me this plaque and the desk and the chair where I wrote the little prayer that I used at the Inauguration some three years and more ago. I was seeking some way to impress upon the audience at that moment that all of us realized a new Chief Executive was being inaugurated over a nation that was founded on a religious faith.
>
> Our founding documents so state. In explaining . . . our government and what we intended to do in the Declaration, our founding fathers held it was our Creator that gave us certain rights, and this government was set up to sustain them . . . it was with some astonishment that . . . Literally thousands of messages

4. Keller, "Intellectuals and Eisenhower," 261.

5. Moore, *One Nation under God*, 336.

6. Keller, "Intellectuals and Eisenhower," 259.

7. Moore, *One Nation under God*, 336.

8. Graham, "General Who Became," 203.

9. Keller, "Intellectuals and Eisenhower," 298.

10. Keller, "Intellectuals and Eisenhower," 298.

coming in, some of them from people who did not particularly think I was the man to occupy that place that day, still applauded that act.

. . . very few men . . . tell me they are atheists or they are even agnostics, but we find among the laity a curious diffidence in merely stating the fact that they believe there is a God and He is more powerful than I, and I am dependent upon Him . . . by announcing to the world that we come up as laymen and meet, making the same acknowledgments that are made in that prayer, . . . we are telling people that this nation is still a nation under God.

This is terrifically important today. There has been too much of the world that believes the United States to be completely materialistic, boastful, proud and arrogant . . . poll after poll have reported the same thing.

It is such meetings as this . . . that help to dispel this very great and dangerous delusion. It still is a nation that is grounded on the religious faith, with great concern for the sentiments of compassion and mercy that Mr. Hilton so eloquently spoke about. That is what we want others to think about when they think of the United States . . . was truly trying to follow in the footsteps of the Prince of Peace, and to establish a just peace for the world.

. . . the Bible says "When the strong man armed keepeth his palace, his goods are in peace"—we intend to remain that strong, but let us always do it with certainty that anyone who will come in integrity, observing the moral values that we know are imbedded in this great religious faith, that he will be received as a friend and taken with us down the road to the future in peace.

THE NATIONAL DAY OF PRAYER

Neither Eisenhower nor his administration began the National Day of Prayer, but they helped to establish it, and set July 4 as the date of its first national observance, a date later changed to May 1. Keller noted the wording of the National Day of Prayer text was "given special attention" by the White House and the State Department, and while the proclamation was originally mandated by Congress, the White House had received over fifty thousand communications requesting the president set aside one day of the year for penance and prayer. This massive response was driven in part on May 5 by a national television broadcast of Bishop Fulton Sheen. Sheen wrote to Eisenhower requesting his support for a National Day of Prayer "and Fasting and Reparation for our sins, for the peace of the world."[11] After pointing out

> that Lincoln saw the Civil War as punishment for U.S. sins, Sheen suggested that the nation confess its sins and pray for forgiveness in a "National Day of Expiation." The initial draft letter to be sent to Sheen from the White House did not include the words "expiation," but speech writer Emmet Hughes, a liberal Catholic, added the word to the Eisenhower draft.[12]

This work was continued by Eisenhower's personal secretary, Ann Whitman, who requested staffer Bernard Shanley improve the draft and determine its accuracy. An example is if the word "expiation" should be changed and, if so, to what different word? Shanley noted, as a non-Catholic, he did not know for sure what "expiation" meant and concluded that a day set aside that uses

> "such a strictly Catholic word in its title might be resented by other denominations." Shanley wrote a gloss on the side: "Neither do the Catholics [know what the word means]! Except I hope in practice. The word was used in the old testament much more so than today." . . . Sheen countered . . . writing the nation needed to avoid pretensions of innocence: "expiation admits that cold wars could be as Lincoln saw the Civil War: 'a punishment inflicted upon us for our presumptuous sins, to the needful end of our national reformation as a whole people.'" Maxwell Rabb responded on behalf of Eisenhower conveying to Sheen that the NDP would simply be one of prayer and humility.[13]

The reason for the many date changes (for example, sometimes it was in September and other times in October) was partly linked to a desire to assign a date not coinciding with an established religious holiday. Another factor was the Rev. Elson opposed scheduling the National Day of Prayer during either July or August because church attendance is normally down during these summer months. In 1958, at the suggestion of the Rev. Fox, President Eisenhower agreed to set the National Day of Prayer on the first Wednesday in October for the remainder of his second term as president in order to allow the American government and the various

11. Keller, "Intellectuals and Eisenhower," 263.

12. Keller, "Intellectuals and Eisenhower," 263.

13. Keller, "Intellectuals and Eisenhower," 263.

religious officials sufficient time to properly prepare for the occasion. In Fox's mind, this placement would accentuate two things:
the NDP as a day to pray for "spiritual blessing," and, Thanksgiving
as the day to pray in gratitude for the nation's "material blessing."
The second NDP was scheduled for September 22, 1954, and was
closely coordinated with the Department of State. At the suggestion of Walter Beddell Smith, acting Secretary of State, Eisenhower
agreed to use the NDP as an occasion to extend an invitation to
the peoples behind the "Iron Curtain" to join the United States in
prayers for world peace.[14]

The Department of State originated the first National Day of Prayer during
the first four years of Eisenhower's administration, but the event actually
first began in 1955 when Dr. Elton Trueblood, Chief of Religious Information at the U.S. Information Agency, completed the first draft. Dr. McCann
worked very closely with Elton and several other religious leaders during
the early National Day of Prayer events, both to determine the best time
for the observance and to polish the final draft. Afterward, at the behest of
Fox, several prominent clergy were called on to draft a new prayer for the
succeeding years. These clergy included the following:

> Chaplain Ivan Bennett, Director of the American Bible Society
> (1958); Reverend Henry Pitney Van Dusen, President of Union
> Theological Seminary (1959); and, the Very Reverend Francis B.
> Sayre, Jr., Dean of the Washington National Cathedral (1960). By
> the fall of 1957, however, Eisenhower . . . called upon Fox and the
> Department of State to develop a means for wider publicity and
> participation.[15]

The Supreme Court, quite in contrast to today's court rulings, openly entered into the spiritual domain when the majority ruled in the *Zorach v.
Clauson* case, as stated in an opinion ironically written by liberal Judge William Douglas that "We are a religious people whose institutions presuppose
a Supreme Being."[16]

---

14. Keller, "Intellectuals and Eisenhower," 263–64.
15. Keller, "Intellectuals and Eisenhower," 263–64.
16. Moore, *One Nation under God*, 335.

PERSONAL PRAYER

It was not only during his World War II campaigns that Dwight constantly asked for "God's guidance in making the right decision," but he likewise relied on God's guidance during the eight years he was president.[17]

In his letters, Ike often discussed the "importance of religion in our national life."[18] When Norman Vincent Peale and Mrs. Peale spent the night in the White House, Dr. Peal asked the president if he prayed regularly. Ike responded "Yes, I do. I do most of my praying at night, just before I go to sleep, and every morning as soon as I rise. At night I say, 'Dear God, I have done the best I could today, so won't You please take over until tomorrow morning?'"[19]

In another situation, Secretary of the Interior Fred A. Seaton walked unannounced into the president's White House office in 1957, finding "President Eisenhower on his knees in prayer beside his desk. Seaton apologized profusely, but Ike quietly waved his apology aside, explaining he was making a crucial decision that could mean war or peace in the Far East. He was praying for guidance in helping him choose the right course."[20] One prayer of note that Eisenhower wrote while in office is as follows:

> Before all else, we seek, upon our common labor as a nation, the blessings of Almighty God. And the hopes in our hearts fashion the deepest prayers of our whole people. May we pursue the right—without self-righteousness. May we know unity—without conformity. May we grow in strength—without pride in self. May we, in our dealings with all people of the earth, ever speak truth and serve justice . . . And so the prayer of our people carries far beyond our own frontiers, to the wide world of our duty and destiny.[21]

Morin notes on "more than one occasion, in moments of adversity," Dwight said he "felt the need for divine assistance. The instinct for prayer was deeply ingrained. 'Freedom itself means nothing unless there is faith,' Eisenhower often said."[22]

---

17. Quoted in Gammon, *All Believers Are Brothers*, 3; see also Patterson, letter to Jerry Bergman.

18. Letter to his physician, Dr. Syder, 1. Copy in the author's files.

19. Hutchinson, "President's Religious Faith," 362.

20. Jameson, *Heroes by the Dozen*, 151.

21. Quoted in Moore, *One Nation under God*, 314.

22. Morin, *Dwight D. Eisenhower*, 13.

The role of religion in Dwight's life was evidently so central, even as president, that "again and again," as he wrestled with the requirements of the presidency, his religious upbringing showed through. Fortunately, most of the time it helped to "steady his thinking and give his leadership confident direction. Occasionally, it betrayed him into a belief that some problems are simpler than they" actually are.[23]

According to Milton Eisenhower, Dwight believed America was more than just a religious nation, but that "all of our basic documents are political expressions of certain cardinal religious concepts."[24]

23. Hutchinson, "President's Religious Faith," 362.
24. Quoted in Kornitzer, *Great American Heritage*, 137.

18

The Presidency and Religion

Each year the Committee on Religion in American Life reminds us of the importance of faithful church attendance. It urges full support of religious institutions to the end that we may add strength and meaning to the religious virtues—charity, mercy, brother love, and faith in Almighty God. These spiritual concepts are the inspiration of the American way. It was once said, "America is great because America is good—and if America ever ceases to be good, America will cease to be great." By strengthening religious institutions, the Committee on Religion in American Life is helping to keep America good. Thus it helps each of us to keep America great. I earnestly hope that during November, and throughout this and every year, each American citizen will actively support the religious institution of his own choice.[1]

DWIGHT COMMONLY DISCUSSED THE importance of God in his presidential speeches and lectures. Three examples follow:

> We are one nation, gifted by God with the reason and the will to govern ourselves, and returning our thanks to Him by respecting His supreme creation—the free individual[2].

1. Dwight Eisenhower, Statement for the Committee on Religion in American Life, October 31, 1953.

2. Speech to Republican Party, Boston, Massachusetts, September 21, 1953.

> Without God there could be no American form of government,
> nor an American way of life. Recognition of the Supreme Being is
> the first—the most basic—expression of Americanism. Thus the
> founding fathers of America saw it, and thus, with God's help, it
> will continue to be.[3]

> Oceans and great distances do not divide the human family in the
> sight of our Divine Creator. We are all His children. He teaches us
> to cherish and sustain one another.[4]

On July 16, 1956, Princeton-educated (BA from Princeton, BD from Union Theological Seminary) Congregational minister Rev. Frederic Fox became part of the White House staff and served the president until January 20, 1961. His title was "Special Assistant," and one of his informal jobs was to serve as an advisor to President Eisenhower and his staff on matters related to religion. His tasks included checking the Scriptures used in White House written statements and helping to answer the president's mail.[5] Few presidents had a religious "special assistant." A major reason given for selecting the Rev. Fox for this position was his writing skills, but the person who facilitated Fox's hiring into the administration, Dr. Kevin McCann, also held strong Christian religious beliefs and wanted to appoint someone who shared them.

Before his special appointment, Fox was active as a minister, encouraging his congregation to become involved in the political process, and his writings in this area were no doubt important in helping him to obtain his position in Eisenhower's administration. Fox believed we can "see God's hand in all [of] our affairs."[6] Fox's role as a religious advisor, in fact, went beyond advisor and even involved lacing Eisenhower's political pronouncements with biblical quotes and references to accentuate his arguments. In a memo to Eisenhower, Fox suggested that before Gabriel Hauge left the White House the president could give him "this old coin" which said, "Render to Caesar the things that are Caesar's and to God the things that are God's (St. Mark 12:13–17)."[7]

---

3. February 27, 1955, speech marking American Legion's "Back to God" movement.

4. Speech at Tenth Colombo Plan Meeting, Seattle, Washington, November 10, 1958; from Eisenhower, *Quotable Eisenhower*, 85–86.

5. Keller, "Intellectuals and Eisenhower," 299.

6. Quoted in Keller, "Intellectuals and Eisenhower," 301.

7. Keller, "Intellectuals and Eisenhower," 305.

The Rev. Fox believed "the president was the 'Defender of the Faith' and in many ways a 'pastor of his people.'" Furthermore, Fox believed all of Eisenhower's White House assistants should be "assistant pastors." Keller concluded each of these roles fit into Fox's "broader scheme of civil religious life" to the extent that Fox believed the church should function as a "wheel" within the wheel of government, acting as a "modern gyroscope" to "provide direction and stability for the responsibilities of government, thereby protecting against the rise of a totalitarian state." Fox even "repeatedly called for a spiritual revival and a moral crusade to remedy the nation's ills.[8] Considerable evidence exists that this goal was a result of Eisenhower's deep belief in the power of prayer.[9] The public ultimately would underwrite this scheme for civil religious governance."[10]

In spite of his frequent public expressions of religiosity, so many persons assumed Dwight was irreligious that the Rev. Frederic Fox was more than once called on to defend

> Eisenhower's personal and political religiosity in the face of public criticism. Sometimes Fox simply promoted Eisenhower's faith, and on other occasions he actively defended it. For example, early in his tenure, Fox sought to publish through the *Religious News Service* a prayer a citizen had written for Eisenhower. Alternatively, he drafted an unsent reply to the journal *Christian Century* critiquing the articles of Ernest Lefever about the candidate's religious beliefs:
> "Mr. Lefever was too partisan to mix the politics of the 1956 presidential campaign. He is too madly for Adlai . . . He tries to make Mr. Stevenson look like a modest, yet profound, follower of Reinhold Niebuhr and he tries to make President Eisenhower look like a boastful, superficial follower of Billy Graham. In both instances, nothing could be further from the truth . . ."
> Fox argued that . . . while Eisenhower's faith was simple, it was better compared with that of King David than Norman Vincent Peale's.[11]

In another case, Fox defended both Eisenhower's participation in prayer breakfasts and "the depths of the president's faith" in a private letter he sent

8. Smith, *Faith and the Presidency*, 222.

9. Smith, *Faith and the Presidency*, 227.

10. Keller, "Intellectuals and Eisenhower," 309–10; Pierard, *From Evangelical Exclusivism.*

11. Keller, "Intellectuals and Eisenhower," 307.

to *Christianity Today* in which he said he questioned the author's standard for

> measuring 'the depth of the president's spiritual experience.' You used three yardsticks: 1) His Church attendance, 2) His (Christian) references in speeches, 3) His attitude toward religious functions." Fox concluded that these standards were utterly inadequate. Even in the articles focusing on Fox, the White House staffer was certain to promote and validate the authenticity of the president's beliefs. Indeed, Fox was so sensitive to Eisenhower's faith that he sought to protect him even in matters of association. (The question of plagiarism arose in the planned publication of Elson's book *And Still He Speaks,* and Fox believed Eisenhower's reputation could be besmirched.) [12]

Although some atheists have even claimed Eisenhower was an atheist, one event almost completely dispels this rumor by itself. *Chicago Daily Tribune* reporter Clay Gowran reported Ike told the Nebraska delegates that there exists in this nation a strong need to "return to religion and deep honesty in all branches of government . . . One of the ways in which the French have gone so far astray is that they now brag that 50 percent of them are either agnostics or atheists . . . It takes no brains to be an atheist. They have reached the point where their moral fiber has disintegrated."[13] The result of this report was a nightmare for the Eisenhower staff, resulting in the embarrassment of the officials in Eisenhower's French headquarters

> by the repercussions to General Eisenhower's critical remarks earlier this week about Frenchmen. Many letters and telegrams have been sent to the general protesting this statement. What the general said was that "one place where France has gone astray is that they have 50 percent of their people agnostics or atheists . . . It takes no brains to be an atheist."

This casual remark was made at a small gathering of delegates who came to see General Eisenhower. One of the delegates

> asked the general about his emphasis on the need for a spiritual re-vival in the nation. He replied that he believed true democracy was the political expression of a religious concept of life and that unless we carried this spiritual and moral concept in to our political life the nation would surely decline. He then pointed to France as one

12. Keller, "Intellectuals and Eisenhower," 308.

13. Smith, *Faith and the Presidency,* 227.

example of a nation that . . . emphasized the concept of "reason" to the detriment of religious faith.[14]

Interestingly, another claim, noted above, was that Dwight was here putting on a show to win political points, a show called civil or cultural religion, as is common among presidents.[15] Looking at his whole life and the statements made by those who knew him well, such as Andrew Goodpaster, this view is also not viable.

USE OF CIVIL RELIGION

Toolin, in a study of forty-nine inaugural addresses of United States presidents, found a civil religious dimension in all inaugural addresses focusing around the themes of sacrifice, destiny, under God, exodus, and international examples.

Although the church and state are separate in the United States, the political realm still contains a major religious dimension that runs parallel to, and sometimes finds expression through, formal religion. Civil religion is an understanding of the universal and transcendent religious reality as seen in, or revealed through, the experience of the American people.[16] Civil religion performs many functions, including culture building, culture affirmation, and, most importantly, legitimation.

Civil religion also provides a frame of reference helping citizens both understand and interpret their life experiences. American civil religion draws on the religious ideologies and common historical experiences of the American people, unifying a very diverse people into one largely harmonious society, plus interpreting and giving meaning to their shared existence by putting their existence into a common American frame of reference.[17] Before this time, like his predecessors, Eisenhower did not have general guideline for dealing with church-state relations to follow. Consequently, they lacked a plan to help coordinate a working relationship between the White House and the various religious groups.

Before Fox's appointment, people from a wide variety of religious backgrounds made many of the presidential decisions related to religious

14. *New York Times*, July 11, 1952, 10.

15. Pierard and Linder, *Civil Religion*; Smith, *Civil Religion and the Presidency*.

16. Bellah, and Hammond, *Varieties of Civil Religion*.

17. Hendon, and Kennedy, "Civil Religion."

issues. This included Eisenhower's chief of staff, Sherman Adams, and his press secretary, James Hagerty. Evangelical and Reformed leader Kevin Mc-Cann wrote many of the president's religious proclamations and speeches. Emmett Hughes and Bernard Shanley, both active Catholics, oversaw the communications with the various Catholic organizations, and a Jew, Maxwell Robb, served the same function with Jewish groups.[18]

SOME EXAMPLES OF EISENHOWER'S RELIGIONS INFLUENCE

Author Paul Blanshard concluded the "enormous increase in church membership" that occurred during the 1950s was, in part, due to the activities of President Eisenhower in support of religion.[19] Gustafson claims one evidence of the effectiveness of Eisenhower's religious promotion activities was that, within only a few months after taking the oath of office, his policies made Eisenhower the "most religious president in our history." Examples of Eisenhower's religious actions that earned him this title include helping to "sponsor a nationwide moral crusade and religious revival," in order to further the basic goals of the religious interests in America:

> During his administration the highly publicized Prayer Breakfasts were begun and "Under God" was placed in the pledge of allegiance to the flag. He proclaimed Days of Prayer for the nation [a tradition followed by every president since], backed the organization known as Foundation for Religious Action and invited Billy Graham and other prominent religious leaders to the White House. And he delivered hundreds of messages, both written and oral, to religious organizations.[20]

Eisenhower and his administrative team also "took Communion before the opening of each new session of congress."[21] Eisenhower was also the first president to mail presidential Christmas cards. His 1953 mailings totaled 1,100 cards; in comparison, President George W. Bush mailed close to one million cards.[22] Other religious actions of Eisenhower's administration in-

18. Smith, *Faith and the Presidency*, 239.

19. Blanshard, *God and Man*, 13.

20. Gustafson, *Religion of a President*, 610–13.

21. Smith, *Faith and the Presidency*, 226.

22. August and Burovick, *1 Million*, 21.

cluded the "pray for peace" mail cancellation stamp, and inclusion in the 1953 inaugural parade of a "church" float titled the "God Float," on which "in God we trust" and "freedom to worship" was printed in bold letters.[23]

Soon after this event, the postmaster general issued a stamp bearing the motto "In God We Trust," which was shortly thereafter printed on all U.S. paper currency. The inclusion of religion in government was so great during Dwight's presidency that some historians have concluded "the extent of the mixing of politics and religion during the era" was greater than ever before in history.[24]

Holl opined the "U.S. constitution prohibits the establishment of a national church" but does not prevent "Americans from adopting a public civil religion."[25] For example, as part of the American Legion "Back to God" program broadcast from the White House on February 7, 1954, Eisenhower said this:

> As a former soldier, I am delighted that our veterans are sponsoring a movement to increase our awareness of God in our daily lives.
>
> In battle, they learned a great truth—that there are no atheists in the foxholes. They know that in time of test and trial, we instinctively turn to God for new courage and peace of mind. All the history of America bears witness to this truth.
>
> Out of faith in God, and through faith in themselves as His children, our forefathers designed and built this Republic. We remember from school days that, aboard a tiny ship of destiny called the Mayflower, self-government on our continent was first conceived by the Pilgrim Fathers. Their immortal compact began with the words, "In the name of God, Amen."
>
> We remember the picture of the Father of our Country, on his knees at Valley Forge seeking divine guidance in the cold gloom of a bitter winter. Thus Washington gained strength to lead to independence a nation dedicated to the belief that each of us is divinely endowed with indestructible rights.
>
> We remember, too, that three-fourths of a century later, on the battle-torn field of Gettysburg, and in the silence of many a wartime night, Abraham Lincoln recognized that only under God could this Nation win a new birth of freedom . . . America's

23. Miller, *Piety Along the Potomac*.
24. Keller, "Intellectuals and Eisenhower," 312.
25. Holl, *Civil Religion*, 123.

freedom, her courage, her strength, and her progress have had their foundation in faith.

Today as then, there is need for positive acts of renewed recognition that faith is our surest strength, our greatest resource. This "Back to God" movement is such a positive act. As we take part in it, I hope that we shall prize this thought:

Whatever our individual church, whatever our personal creed, our common faith in God is a common bond among us. In our fundamental faith, we are all one. Together we thank the Power that has made and preserved us a nation. By the millions, we speak prayers, we sing hymns--and no matter what their words may be, their spirit is the same—"In God is our trust."

This "civil religion" was also reflected in various proclamations Dwight issued that were clearly religious in content. For example, in his Thanksgiving Proclamation on November 6, 1954, Dwight wrote that early in American history our pilgrim fathers began the "custom of dedicating one day at harvest time to rendering thanks to Almighty God for the bounties of the soil and for His mercies throughout the year," adding we are grateful our country was settled by forebears that were seeking religious freedom, a goal that remains strong today to allow each of us to

worship God in his own way, according to the dictates of his conscience. We are grateful for the innumerable daily manifestations of Divine goodness in affairs both public and private, for equal opportunities for all to labor and to serve, and for the continuance of those homely joys and satisfactions which enrich our lives.

In his Thanksgiving Proclamation of November 12, 1956, Dwight wrote Thanksgiving is a time when people's minds

and hearts turn to Almighty God in grateful acknowledgment of His mercies throughout the year. It is also fitting at this season that we should consider God's providence to us throughout our entire history. . . the Pilgrim Fathers who, fleeing from religious oppression, landed on a bleak, forbidding shore and began to carve out what became this great Republic which it is our happy destiny to love and serve. For their foresight, their courage, and their idealism let us give thanks to the Power which has made and preserved us a Nation. . .let us pray this year not only in the spirit of thanksgiving but also as suppliants for God's guidance, to the end that we may follow the course of righteousness and be worthy of His favor. Now, therefore, I, Dwight D. Eisenhower, President of the United States of America, . . . do hereby proclaim Thursday, the twenty-second day of November of this year, as a day of national thanksgiving. On that day let all of us, of whatever creed, foregather in our respective places of worship to give thanks to God and prayerful contemplation to those eternal truths and universal principles of Holy Scripture which have inspired such measure of true greatness as this Nation has achieved. And let us, as the beneficiaries of this greatness, give a good account of our stewardship by helping those in need and by rendering aid, through our religious organizations and by other means, to the ill, the destitute, and the oppressed in foreign lands.

Although the Rev. Fox did the research for many of these spiritual speeches, Eisenhower "supplied the numerous religious references."[26]

One of the primary Watchtower teachings Eisenhower evidently did accept later in life was the value of the Bible as a source of wisdom. Professor Pinkley concluded that Ike's faith was much like that of Lincoln, who had

> a deep, quiet faith in God. It was a private and precious thing to him. Wherever he was quartered or headquartered, I never saw Ike Eisenhower without a Bible somewhere in sight—on his desk, in a bookcase nearby, or on a table in his office. It was a Bible for use, as the well-worn pages showed. He once said, "Like stored wisdom, the lessons of the Bible are useless unless they are lifted out and employed. A faithful reading of . . . Scripture provides the courage and strength required for . . . our time." One gift that seemed to please him above others was the 500 millionth copy of the Scripture disseminated by the American Bible Society—a nine-pound King James Version family Bible bound in red Morocco.[27]

Dwight once stated, "If each of us in his own mind would dwell upon the simple virtues—integrity, courage, self-confidence, and unshakable faith in his Bible—would not some of our problems tend to simplify themselves?"[28] According to Princeton PhD General Andrew Goodpaster,[29] Eisenhower often noted the major importance of what he called the "spiritual factor" in our society and stressed "security is the product of economic, political, military, and spiritual strength." As a key aid to Dwight (as well as Kennedy,

26. Smith, *Faith and the Presidency*, 240.

27. Pinkley, *Eisenhower Declassified*, 378.

28. Fuller and Green, *God in the White House*, 216.

29. Goodpaster, personal interview.

Johnson, and Nixon), Goodpaster was in a good position to judge Dwight's religiousness and especially his sincerity.

FIGHTING FOR "MORAL AND RELIGIOUS" GOALS

A major thrust of Eisenhower's presidency was to fight for "moral and religious" goals.[30] Eisenhower's former speechwriter, Stanley High, concluded Dwight had "hoped to inspire a spiritual reawakening in America."[31] His specific goal for America was that a "moral and spiritual" revival would produce a rededication to the Christian religious faith and values.

Eisenhower expected all of his cabinet members and their families be active in a church and "stressed that the founding fathers wrote their religious faith into our founding documents, stamped their trust in God on the face of their coins and currency, and put it boldly at the base of our institutions."[32] The pastor of the church Eisenhower attended in Washington, DC, Edward Elson, stated that Dwight gave powerful testimony by both "personal example and public utterance," to America's spiritual foundation.[33]

Eisenhower once said he believed one of the reasons he was elected president was "to lead this country spiritually" because at this time in history "we need a spiritual renewal."[34] He believed our nation's founders taught our government is the result of "a political expression of a deeply felt religious faith," and America will be "governed by our own consent" and anyone who believes he is above politics forgets the meaning of the word politics, which is

> the business of the people. Nothing is more important to preserve those great values that are derived from religious conceptions, that is—the freedom of men—you are just as free as you can possibly be as long as you do not transgress the equal rights of others. You are free to fulfill your highest ambitions, no matter what they may be, as long as they are noble and decent . . . Now, if we recognize always this relationship between a deeply felt religious faith and your duty as a citizen of the United States, personally, I think there

30. Gustafson, *Religion of a President*, 612.

31. High, *What the President Wants*, 1; Miller, *Piety along the Potomac*, 18.

32. High, *What the President Wants*.

33. Elson, *America's Spiritual Recovery*, 1.

34. Hendon and Kennedy, *Civil Religion*, 390–91.

will never be any difficulty as you approach the problems, whether they be those of space, handling and battling Communism—all of these problems that we know about and have to meet begin to lose some of their terror as you just keep hold of that one simple truth.[35]

To lead this renewal, Dwight "hammered so hard on the importance of religion" it became a constant theme of his presidency.[36] Eisenhower's stress on religion was so great, Perret claimed, that soon after he was elected president, Eisenhower became convinced the United States government "was based on religious belief, a conclusion that would have surprised the eighteenth-century men of the Enlightenment who considered faith a strictly private affair."[37]

In 1952, columnist Drew Pearson reported Eisenhower once stressed his idealism by pulling a coin from his pocket he was given by someone in Kansas years ago, and handing it to Pearson. The coin "had a cross on one side with the word 'freedom,' and the word 'God' on the other side ... 'That coin [Ike said] represents my religion."[38] In 1956 "In God We Trust" became the national motto by law, printed on all U.S. paper currency (it was already on all coinage) to remind us of this creed.[39]

Eisenhower firmly believed "the United States rested on a firm religious foundation" and "religion and democracy were closely related,"[40] and for this reason selected active Christians reflecting this belief to be part of his administration. He chose an active Mormon apostle, Ezra Taft Benson, as his Secretary of Agriculture; an active Methodist, Arthur Fleming, as his Secretary of Health, Education, and Welfare; and Robert B. Anderson as his Secretary of the Treasury. Douglas McKay, a member of the National Presbyterian Church, was his first Secretary of the Interior, and an active Episcopalian, Fred Seaton, was his second. One of America's leading Protestant laymen, John Foster Dulles, was selected as Secretary of State. Dulles "consistently sought to apply moral law to international relations and bring 'the force of Christianity' to bear on global problems."[41]

35. Eisenhower, commencement address, Messiah College, May 29, 1965.
36. Hutchinson, "President's Religious Faith," 362.
37. Perret, *Eisenhower*, 429.
38. Pearson, *Drew Pearson Diaries*, 211.
39. Moore, *One Nation under God*, 337.
40. Smith, *Faith and the Presidency*, 227.
41. Smith, *Faith and the Presidency*, 226; Nannes, *President and His Pastor*.

Eisenhower's openly moral and religious campaign to Christianize America would seem to have caused an outcry from the ACLU (Americans for the Separation of Church and State) and similar groups, but "Eisenhower's zeal in promoting interest in religion raised no church-state conflicts" in either the courts or the press.[42] The only persons that objected were atheists.[43] This fact indicates how radically the American nation has changed since the 1950s. The ACLU and other groups are now very active, ensuring any and every display of religion by the government is kept out of the public square.[44]

Nonetheless, most of the practices began by President Eisenhower still persist today. Furthermore, every president since Eisenhower "has actively encouraged the country to pray, believing that doing so remains a powerful unifying force, and is very much in keeping with the wishes of the Founding Fathers."[45] Eisenhower agreed with this position because he firmly believed not only America, but all of Western society rested on a religious foundation. The founding fathers "wrote their religious faith into our founding documents, stamped their trust in God up on our coins and currency, [and] put it squarely at the base of our institutions." They strove to obey God's commandments, live in freedom, and create a prosperous country.

Eisenhower firmly believed the "knowledge that God is the source of all power" and had given birth to, and sustained, the nation since its founding. The concept of free government depended on the conviction that God had endowed all people created in his image "with certain rights." Human dignity sprang from these rights, as so "eloquently stated" in the Declaration of Independence. Those who first settled in America, Eisenhower asserted, had "faith in a Provident God whose hand supported and guided them; faith in themselves as the children of God, endowed with purposes beyond a mere struggle for survival," and believed the principles of freedom and justice were of "divine origin."[46]

42. Gustafson, *Religion of a President*, 612.

43. Smith, *Faith and the Presidency*, 228.

44. Smith, *Faith and the Presidency*.

45. Moore, *One Nation under God*, 418.

46. Smith, *Faith and the Presidency*, 229–30.

19

The Pledge of Allegiance
and Civil Rights

PRESIDENT EISENHOWER WORKED WITH Congress to ensure the words "under God" were added to the Pledge of Allegiance.[1] The form used today was originally written by Baptist minister Francis Bellamy. His words became the nation's official pledge during World War II. The decision to add "under God" to the official Pledge of Allegiance was signed into law by President Eisenhower on Flag Day, June 14, 1954. One impetus for this change was a sermon by Scottish-born minister Rev. George Docherty, given on February 7, 1954. President Eisenhower and several members of Congress were in the audience when the sermon was given. Keller recounts the gist of the sermon as follows:

> Docherty shared his conclusion that something seemed to be missing from the pledge; he argued that apart from the naming of this nation, the pledge could be recited in any republic. Indeed, Docherty stated: "I could hear little Muscovites repeat a similar pledge to their hammer and sickle flag in Moscow with equal solemnity. Russia is also a Republic that claims to have overthrown the tyranny of kingship . . . What was missing, the minister proclaimed, was the U.S. belief in God. That belief clearly was seen as separating this country from the Soviets and would serve as the basis for moral and spiritual education.[2]

1. Moore, *Faith and the Presidency*, 336.
2. Keller, "Intellectuals and Eisenhower," 319–20.

149

Numerous politicians agreed with the minister, and only five days later several congressmen, including U.S. Representative Charles G. Oakman (R-MI), called on his colleagues to support a measure to add "under God" to the pledge. Oakman chose Lincoln's Birthday (February 12) to broach the matter to his colleagues, stressing the words were added to remind Americans of the nation's religious heritage. The specific words "nation under God" was also inspired partly by the Gettysburg address: "That we here highly resolve that these dead shall not have died in vain, that *this Nation under God* shall have a new birth of freedom, and that government of the people, by the people, for the people shall not perish from the earth."[3]

Representative Oakman also used the example of the motto "In God we trust" that was engraved on our money to support the measure. Oakman's reasoning was that because this recommendation was followed in a material symbol, such as on our coins, the same idea was even more appropriate as an example to support adding the phrase "under God" to the Pledge of Allegiance to our flag and country because "The Pledge of Allegiance is not a confession of faith. It is an affirmation of loyalty to a nation symbolized by its flag." Freedom and religious faith were often seen as inseparable by President Eisenhower. He once even said, "Freedom itself means nothing unless there is faith."[4]

While Oakman argued for adding mention of the deity in the pledge, he stressed that the recitation of the pledge itself was "not a religious act," because the phrase "under God" was "referential not reverential." Acceptance of this standard was obviously separate from the early 1900 religious flag rituals. The wording of his resolution, House Joint Resolution 371, was designed to alter the phrasing in the pledge to add: "one nation, under God, indivisible." Oakman

> specifically mentioned Eisenhower's presence at Docherty's service, noting that he sat at the same pew reserved for Lincoln when the latter was a member of that congregation. After his attendance, Eisenhower attended an American Legion event, which was attended by leaders of the three faiths, to dedicate the organization's "Back to God" campaign.[5]

In view of the 2004 court ruling declaring the pledge "unconstitutional," it is noteworthy that members of Congress were cognizant of the level of

3. Keller, "Intellectuals and Eisenhower," 302–21, emphasis added.
4. Quoted in Morin, *Dwight D. Eisenhower*, 13.
5. Keller, "Intellectuals and Eisenhower," 320–21.

popular support for adding the word God to the pledge in deciding to support the act: "Numerous members of Congress testified to the effect that not only was support of the measure massive and across religious lines but that opposition was non-existent."

When President Eisenhower signed the bill into law, he noted that by adding the words "under God" to the pledge, they were "reaffirming the transcendence of religious faith in America's heritage and future; in this way we shall constantly strengthen those spiritual weapons which forever will be our country's most powerful resource in peace and war."[6] The statement made by the president when signing the bill[7] to include the words "under God" in the pledge on June 14, 1954, are as follows:

> From this day forward, the millions of our school children will daily proclaim in every city and town, every village and rural school house, the dedication of our nation and our people to the Almighty . . . nothing could be more inspiring than to contemplate this rededication of our youth, on each school morning, to our country's true meaning.

He added that this is especially meaningful in view of the violence in

> today's world. Over the globe, mankind has been cruelly torn by violence and brutality and, by the millions, deadened in mind and soul by a materialistic philosophy of life. Man everywhere is appalled by the prospect of atomic war. In this somber setting, this law and its effects today have profound meaning. In this way we are reaffirming the transcendence of religious faith in America's heritage and future; in this way we shall constantly strengthen those spiritual weapons which forever will be our country's most powerful resource, in peace or in war.

Representatives of all the three major American faiths, Protestantism, Catholicism, and Judaism, were all openly supportive of the measure. Among the very few exceptions included John G. MacKinnon, president of the Unitarian Ministers Association, who wrote his organization held "that it is an invasion [sic] of the principle of religious liberty to alter the Pledge of Allegiance to the Flag by injecting a theological term 'under God.'"

Congress's motivations for passing the bill, besides the need to set the United States apart from the Soviet Union during the heat of the Cold War, included to

6. Moore, "Intellectuals and Eisenhower," 337.
7. Public Law 396, 83rd Congress (68 Stat. 049).

affirm the spiritual basis of the United States amidst material wealth and the specter of atomic war; and, to create an educational tool for children for the basis for citizenship training. The overall assessment was the need to augment U.S. defense with a spiritual dimension. Indeed, during a Senate Judiciary Committee hearing, Ferguson stated, "we cannot defend ourselves by ships and guns and planes alone. . . it is the souls of our people that are going to defend us." . . . Ferguson and others were suggesting that reliance upon a divine creator lent citizens and leaders a moral orientation, but equally, some were suggesting that belief in God would provide protection almost as a reward for maintaining the dictates of faith.[8]

IKE'S EFFORTS TOWARD IMPROVING CIVIL RIGHTS

Eisenhower's religious convictions were also expressed in his civil rights efforts. Although he declared in his first message to Congress, presented in February 1953, that if "we expect to make true and rapid progress in civil rights," we must adopt a gradual approach in order to steer "between extremist firebrands and extremist diehards." Moving too rapidly could have caused the South to erupt into riots and bloodshed. Inflamed by the 1954 *Brown v. Board of Education* Supreme Court decision, Southerners began organizing White Citizens Councils, which, by 1956, had 250,000 dedicated members working to prevent integration. The president then

> asked Billy Graham to help convince Southern ministers to support a "moderate," "sensible course of action" that steered a path between "the . . . extremists on both sides . . ." He hoped the clergy would promote and publicize black progress and prevent quarrels rather than simply help pick up the pieces after "an unfortunate fight." . . . Eisenhower wrote Graham that conciliation could produce "more lasting and stronger" results than could "force and conflict." He asked the evangelist to consider ways to increase the number of qualified blacks elected as city and county commissioners and school board members, to prod universities to base entrance to their graduate schools strictly on merit, and to develop plans to seat blacks and whites more efficiently on public transportation.[9]

8. Keller, "Intellectuals and Eisenhower," 324–25.

9. Smith, *Faith and the Presidency*, 250–52.

Eisenhower and the Rev. Billy Graham both felt ministers should stress in their pulpits the need to help solve the civil rights problem. He applauded the Louisiana archbishop who had courageously and successfully desegregated all New Orleans parochial schools. Dwight also recognized the progress the border states were making in improving race relations. He felt stressing these facts, and others like them, would serve to pressure judges to make decisions promoting racial justice.

As a result of these efforts, in June the Rev. Billy Graham "reported to Eisenhower that he had met with numerous prominent black and white pastors to persuade them to 'take a stronger stand' for desegregation . . . He had asked Southern religious leaders to . . . promote racial reform. If the Supreme Court went slowly and 'the extremists on both sides' quieted down, Graham concluded, the nation could achieve a 'peaceful social readjustment' within ten years."[10]

In a letter to Graham, Eisenhower also suggested they needed to work to insure the election of more qualified blacks to school boards and to various positions in government and in universities.[11] Billy Graham repeatedly exhorted numerous religious, civil rights, and even business leaders to "encourage Americans to strive to better understand blacks and work to end discrimination" by "education, persuasion, and personal example."[12] Dwight

> rarely used his personal popularity or the prestige of his office to directly challenge citizens to work for racial justice. Instead, he urged blacks to be patient in their crusade for equal rights. Eisenhower hosted black leaders only once during his presidency. In their brief meeting with him in June 1958, Martin Luther King Jr., Roy Wilkins, and others failed to convince Eisenhower to use his "moral authority to persuade his fellow Americans that integration was right and just.[13]

DiCianni wrote that, in order to help destroy the idea of "second-class citizens" based on race, Eisenhower "desegregated the armed services and continued the desegregation of schools even to the point of sending troops into Little Rock, Arkansas, to enforce court-ordered integration."[14] One example

10. Smith, *Faith and the Presidency*, 250–52.

11. Copy in Burns, *Ike Files*, 145–46.

12. Smith, *Faith and the Presidency*, 250–52.

13. Smith, *Faith and the Presidency*, 250–52.

14. DiCianni, *Faith of the Presidents*, 147.

where Ike stepped in to enforce civil rights was in 1958 when Arkansas Democrat Governor Orval Faubus ordered the Arkansas National Guard to prevent black students from enrolling in Little Rock Central High School. In response, Eisenhower sent troops from the 101st Airborne to enforce the court-ordered desegregation. Faubus's response was to block Eisenhower's order by closing all Little Rock government high schools for the 1958–1959 school year. From our perspective today, it is easy to conclude Ike could have done much more in support of civil rights, but the fact is he did more than most all presidents before him.

IKE'S MORAL CODE

In a study of Dwight's religion, Gustafson concluded that the Witnesses "undoubtedly had some effect on Dwight"; specifically, they helped to "shape his religious philosophy."[15] An example is that Ike "was more likely to pin hope for peace on individual moral and religious reform" than other factors, such as the government, both Witness and Brethren teachings.[16]

Their major influence was in the area of morals—a central Watchtower teaching is the importance of morality. More than most religious sects, the Watchtower Society stresses the importance of maintaining high moral standards in all areas of life, including sexuality, honesty, morality in leisure, business, work, school, and the home.[17] Their moral code is strictly enforced and violators are disfellowshipped, meaning the offender is permanently prevented from associating with most Witnesses until they repent and petition to be accepted for fellowship again. Each year thousands of Witnesses are disfellowshipped, mainly for immorality, especially for sex before marriage, an act called fornication.

Eisenhower biographer Alden Hatch, in support of this fact, noted, "West Point did not teach Ike not to lie and cheat—his mother's upbringing did that."[18] Professor Chernus added, "Eisenhower was careful to locate the solution to all human problems in a generic concept of religion, 'no matter what the faith.' Although he assumed that all people had some taint of sin, he also assumed that anyone could choose to overcome the power of sin through education and a strenuous effort of the will."[19]

15. Gustafson, *Religion of a President*, 610–11.

16. Chernus, *General Eisenhower*, 59.

17. Bergman, *Jehovah's Witnesses: A Comprehensive*.

18. Hatch, *Young Ike*, 98.

19. Chernus, *General Eisenhower*, 91.

20

Ike's Final Battles

ON SEPTEMBER 23, 1955, when Dwight was only sixty-five years old, he suffered his first heart attack. Dwight's personal physician, Dr. Major General Howard McCrum Snyder, and several specialists were immediately called in to provide the best care available to him at that time. Fortunately, he had sustained only a moderate myocardial infarction and was able to resume his duties as president in a few weeks. Nonetheless, Dwight's heart specialist, the world-famous cardiologist Dr. Paul Dudley White, had tried in vain to persuade the president not to run for reelection in 1956.

White wrote that Dwight's "major aim in life was to promote world peace," and for this reason he was willing to sacrifice his health to help achieve this goal.[1] No doubt his upbringing, as well as his experiences during World War II, influenced this major goal in his life, but his illness vividly introduced into his life the reality that he was not invincible. Lasby noted that his friend Arthur Wilson wrote that some things are worse than bad hearts and "I can't help but feel that it is a God-given warning" to reduce the president's awful responsibility

> despite the fact that the world needs you." One friend who saw God's hand at work was the Reverend Billy Graham, who wrote on 8 October to commiserate about the "terrible dilemma" the president faced. "I want to withdraw my urgent request of a few weeks ago that you run again," he wrote. "I think you have given enough to your country, and you deserve some peace and quiet."

1. White, *My Life and Medicine*, 188.

> The famous minister then engaged in a bit of advice; "None of us
> can understand why God allows these things to come into our lives
> and change our plans, programs, and ambitions—but he does! We
> must accept it as from God and realize that he knows better than
> we what is best for us as individuals and as a nation."[2]

On June 8, 1956, President Eisenhower had again been hospitalized, this
time with bowel obstruction, evidently due to a long-term problem with
chronic ileitis, a condition now termed Crohn's disease. The public often
prayed for his heath, and Eisenhower "frequently expressed his deep ap-
preciation for those who prayed for him."[3]

Then, on November 25, 1957, when Dwight was sixty-seven, his secretary noticed he could not speak clearly and called Dwight's physician,
Dr. Snyder, plus his close friend General Goodpaster.[4] After Dr. Snyder
examined him, he consulted with five other doctors, including leading
brain researcher and Columbia University professor Dr. Francis Forester.
All of these experts confirmed Snyder's diagnosis—a mild stroke caused
by a blockage in a branch of a cerebral artery. Although confined to his
bed, three days later Dwight "insisted on going to church with Mamie."[5]
Dwight again recovered, and he was well enough to attend a NATO conference in Paris two weeks later.

PEACE AND QUIET

In 1951, the Eisenhowers purchased the Redding Farm, the only home
they owned in their fifty-three years of married life.[6] On January 20, 1961,
Dwight and Mamie left the White House to retire to Gettysburg, where
they lived until their deaths. One reason Gettysburg appealed to Dwight
was, as a military history buff, the farm was adjacent to the Gettysburg
Civil War battlefield. The farm buildings were completely remodeled and
served as a retreat as well as a place the Eisenhowers could relax and meet
with world leaders.

On his visit to the Eisenhower farm in Gettysburg on November 25,
1955, Dr. Elson recounted that the Eisenhower grandchildren joined the

2. Lasby, *Eisenhower's Heart Attack*, 146.

3. Smith, *Faith and the Presidency*, 228.

4. White, *My Life and Medicine*, 191.

5. Johnson, *Life and Times*, 150.

6. Cohen, *Gettysburg's First Family*, 4.

group after lunch in their cozy drawing room that was beautifully furnished with numerous mementos and gifts given by leaders from many parts of the world. When they were all settled in, Ike "related how both he and Mrs. Eisenhower had been reared in the presence of an open Bible, revered as the Word of God, and with family prayers as a daily practice. They had lived in many dwellings in their long association with the Army . . . but this was the first house that they could call their very own. For this reason, it "seemed proper to dedicate their home to God."[7] Elson added that, as soon as Dwight said, "Let us pray,"

> the president's grandchildren—Dwight David, Barbara Anne, and Susan Elaine—spontaneously knelt down at a low, carved-ebony table, the gift of President Syngman Rhee of Korea. There was something profoundly moving about the spirituality of the occasion—not only because it was the President of the United States with his family, worshiping together in their very own home after the anxiety of a serious illness, but because this was a good Christian family and an exemplary American household.[8]

In Gettysburg, they faithfully attended the Gettysburg Presbyterian Church where Ike's pew is still marked with a plaque. Ike and his wife formally joined a church on February 1, 1963.

IKE'S DEATH

Unfortunately, Ike was struck with his fourth coronary thrombosis in May of 1968 and admitted to Walter Reed Hospital. Dwight's health was so poor that Lasby wrote the

> physicians who served Eisenhower during these later years were understandably proud of their ability to keep him alive for so long. "There was the satisfaction that, with our help and the grace of God," Dr. Mattingly wrote, "we had provided the general with an additional four years."

As he lay dying, Eisenhower was surrounded by his family, and holding his wife's hand, his last words were, "I want to go, God take me!"[9] He died on March, 28, 1969, at Walter Reed Army Medical Center in Washington,

7. Elson, *President's Dedicated Home*, 12–13.

8. Elson, *President's Dedicated Home*, 13.

9. Sinnott, *Mamie Doud Eisenhower*, 92; Perret, *Eisenhower*, 608.

DC, and was buried in Abilene next to his first son in a plain eighty-dollar military coffin.[10] A ten-car special train transported Dwight's body on the 379-mile trip from the hospital in Washington, DC, to Abilene. Of note is the fact that Eisenhower predicted the date of his own death in 1954, and was off by only a matter of months.[11]

On the way, thousands gathered to sing Ike's favorite hymns, including "Onward Christian Soldiers," "A Mighty Fortress Is Our God," and "Lead Kindly Light."[12] In Abilene, then a town of 7,400, an estimated 100,000 visitors traveled there to pay their last respects to Ike, and as many as 75 million watched the proceedings on television.[13] Scripture was read and prayers were offered at the simple ceremony in Abilene. President Nixon remarked Dwight spoke from the heart of America,

> not only from its geographical heart, but its spiritual heart. He exemplified what millions of parents hoped that their sons would be—strong, courageous, honest, and compassionate . . . it was the character of the man—not what he did, but what he was—that so captured the trust and faith and affection of his own people and of the people of the world . . . He was a product of America's soil and of its ideals, driven by a compulsion to do right and to do well; *a man of deep faith who believed in God and trusted in His will;* a man who truly loved his country and for whom the words 'freedom' and 'democracy' were not clichés, but they were living truths.[14]

The last words of Ike's service were by Major General Luther Miller, who said, "Unto God's gracious mercy we commend you, old friend."[15]

Just before he had died, Dwight had the following conversation in the Walter Reed Hospital with his close long-time friend and spiritual adviser, the Rev. Billy Graham:

> Then when I reached the doorknob and started to open it, the general raised his head slightly. "Billy, can I ask you one more question?"
>
> "Of course," I said.

10. Nevin, *Home to Abilene*, 25.
11. Holl, *Civil Religion*, 131.
12. Graves, *World's Last Salute*, 50.
13. Graves, *World's Last Salute*, 50–51.
14. Quoted in Graves, *World's Last Salute*. 47, emphasis mine.
15. Nevin, *Home to Abilene*, 34; Graves, *World's Last Salute*, 50.

In a firm, strong voice, he asked, "Can an old sinner like me ever go to heaven?"

"Of course, General Ike. You have made the ultimate decision—the greatest single decision that anyone can make. You have accepted Jesus Christ as your Savior, you'll go to heaven. The moment you stop breathing, you will automatically be in heaven."

As Billy Graham quietly closed the door, he glanced back once more. Tears were streaming down the face of Dwight D. Eisenhower, who had lived, loved and fought as a true Christian.[16]

MAMIE'S DEATH

Mamie, who outlived her husband by a decade, stated she missed him every day since he passed away. She died on November 1, 1979, and was also buried beside Ikky and her husband in Abilene, Kansas. The following prayer was said at Mamie's funeral:

> Dear Lord and Father of us all, we thank Thee for the good and gracious influence of Mamie Doud Eisenhower. We thank Thee for the faith by which she lived, for the home she made and the quiet steadfast service she rendered . . . As coming generations, cherish her memory, may something of her gentleness, her strength, her patriotism and her spiritual power encourage better living and more sacrificial service . . . And now, O Father, who doest all things well, with thankful hearts that Thou has given her to us for a season, we give Thy servant, Mamie back to Thy tender care, until the shadows flee away, and the brighter day dawns, when the visible and invisible are as one in Thy higher kingdom. Through Jesus Christ our Lord. Amen.[17]

When Mamie died, the Rev. Elson stated, "Now Dwight and Mamie Eisenhower are both in that other home whose Builder and Maker is God."[18]

---

16. Quoted in Pinkley, *Eisenhower Declassified*, 379.

17. Elson, *Memorial Addresses*, 15.

18. Elson, *President's Dedicated Home*, 13.

21

Summary

Dwight Eisenhower and his brothers, as occurs in about half of all persons who were raised in the Watchtower sect, did not continue in that faith when they became adults.[1] Nonetheless, the Eisenhower boys were clearly influenced by their Bible study, and to some extent by the early Watchtower belief structure and many of its ideals. By setting high standards and teaching the value of high moral principles taught by the Bible Students, Dwight's parents had given their sons a "quiet strength" that stayed with them for their entire lives.[2]

As is true of many persons raised as Witnesses, though, they never could accept some of the Watchtower's more eccentric teachings. Nonetheless, Dwight once said their mother was "by far the greatest influence in our lives," and *her* source of strength and wisdom was the Bible.[3] Dwight attributed his success, as well as the success of his brothers, to the genuine love of their parents and their strict, extensive moral religious teaching.[4] While growing up, everyday events commonly became a focus for a moral object lesson. In summing up his mother's temperament, Edgar said, "Mother had the fire. Mother had the ambition. Mother had the personality. She had the joy. She had a song in her heart."[5]

1. Stark, *Rise and Fall*.
2. Neal, *Eisenhowers*, 13.
3. Gullan, *Faith of Our*, 206; Eisenhower, *At Ease*, 52.
4. Eisenhower, *At Ease*, 37.
5. Ambrose and Immerman, *Milton S. Eisenhower*, 15.

As Eisenhower once said, "A lifetime of soldiering and public service confirms my conviction that nobody can go through six years of war and two terms of the Presidency without faith" in God.[6] This expression of religiousness was not unique to Dwight—other former presidents expressed it as well. For example, President Wilson believed "it was God, not the Democratic Party, who had placed him in the White House."[7] President Franklin Roosevelt also had a "strong belief that God directed the world's affairs . . . and saw World War II as a God inspired crusade to protect democracy and religion against the Axis tyranny."[8] Dwight, though, expressed his religious feelings more often and more openly than most presidents, both before and after him.

Dwight Eisenhower achieved a great deal to further the cause of theism, specifically Christianity, in the United States, especially during his presidency. His upbringing was steeped in religion and he was reared with a firm basis on which to build his religious worldview. God was critically important in his life and clearly influenced many of his decisions, both as a general and later as president. As president, he believed that in order to work, our form of government must be "grounded in a deep religious faith."[9] In Eisenhower's own words,

> Like stored wisdom, the lessons of the Bible are useless unless they are lifted out and employed. A faithful reading of Scripture provides the courage and strength required for the living of our time . . . I believe this made a dramatic symbol of America's effort to speak to our neighbors everywhere in the voice of hope and charity. That tiny star has long since been consumed in the atmosphere, but the model for it, as described in the pages of the Bible, can never be consumed. The message of Scripture, the commandments and promises of God, remain the same from age to age. They are a constant source of light and strength.[10]

In many ways, he saw himself as a servant of God, doing God's will by defeating the Axis during World War II and becoming the President of the United States to do God's will.[11] This aspect of his life, and of our other

6. Quoted in Gammon, *All Believers Are Brothers*, 2–3.

7. Wallace, *Presidential Courage*, 205.

8. Smith, *Faith and the Presidency*, 229.

9. Quoted in *Civil Religion*, 2007, 120; see also Alley, *Religion and the Presidency*; Boller, *Religion and the Presidency*; Bonnell, *Presidential Profiles*.

10. American Bible Society, *Eisenhower's Bible-Based Legacy*.

11. Pierard, "On Praying."

presidents as well, is generally ignored, often totally, by historians today. To understand the man, this aspect of his life must *not* be ignored, but rather fully explored and understood. This was the goal of this study. Religion and beliefs about God have always been a major motivator in the lives of most humans, and no person can be completely understood without carefully evaluating this critical area of their life. As this study documents, this is especially true of Dwight Eisenhower.

In Eisenhower's farewell address to the nation, he urged all Americans to remain strong in their faith in God because we must

> be strong in our faith that all nations, under God, will reach the goal of peace with justice. May we be ever unswerving in devotion to principle, confident but humble with power, diligent in pursuit of the Nation's great goals.
>
> To all the peoples of the world, I once more give expression to America's prayerful and continuing aspiration.
>
> We pray that peoples of all faiths, all races, all nations, may have their great human needs satisfied; that those now denied opportunity shall come to enjoy it to the full; that all who yearn for freedom may experience its spiritual blessings; that those who have freedom will understand, also, its heavy responsibilities; that all who are insensitive to the needs of others will learn charity; that the scourges of poverty, disease and ignorance will be made to disappear from the earth, and that, in the goodness of time, all peoples will come to live together in a peace guaranteed by binding force of mutual respect and love.[12]

Professor Chernus, after stating that Dwight's "parents, particularly his mother, later became involved with the Jehovah's Witnesses," opined, "Jerry Bergman has suggested a strong influence of the latter tradition on Eisenhower, but his argument adduces no substantial evidence. The evidence for direct influence of these traditions on Eisenhower is so slim and inconclusive that it has not seemed to me worthwhile to speculate on it."[13]

As this work makes clear, Ike rejected many unique Watchtower teachings—but was highly influenced by many, if not most, of the *basic* core Bible Student biblical teachings. As Ambrose and Immerman concluded, Dwight's breaking with his past did not mean abandoning Christianity but only certain Watchtower teachings, especially those developed under Rutherford.

12. Quoted in DiCianni, *Faith of the Presidents*, 148–49.
13. Chernus, *General Eisenhower*, 309.

Indeed, as Milton recalled, "Religion was as much a part of our home life as eating or sleeping."[14] Long-time family friend Henry Jameson claimed Dwight was a "sincere, patient, religious man . . . Ike was proud of his church background."[15] Many Eisenhower scholars have endeavored to determine the source of Dwight Eisenhower's greatness. Professor Kornitzer concluded from his research that Dwight's greatness came from his family and their values, especially those of Ida, who was both the more compassionate and the stronger of his two parents.[16]

14. Ambrose and Immerman, *Milton S. Eisenhower* , 13.
15. Jameson, *They Still Call Him Ike*, 14.
16. Gullan, *Faith of Our*, 223.

Appendix I
Brief Review of Watchtower History

SOME BACKGROUND ON THE religion in which Ike was reared is required to understand the Watchtower's influence on him. It is critical to stress that the religion in which Dwight was reared was very different than the Jehovah's Witnesses of today because, although the Bible Students would later be known as Jehovah's Witnesses, many differences exist between them.

HISTORY OF THE MOVEMENT

The Watchtower movement was formally founded in 1879 by Charles Taze Russell (1852–1916). Born on February 16, 1852, in Pittsburgh, Pennsylvania, of Scottish-Irish Presbyterian parents, Russell was a former Congregationalist who, while a young man, drifted into agnosticism. Russell's faith was revived by the Second Adventists, a church related to the modern Seventh Day Adventists.

Russell was, at first, one insignificant member of a large movement within Christianity that consisted of many individuals, including ministers from different denominations such as the Lutheran and Calvinist branches of Protestantism. The writings of men such as George Storrs, William Miller, Joseph Seiss, J. H. Paton, Nelson H. Barbour, and others were the real intellectual backbone of the Bible Student movement created by Russell.

In developing his own theological system, Russell borrowed many Adventist doctrines, such as stressing the return of Christ, the belief that we are living in the end times, and the importance of creationism. He also developed his core teachings around the imminent return of Christ Jesus. Russell, however, was not only influenced by conservative churches, but also by the Universalists, the Unitarians, and even the Plymouth Brethren and Mennonites.

Russell, in effect, began his movement (the Watchtower Society) as a mail-order publisher, and the printed page has played a critical part in the movement ever since. According to Russell, the Watchtower Society itself was originally "nothing more than a publishing house," but in time became "God's organization, the only ark of salvation," and the Witnesses now believe one must be firmly inside of that ark in order to be saved.[1]

The various Bible Student study groups were at first only loosely affiliated with Russell, and each "ecclesia" was largely independent. Many met to discuss the ideas in *Zion's Watch Tower.*[2] The ecclesia (Greek for "church") were loosely held together primarily by Watchtower representatives called "pilgrims." Gradually Russell and his followers also became more rigid in their beliefs. The stress at first was on Bible study and character development. In time, a formal organization developed. Dwight concluded a kind of loose worship association eventually developed "with similar groups throughout the country . . . chiefly through a subscription to a religious periodical, *The Watchtower.* After I left home for the Army, these groups were drawn closer together and finally adopted the name of Jehovah's Witnesses" in 1931.[3]

By 1880, scores of congregations existed in most Eastern states and several in the Central states, all of which developed from the one small Bible study Russell began in the early 1870s. In 1881 Zion's Watch Tower Bible and Tract Society was formed and was legally incorporated in 1884 with C. T. Russell as its first president. The Watchtower claimed 50 full-time workers in 1888 (a number that grew to over one million in the U.S. alone by 2018). In 1909, the headquarters moved from Allegheny, Pennsylvania, to Brooklyn, New York, partly because Russell wanted to "start over" after several embarrassing events in Allegheny, including his messy divorce trial.

The Watchtower Bible Society, their legal organization, has grown from a handful of followers in 1879 to 8.45 million active members worldwide in 2017 in 120,053 congregations.[4] In 2017, almost 20,175,477 persons worldwide attended their most important annual religious celebration, held at their churches, called "kingdom halls": the memorial of Christ's death. The

1. Franz, *Aid to Bible.*

2. Rogerson, *Millions Now Living*, 12.

3. Eisenhower, *At Ease*, 305.

4. See *2018 Yearbook of Jehovah's Witnesses*, 38.

20 million number includes mostly active Witnesses, but some interested persons, inactive Witnesses, and Witnesses' relatives.

The Watchtower structure gradually became more and more autocratic until today. In many countries, the Society owns all of the local congregational properties, and individual "congregations," as they are now called, exercise virtually no independence. They are required to strictly follow all of the instructions issued by the Watchtower Society headquarters in Brooklyn, New York. The "meetings," as their religious services are now termed, are conducted with only very slight variations the world over. Almost every congregation studies the same Watchtower lesson and even sings the same songs on the same Sunday throughout the world.

The primary advantage Russell had was the money required to widely propagate his message before the public. He and his father owned a chain of clothing stores that made Russell a very wealthy man. He was one of the few men who had the money (over a quarter of a million dollars from the business that he and his father started), the drive, and the determination required to propagate his ideas.

His success helps to explain why this movement became permanently entrenched in the American religious scene. Unfortunately, Russell made several predictions that failed. The most well-known was his 1914 prediction of Christ's return—a prophetic failure that caused David Eisenhower to leave the Watchtower fellowship.

That being said, a major reason for their growth, and an important aspect of Eisenhower's background, is that the Witness community offers a highly supportive social network. Their support of each other includes helping fellow members deal with the mundane tasks of living and with personal problems. Many find their high moral ideals, including their prohibition against sexual immorality, smoking, and excessive drinking, very appealing. Divorce is allowed only in the case of adultery, and all forms of sexual immorality are condemned. As a result, illegitimacy and sexually transmitted diseases are lower than among non-Witnesses, and most of the problems of unwed or single mothers are avoided.

The Bible Students stressed Bible reading and study as well as Christian charity, the importance of helping others, kindness to all including loving your enemies, the harm of gossip, and the general wisdom found in the Scriptures. The Eisenhower boys all rejected the more controversial Watchtower ideas but accepted many of their core, more orthodox teachings.

Although nominal followers exist in all faiths, most Watchtower followers have always had a level of commitment that other denominations envy; in 2017, worldwide they spent over two billion hours in the proselytizing work. Witnesses are known internationally for distributing millions of books and magazines from door to door and on the street corners of most big cities.

Most of their publications have print runs in the multi-millions and in hundreds of languages. Over 45 million copies of each Watchtower issue were printed in 240 languages in 2017.[5] They do most of their own printing and operate one of the largest publisher establishments in the world. Until recently, Witnesses formally met for two hours on Sundays, two hours on Thursdays, and an hour on Tuesdays. Additionally, they also met two nights a week, usually in their "kingdom halls," to study Watchtower publications and hone their proselytizing skills. In Ike's day, they usually met in homes or rented halls for their services.

The number of college graduates in the group has always been very small. Today it is around 5 percent, compared to 46.7 percent among Jews and 49.5 percent among Unitarians. This is partly because the Watchtower has, until very recently, strongly discouraged pursuing post-secondary education. Since discouragement of higher education has softened in the past few years—but still exists[6]—the educational level will no doubt rise in the future.

When the Eisenhowers were involved in the Watchtower, the ethnic composition was largely white European, but recently the percentage of minority persons, especially blacks, has grown enormously. Part of the reason for this is due to the Watchtower teaching all races are literal descendants of Adam and Eve and, consequently, all persons are equal before God. In the United States, minority members are now a majority (over 52 percent of Witnesses are African American or Latino) and their growth has been especially large in Africa.

The Witnesses also endeavor to effectively present their message to a non-Western, non-white audience. Their publications now regularly feature illustrations of black and Asian members from many nations. Growth in the past decade has been most rapid in Third World countries and former

5. https://www.jw.org/en/jehovahs-witnesses/activities/publishing/watchtower-awake-magazine/. See also https://www.businessinsider.com/the-most-widely-read-magazine-in-the-world-is-the-monthly-pub-of-jehovahs-witnesses-2010-9.

6. See *Watchtower*, October 15, 2005.

communist nations, including Russia. Most converts were raised in a Christian denomination, primarily Protestant and Catholic; the Witnesses have had very limited success converting Hindus, Muslims, or Buddhists.

Witnesses today still stress the need to proclaim to the world the impending battle of Armageddon, which they believe will soon destroy all wicked humans (i.e., in general, all non-Jehovah's Witnesses). Persons who survive Armageddon will live forever on a paradise Earth where no pain, sorrow, or sin will exist, and a select 144,000 persons will spend eternity in heaven with Christ Jesus to rule those persons on Earth.

Russell's untimely and unexpected death on October 31, 1916, in Pampa, Texas, was a blow to the movement that should have been anticipated. His health was always somewhat poor, but in his role as the man to restore early Christianity, he tended to feel his life was shielded by God, so Russell evidently did not properly take care of himself. Toward the end of his life, he even neglected necessary medical treatment. Russell was buried in United Cemetery in Millvale, Pennsylvania, near Pittsburgh.

When Russell died, his organization was thrown into turmoil resulting in many splinter groups, most of which insisted on following Russell and not the Watchtower Society's new president, J. F. Rutherford. Russell was seen by many of his followers as "the faithful and discreet slave," God's only spokesman on Earth today. The changes made in policy and doctrine after he died were so drastic that many scholars now consider the modern Jehovah's Witnesses to be an offshoot of the original movement that Russell began. The several movements claiming to be "faithful" followers of Russell's teachings still call themselves Bible Students today.

EARLY OPPOSITION TO THE BIBLE STUDENTS FROM THE ESTABLISHED CHURCHES

Russell vehemently insisted on the correctness of his teachings, and because his position on several major issues conflicted with the orthodox churches, many persons in the religious world intensely disliked him and his movement.

The influential Eastern newspaper *The Brooklyn Daily Eagle* constantly criticized Russell, his personal practices, his religion, and his followers. Some sample *Eagle* headlines illustrate the flavor of the attacks: "Girl Kissed Pastor and Sat on His Knee" (October 29, 1911), "Pastor Silent to His Wife for Months" (October 31, 1911), "Give Up Their Homes,

Following Russellism" (December 26, 1911), "Russell's Latest Outburst" (May 1, 1912), "Sold House for $50.00 to Defy His Wife" (November 27, 1911). One article provides a particularly good example of the religious opposition that Russell faced:

> One N.H. Barbour, called Dr. Barbour, with his confreres, J.H. Paton and C.T. Russell, is traveling around the country, going everywhere that they can find Adventists, and preaching that Jesus has come secretly, and will soon be revealed and mingling in their lectures a lot of "Age-to-come" trash, all to subvert their hearers. They are not endorsed by Adventists, "Age-to-come" folks, or anybody else, yet having some money and a few sympathizers they will probably run awhile . . . We are credibly informed that one of them boasted in Union Mills, Ind., a few days since, that they would break up every Advent church in the land. We guess not. Their whole work is proselytizing. The Lord never sent them on their mission. Give them no place, and go not near them or countenance them.[7]

Abrams described the Russellites as a thorn in the flesh of the larger denominations, and their conflicts with the state and society became far worse after Russell died.[8] After 1918 some even argued that the state should arrest the Russellites, and after "similar pleas by the hierarchy of the orthodox churches, the Russellites began to be arrested."[9] The "churches and the clergy were originally behind the movement to stamp out the Russellites," and the state continued to oppress them for decades; in many parts of the world it still does.[10]

DOCTRINAL POSITIONS OF RUSSELL

Although most Watchtower beliefs are similar to mainline Protestantism, since Russell's day they have deviated from mainline Christianity in several major areas. However, Russell became famous (or, more accurately, infamous), not so much for what he believed, but for what he did *not* believe. Among the orthodox Christian doctrines that he denied, as is still true of the Jehovah's Witnesses today, are the immortality of the soul, the bodily

7. *Advent Christian Times*, July 18, 1877.

8. Abrams, *Preachers Present Arms*, 182.

9. Abrams, *Preachers Present Arms*, 183.

10. Abrams, *Preachers Present Arms*, 183–84.

resurrection of Christ, the full deity of Christ (Christ was believed to be a god, but a lesser god than the Father), the personality of the Holy Spirit, and the legitimacy of the church and all its branches after the apostles died.

Witnesses also reject the Trinity, teaching that the Son is a created being[11] and that the Holy Spirit is God's active force. They also reject the concept of hell as a place of eternal torment. Instead, they teach that hell is the grave, from which people can be resurrected.[12] They share several of these teachings with other Protestant sects such as The Way, the Mormons, and others. Russell's followers came to believe the churches in general had become corrupt and that God used Russell to lead his people back to Christian foundations.[13]

The Witnesses' primary commitment is to both the Old and New Testaments, but they are also required to accept current Watchtower teachings and policy. Disagreement with this policy can be grounds for disfellowshipping. Some are even disfellowshipped for challenging the Watchtower's interpretation of Scripture, often on issues outsiders view as minor.[14]

Obviously, this prohibition creates serious problems when a spouse, child, or other family member is disfellowshipped. Much more latitude in belief and requirements was allowed in the early Watchtower movement. For example, during Russell's presidency, Watchtower policy required baptized members "seek to be excused" from military service and, failing that, to seek non-combatant positions such as nurses and medics.[15] After Rutherford became president, and until very recently, Watchtower policy required disfellowshipping baptized members who became involved in the military, even indirectly, such as working as an employee for a war armaments plant.

Witnesses were required to go to prison rather than submit to conscription and were the largest group of persons jailed for refusing conscription. Today, disfellowshipping is used to force dissenters to either toe the line or be forced out. Once forced out, they are labeled apostates, and Witnesses are warned to have nothing to do with them or their writings. One might believe their staunch opposition to Darwinism and evolution

11. Rev 3:14.

12. Rogerson, *Millions Now Living*, 10.

13. Rogerson, *Millions Now Living*, 10–11.

14. Harrison, *Visions of Glory*.

15. See *Zion's Watch Tower*, August 1, 1898, 231–32, and *Reprints of the Original Watchtower*, 5:2345.

would cause more problems, but this is rarely the case. Generally, people who leave the fellowship do so as a result of interpersonal conflicts or their own Bible study and theological research that have caused them to believe the Watchtower's doctrinal interpretations are incorrect.

When the Eisenhower boys were reared in the Watchtower at the turn of the century, close to 90 percent of the Watchtower's teachings were in harmony with mainline Christianity. The Watchtower openly relied heavily on mainline Protestant literature to formulate its doctrine. Even unique Watchtower teachings not held by mainline Christianity were found in some Christian and para-Christian denominations.

For example, opposition to war is taught by the Quakers, Seventh Day Adventists, Mennonites, Doukhobors, Anabaptists, and Amish, among other peace churches. Even the more controversial doctrinal views of the Watchtower, such as rejection of the Trinity, is also in part taught by The Way (since 1958), certain Messianic Jews, Unitarians, and many independent churches including several Pentecostal groups. Other differences, including the Watchtower's teaching that hell is the grave and two classes of people exist (the earthly class and the heavenly class), are taught by certain small sects.

As noted, many of the controversial Watchtower teachings were developed *after* the Eisenhower boys left home. Most of the beliefs and doctrines separating Witnesses from mainline Christianity—prohibition against voting, political involvement, blood transfusions, celebration of birthdays, Christmas, and attending non-Witness religious services—actually came much later. It is not unusual for persons raised as Witnesses to leave the faith and associate with mainline conservative Christianity—some even becoming ministers or leaders in major Christian groups. A few well-known examples include Charles Trombly, the Rev. Paul Blizzard, and Duane Magnani.

THE FUEL FOR PERSECUTION: RUTHERFORD'S WRITING

One factor involved in stirring up persecution was the attitude and teachings of the Watchtower. During the presidency of J. F. Rutherford, many articles in Watchtower publications were deliberately written to stir up trouble. Rutherford's vitriolic attacks were not only against the government, but also against the clergy, especially Roman Catholic priests, who he believed were not following the Bible's teachings. He repeatedly called them "scum," "roosters," "jackasses," "harlots," "SOBs," and worse. Many of his articles would today, no doubt, engender legal action against the Watchtower, claiming they incited religious hatred. And the claimants would likely prevail, at least in American courts.[16] Conversely, individual Witnesses were often caught in between their governing bodies' regulations and the states' laws.[17]

In a letter to Watchtower attorney O. R. Moyle dated February 28, 1937, Rutherford requested his opponents to debate him in a "national" affair, not letting his adversaries "sneak off into some isolated corner and spitting out their stuff by an insignificant rooster." In a letter to Moyle about the assault cases against Witnesses dated April 22, 1939, Rutherford advised showing a "little fight and peel someone's head for him" may help the Witnesses solve their problems. Rutherford may have been blunt and cross, but the vast majority of Witnesses were hard-working, tactful, meek persons who went about their business with seriousness and purpose.

In another letter dated March 31, 1939, Rutherford requested Moyle to file a lawsuit against everyone involved in one case, including the city, the city manager, the commissioner, the mayor, the Catholic priest, and "every other SOB that incited the mob." Articles in the *Golden Age* and *Consolation* pictured Catholic priests in the vilest of terms, and numerous illustrations shown, especially of Catholics, were close to slanderous.[18]

Shortly after Rutherford wrote the above letter, he gave a talk at Madison Square Garden titled "Government and Peace." At this rally, he was seemingly trying to stir up trouble when he made statements such as, "The Catholic Church, no matter what anybody tells you, supports Hitler." The response of some in the audience, evidently mostly Catholics who attended solely for the purpose of disrupting the meeting, began booing and hissing Rutherford. In response,

> Witnesses, acting as ushers and armed with canes, rushed over to the trouble spot and began cracking their sticks against heads . . . Other knots of anti-Rutherfordites popped up throughout the audience and pelted the speakers' platform with rotten eggs. By the time the police had dashed in from the street it was a huge free-for-all. Among the four persons injured was a woman of

16. Mazur, *Americanization of Religious Minorities.*

17. Bergman, *Mandatory Flag Salute.*

18. For photocopies of letters see Magnani, *Danger at Your Door,* 196, 197, and 245.

42 and a girl of 14, thrown down a staircase and trampled. When
the war was over, police . . . arrested . . . three Witnesses' leaders.[19]

The Watchtower Society, as the above incident illustrates, caused many of
its own problems, but this does not in any way justify the violence that
was meted out to innocent Witnesses. Unfortunately, the average Witness
suffered because of both the Watchtower policies and the reaction of the
people and the state to these policies.[20] One of the most controversial policies is the refusal to salute the American flag.

REFUSAL TO SALUTE

After the Watchtower lost the 1940 *Minersville School District v. Gobitis*
Supreme Court case,[21] involving the right to expel Witnesses from school
for refusing to participate in compulsory daily flag salute exercises, a wave
of persecution followed that many concluded was close to without equal in
American history.[22] The beatings and murders shocked the legal establishment and, as a result, most journalists severely criticized the court decision.
In Newton's words, "expulsion of Witness children from public schools
became commonplace, and efforts to force individual Witnesses to salute
the flag abounded. Vigilantes undertook massive assaults on Witnesses
throughout the land, burning their homes, destroying their literature, and
physically abusing them, often encouraged, or at least overlooked, by law
enforcement officials."[23]

Many felt that the Supreme Court flag salute ruling was largely re-
sponsible for the mayhem that followed their ruling against the Witnesses
and was a factor in overturning this decision and ruling in favor of the
Witnesses in other cases. After a series of court cases, the Gobitis flag case
was overturned in 1943 by the Supreme Court.[24]

---

19. *Newsweek*, July 3, 1939, 14.

20. Slater, *Ike I Knew.*

21. 310 U.S. 586 (1940).

22. Mazur, *Americanization of Religious Minorities.*

23. Newton, *Armed with the Constitution*, 79–80.

24. See *Taylor v. Mississippi*, 319 U.S. 583 (1943); *West Virginia State Board of Education v. Barnette*, 319 U.S. 624 (1943); *Mathews v. Hamilton*, 320 U.S. 707 (1943).

CHURCHES AND GOVERNMENT GROUPS

The Witness problems have often occurred with the cooperation—and even the open approval—of both the churches and various government officials.[25] White summarizes some of the many attempts to block the Witnesses from assembling together as a group in the 1940s, noting the American Legion, the Veterans of Foreign Wars, and various Catholic groups were the main groups that tried to block their conventions.

Besides the Watchtower requirement that Witnesses not salute the flag of any country, their problems during wartime were because they were not in any way to support the war effort, even buying war bonds, because of their opposition to war.[26] An incident typical of this time occurred at Klamath Falls, Oregon, when the American Legion began to harass the Witnesses assembled over their refusal to salute the flag or buy war bonds. Eventually, they attacked the Witnesses and besieged the hall, breaking windows and tossing stink bombs, ammonia, and burning kerosene rags into the building in which the Witnesses were inside.

Some tried to get in the hall through the broken windows, only to be hit with broken benches by Witnesses inside. The Witnesses' automobiles were all disabled, and many were overturned. Only the militia that was called out by the state's governor finally quelled the mob, which numbered one thousand at its peak."[27]

In Salt Lake City, Utah, two men forcibly entered the home of a Witness and beat him, inflicting cuts, bruises, and a fractured hip. When the Witness's friends attempted to file an appeal bond, a mob attacked the Witnesses, injuring them.

The extent of the mob rule that continued unabated in the mid 1940s included on April 25, 1942, a mob that attacked three Witnesses advertising their literature on the street. One attacker pinned a Witness's arms behind his back while a mobster struck him until he was close to unconscious. In response, the police threatened to arrest the Witness! On May 23 of the same year, a sixteen-year-old Witness was severely beaten for refusing to salute the flag. In Topeka, Kansas, two Witness children, aged fourteen and

25. Mazur, *Americanization of Religious Minorities*.

26. Sibley and Jacob, *Conscription of Conscience*.

27. White, *A People For*, 330.

nine, refused to salute the flag, and as a result were made wards of the court. The judge sentenced their mothers to a year's imprisonment.[28]

In Little Rock, Arkansas, a group of about a hundred pipeline workers formed a mob and, armed with guns and pipes, attempted to break up the Witness assembly currently in progress there. Some mob members entered the convention grounds and, brandishing their weapons and firing shots, dragged the Witnesses out into the streets. After they refused to salute the flag, their attackers beat them and threw the Witnesses into a ditch.[29] White, a Stanford University PhD, ends the story by noting, "No arrests of the mobsters were made."

One example that occurred in Biloxi, Mississippi, involved a Witness who was advertising Watchtower literature. In response to taking a photo of a Catholic priest who was heckling a Witness, the priest had him arrested. Then the Witness asked Chief of Police Alonzo Gabrich to preserve the camera as proof of the priest's illegal behavior, but instead the police destroyed the camera and, while a policeman held him, the Witness was struck in the face.

In another case that occurred in Connersville, Indiana, the sheriff jailed seventy-five Witnesses on a charge of criminal syndicalism. The court set their bail at a level impossible for Witnesses to pay, $225,000.

One key convention city selected by the Watchtower was Columbus, Ohio, but their officials were forced to cancel the contract due to pressure from the public. In response to this action, Witnesses circulated a petition, which was signed by 2,042,126 persons, and 350 "Witnesses showed up at the Governor's house, each bearing a parcel with about 6,000 signatures." In spite of this support, the governor refused to do anything to help the Witnesses because, he said, they didn't salute the flag. The Catholic bishop James J. Hartley reportedly caused the cancellation, so N. H. Knorr, the Society's second in command then, "invited him to speak to the assembled Witnesses on 'Religion as a World Remedy,' the same subject Rutherford" was scheduled to speak on. He never replied.[30]

The Watchtower decided to hold the aforementioned convention in Detroit, but it turned out that the situation was not much better there. The convention hall owner was told if he allowed the Witnesses to meet, his tax assessment would increase. They assembled anyway, and on July 20, 1940,

28. White, *A People For*, 327–30.

29. White, *A People For*, 327–30.

30. White, *A People For*, 326–27.

thirty-seven Witnesses were jailed, and at least twelve persons, including several women, were attacked by opposers. One priest tore both a sign and part of the clothing from a female Witness who was advertising the convention.

By the time the convention concluded, instead of coming to the Witnesses' aid, the police put fifty Witnesses in jail. Similar events occurred in other convention sites. For example, over twenty-five "Witnesses were arrested at Boston, Massachusetts . . . Twenty-four were jailed at Las Cruces, New Mexico. At Jackson, Mississippi, a mob of fifty men invaded the auditorium demanding that the Witnesses leave town. When they didn't, the mobsters forcibly made them, and the convention had to be abandoned."[31]

In 1940, the major reason given for arresting Witnesses in the United States was the claim their assembly was in violation of various "ordinances," a ploy that was useless to stop them.[32] Consequently, more serious charges were brought against Witnesses, including blasphemy, ridicule, inciting violence, breach of the peace, and desecration of the flag.

LOCAL LAW ENFORCEMENT

A major cause of the 1940 conflicts was the hostility of citizens, openly condoned by officials who often violated the law themselves, or at the least, approved the mob violence. One 1943 incident of violence against Jehovah's Witnesses involved two Witnesses, Robert Cofer and Osca Lawrence Pillars. The marshal arrested Mr. Pillars but promised him protection only if he would first salute the flag. When he refused, he was turned over to the mob and

> beaten to unconsciousness, revived with water, beaten again, dragged by a rope around his neck to the city hall and hanged to a post. Fortunately, the rope broke. At 12:30 pm he was put in jail again, and a doctor at 3:45 pm said he would have to be taken to a hospital in order to remain alive. By 9:30 p.m. he was in a hospital. The police chief of Greenville, Mississippi ordered all Jehovah's Witnesses out of town by 5:00 p.m. None left. So he herded fifty into jail, leaving a Witnesses' three-year-old child unattended in the rain outside.[33]

31. White, *A People For*, 326--27.
32. Stevens, *The Bible vs. the Flag*.
33. White, *A People For*, 330.

In addition, the police, not uncommonly, openly contributed to the violence, both by condoning it and by their active involvement in assaulting Witnesses. One case involved an African-American Witness who, after he refused to salute the flag, was beaten into unconsciousness by the police. When he gained consciousness, the police beat him again. Two days later he was released from jail, hemorrhaging and suffering permanent brain injuries. In another case on December 5, 1942, while in the door-to-door witnessing work, August Schmidt unintentionally called on the home of Sergeant Ellis of Redondo Beach, California. Ellis dragged him to his car, then forced him to enter his car at gunpoint, and beat him with a blackjack.[34]

The sad conclusion is the United States justice system failed abysmally during this time. Out of many thousands of assaults on Witnesses during the 1940s, the Department of Justice found the courage to prosecute and convict only one offender, Sergeant Ellis.[35] Judge Henry Edgerton once summarized his long experience on the bench, concluding that during World War II the principal threat to civil liberties came "not from the Federal Government but from the activities of local officials and from the terrorism practiced by private persons against the unpopular groups, especially the pacifist sect called Jehovah's Witnesses."[36]

Some of the violence involved local or higher-level officials. One example is the mayor of Harlan, Kentucky, who "ordered the police to loot the home of Witness Louis Beeler" and then arrest him. After trying to force him to salute the flag, the police repeatedly struck him on his face, then jailed him. When Witness Lindell Carr visited him in jail, he was also arrested and jailed. Later, Witness Elihu Hurst attended Beeler's hearing and was also jailed. Soon other Witnesses were arrested and, unable to obtain legal help, remained in jail without a trial for as long as eighty-four days. To keep them in jail longer, their trials were postponed for three months.

At Somerset, Kentucky, Witnesses Frank Speerless and his wife were jailed "for sedition, and Everett Henry for giving him [Watchtower] literature while in jail. Witness Willie Johnson reclined behind bars for six months under an impossible $5,000 bail until charges were dropped."[37] Another case involved Witness Miss Eunice Lamson, who was attacked by a mob that tried to force her to salute the flag. When she called the police,

34. White, *A People For,* 330–31.
35. White, *A People For,* 331.
36. Edgerton, *Freedom in the Balance*; Bontecou, *Freedom in the Balance,* 2.
37. White, *A People For,* 331.

attempting to receive protection, the police arrested Miss Lamson! Her court trial was set for the next day, which did not allow her time to consult a lawyer.

She was convicted on some trumped-up offense and jailed. An attorney was able to have her released, but another Witness, Mina Kinler, was about that time arrested for trespassing and took her place. The state was having difficulty keeping Witnesses in jail under the existing laws, so the Somerset city passed a peddler's license tax ordinance requiring payment of $7.50 per day for the privilege of distributing literature. Few Witnesses then could afford to pay this amount, and most would not pay it if they could.[38]

An excellent example of this antagonism by a high-level court official was related by Harvard professor Alan Dershowitz, who, as a law student at Yale, studied the Supreme Court decision involving the compulsory flag salute case that occurred during World War II. As noted, Jehovah's Witnesses object to saluting the flag on religious grounds. The majority of the court judges agreed with the religious objectors,

> but Justice Felix Frankfurter dissented essentially on the grounds that patriotism during war-time is more important than religious liberty. Frankfurter, a Jew, began his dissent with a remarkable self-characterization: "One who belongs to the most vilified and persecuted minority in history is not likely to be insensible to the freedoms guaranteed by our Constitution." (He, of course, [then] proceeded to be quite "insensible" to the religious freedoms of the Jehovah's Witnesses!) I read the Frankfurter characterization in astonishment.[39]

The Jehovah's Witnesses have now brought over fifty cases to the Supreme Court and won the majority in a series of decisions that form the foundation of freedom of religion, press, and speech in America today.[40] Two of these cases, *Jones v. Opelika* and *Marsh v. Alabama*, dealt with attempts by the government to limit public expression of religious beliefs, and both decisions are again being challenged. These cases are critical to understand both the struggles of religious minorities and the American Watchtower membership today. Ironically, although cases that went to the Supreme Court generally involved white Witnesses, Roscoe Jones was one major

38. White, *A People For*, 331.
39. Dershowitz, *Chutzpah*, 48.
40. Henderson, "Hayden Covington."

exception. White males controlled the Watchtower movement, but women and blacks bore the brunt of Witness proselytizing activity.[41]

The Watchtower has been very involved in religious freedom litigation at least since the turn of the last century. They were not endeavoring to expand the religious freedoms of all Americans, although today they speak with pride about the cases they won that have had an enormous impact on the freedoms of other groups.

They also both strongly encourage and actively support litigation, but only in those areas involving specific rights that the Watchtower deems necessary in order to carry out its activities. One reason for their extensive legal involvement was because the Watchtower's second president, J. F. Rutherford, was an attorney, as was their vice-president then, Hayden Covington, who fought many of their cases. Actually, many of these cases were orchestrated by Watchtower attorneys, who selectively accepted a few and declined most. Those that they declined were often not litigated because few Witnesses had the financial means to hire their own attorney, and many were unable to find sympathetic attorneys to defend them pro bono.

Furthermore, the Watchtower has experienced conflicts in almost every nation of the world—I have been unable to locate a single country where they have not experienced problems. At one time or another they were banned, or their activities severely restricted, in almost every nation of the world, and they are still banned in twenty-six countries, according to their official worldwide activities report published in 2008.

If they were a small inconsequential sect, this would be of far less importance, but, at around 10 million adherents with an income in the United States alone of over $1.25 billion, the Witnesses are now a major religious force. They are now the second largest religious denomination in Poland, Italy, Spain, and Portugal, and have over 100,000 members in many other countries including Britain, Germany, France, Russia, Brazil, Japan, Nigeria, the Philippines, and Canada. They claim over 600,000 members in Mexico, 300,000 in Nigeria, and over one million in the United States. The Watchtower is a large denomination by any standard and continues to experience significant growth compared to most churches today.

Buoyed by its past success, the Watchtower is still extremely active and aggressive in pursuing litigation. A primary focus today is on child custody cases, a concern because many judges are inclined to award custody to the non-Witness parent. The other area is blood transfusion: when a hospital

41. Newton, *Armed with the Constitution*, 9.

administers a blood transfusion in an attempt to save a Witness's life, litigation not uncommonly follows. The Watchtower often tries to litigate these
cases on an assault and battery claim or a violation of religious freedom.
This is true even in cases in which it is quite clear a transfusion was necessary in order to save the Witness's life.[42]

As noted, Witnesses also tend to use the doctrine called "theocratic
war strategy" in an attempt to defend themselves in these court cases.[43] The
Watchtower teaches that Witnesses in court "do not need to give the truth
to those who have no right to know it," and it is not necessary to adhere to
the norms and ethics of the legal profession. Consequently, Witnesses do
not strictly abide by the oath that states they are to "tell the whole truth and
nothing but the truth."

Their less-than-fully-honest testimony in court, and a tendency to
exploit their public image as meek, honest, and peaceable in court, often
serves them well. As Newton notes, in the 1940s Witnesses were "personally well mannered," but their doctrine was "stridently anti-establishment.
Believing the prevailing religious, economic, and political institutions were
ruled by of Satan, Witnesses minced no words in denouncing them, pro-
voking heated and sometimes violent reactions."[44] Nonetheless, this does
not justify the physical violence often meted out to them during this time.

THE SITUATION IN OTHER NATIONS

The situation we have described in America was much the same in many
other nations. Persecution has been a recurrent experience in the Watchtower Society in most nations in which they were active since they were
founded a century ago and "globally, this persecution has been so persistent
and of such an intensity that it would not be inaccurate to regard Jehovah's Witnesses as the most persecuted group of Christians of the twentieth
century."[45]

Reports of violence against Witnesses come from virtually every nation in the world including Canada, but the former communist countries,
Muslim nations, and those under totalitarian governments or with records

42. Louderback-Wood, *Blood Transfusions.*

43. Bergman, *Lying in Court.*

44. Newton, *Armed with the Constitution,* 4.

45. Jubber, *Persecution of Jehovah's Witnesses,* 121.

of human rights abuse tended to experience far more incidents.[46] One example, which occurred in Tanzania in 1984, involved a government order to demolish every kingdom hall in the Western District. In the Sumbawanga District, commissioner Ediddi Mapinda ordered all Witness kingdom halls demolished in response to reports that members of the outlawed sect had refused to participate in certain government-sponsored activities. The Witnesses were banned

> ten years ago for reportedly being "in conflict with the aims" of the ruling party and the government. Since the sect's formation in the 1870s, in the United States, it has come into conflict with the governments around the world because of its beliefs in the coming theocracy and its teaching that all political powers are expressions of Satan's power over humanity. Earlier last year, Bishop Paul Malseo and about seventy other members of the sect in Mwimbi and Mapaina areas of the western district were sentenced to six months in jail for "staying away from socialist activities."[47]

Hefley, in his summary of the persecution of Christians in the modern world, noted a common reason for conflicts in Africa is because of foreign colonial rule. In contrast, the African Witness movement was controlled by native Africans, not foreign whites, and much of the persecution occurred because they "refused to salute the national flag." These events led up to the development of the most recent example of a Hitler-type concentration camp in this century. After persuasion failed, Dr. Banda's government banned the Witnesses. When the Witnesses ignored the ban, soldiers rounded up thirty thousand members of the sect and forced them into

> prison camps. In December, 1975, officials of the Witnesses in other countries protested that adherents in Malawi were being beaten, tortured, and raped with official approval. Malawi is now, in effect, a police state, Dr. Banda is firmly in power for 'life.' . . . [A full story] about the persecution of the Witnesses [is] hard to determine. However, twenty evangelical foreign missions enjoy freedom of operation under the Banda regime. The Presbyterian Church of Zambia, to which the president belongs, has over six hundred thousand members.[48]

Summaries of similar cases could easily fill up a large set of volumes.

46. Yaffee, *Witnesses Seek Apology*; Yaffee and Yaffee, *Secret Files Reveal Bigotry*.
47. Report by *Religious News Service*, March 20, 1984.
48. Hefley and Hefley, *By Their Blood*, 447.

An example is the Watchtower ruling that members were not allowed to buy, under pain of disfellowshipping, an identification card in Malawi, which the government considered no different than having a driver's license.[49] The Watchtower, in contrast, interpreted the card as indicating party membership, something forbidden to Witnesses. The Watchtower teaches politics are corrupt and any direct involvement in politics corrupts those involved. This belief is easy to document: a reading of most any newspaper gives a regular flow of evidence to the charge of government corruption. One wonders if the reason "Eisenhower loathed the partisanship of the political arena and lacked any burning desire to hold public office" was related to Eisenhower's Witness upbringing and his own awareness of the corruption in politics.[50]

Empirical studies have confirmed these attitudes are still common in the United States. For example, researcher Lipset concluded from his study of prejudice toward minorities that the Jehovah's Witnesses were among the most disliked of all religious minorities he researched—the group average showed Americans had *more dislike of them than even the most hated ethnic minorities*. Specifically, an average of a whopping 41 percent expressed open dislike of them.[51] Research by Brinkerhoff and Mackie concluded the religious groups Americans found least acceptable were the so-called new cults followed by the Jehovah's Witnesses, Mormons, and conservative Christians.[52]

King and Clayson found that Jehovah's Witnesses and Jews were rated the most negative in the United States compared to all other religious groups for the population researched. Another study found "that when twelve religious groups were ranked by a national sample in terms of negative feelings, Mormons, Jews, and Jehovah's Witnesses received the most negative evaluations of the twelve groups. Thus, the general public has imputed negative evaluations to these religious groups, so in a sociological sense, Jews and Jehovah's Witnesses can be defined as deviant groups."[53]

Last, a study by the Barna Research Group found a significant number of Americans have unfavorable views of Jehovah's Witnesses; their study polled over six hundred adults and found, among those who had an

49. Franz, *Jehovah's Witnesses*.
50. Pach and Richardson, *Presidency*, 1.
51. Lipset, *Radical Right*, 435.
52. Brinkerhoff and Mackie, *Social Distance*.
53. King and Clayson, *Perceptions of Jews*, 50.

opinion about the Witnesses, only 26 percent said it was favorable, and fully 74 percent were negative.[54] In comparison, 88 percent had a favorable opinion of Protestants and 85 percent of Catholics.[55] The only other group for which this level of antagonism existed was the Hare Karishnas, which 84 percent viewed unfavorably compared to a mere 16 percent favorably. For many religious groups the data was the reverse of the Witnesses—84 percent viewed Jews favorably, compared to only 16 percent unfavorably.[56]

SIMILAR HOSTILITIES EVEN IN THE 1990S

These hostilities were echoed in former President H. W. Bush's comments during his election, relative to Governor Dukakis vetoing a bill that would require mandatory flag salute by students. This bill was contrary to the Supreme Court's ruling that laws *requiring* students to salute in school are unconstitutional. Dr. Robert Maddox, executive director for Americans United for Separation of Church and State (AU), appeared on the Morton Downey television show in 1988 to discuss this issue, and the enormous hostility he experienced is recounted below. Maddox wrote, "in my day I've endured some tough interviews under the harsh television lights. But nothing I have ever done on camera prepared me for the situation I found myself in a few weeks ago sitting on the 'hot seat' of The Morton Downey Jr. Show." He wrote it began when the Pledge of Allegiance issue surfaced

> during the presidential campaign. Americans United issued a press release tracing the history of the problem, pointing out that the constitutional questions involved in the episode stemmed from conscientious objections against reciting the pledge raised by Jehovah's Witnesses. In our release we made it plain that AU does not take positions for or against candidates but simply felt that the shrill hue and cry needed to be addressed with some sanity and accuracy.[57]

The response to this reasonable response was "an avalanche of requests to discuss our views" that, to their

54. See Sellers, *How Americans View Various Religious Groups*, 3.

55. See Sellers, *How Americans View Various Religious Groups*, 2.

56. Sellers, *How Americans View Various Religious Groups*, 3; Haymann, *Unofficial U.S. Census*, 124.

57. Maddox, "Reflections On Surviving," 21.

surprise, a producer of the Downey show also called, asking if I would appear, at Mort's expense, on the program to "discuss" our views . . . I discovered that the audience poses almost as much a threat to the guests as does Morton Downey . . . These folks love Mort, roaring frequent approval of his outrageous pronouncements. Just about anything he says pushes a button with the audience, causing them to unleash a din of approval alongside breathless threats against any guest who dares to disagree with their hero.[58]

He added that, fortunately for him, he was allowed a few uninterrupted seconds to make his

statement about the religious liberty and freedom of speech problems involved in requiring a person to recite the Pledge. My protagonist . . . tore into me for 'denying children the right to say the Pledge of Allegiance.' Over the tumult that broke as the audience stomped their feet and screamed its agreement with him, I insisted that no one had any notion of denying the right to say the Pledge to anyone. The "dialogue" took a decided turn from that point . . . Some in the audience convinced me they would physically attack a person who refused to give the Pledge, even if saying the words violated a deeply held religious conviction. The disturbing fact is that so many in the country . . . have little tolerance for dissenting views and even less understanding of the nuances of religious freedom issues.[59]

58. Maddox, "Reflections On Surviving," 21.
59. Maddox, "Reflections On Surviving," 21.

Appendix II
Separating Fact from Fiction

Researching Eisenhowers religion required separating fact from fiction. Fortunately I had several primary sources that proved reliable. To illustrate this problem, I have provided a few more examples other than those provided in the text.

ATTEMPTS TO CORRECT THE MISINFORMATION ABOUT EISENHOWER

Publications tend to resist correcting misinformation about Dwight's religious upbringing. For example, on April 19, 1999, I wrote the following in a letter to Lars Mahinske at the *Encyclopedia Britannica* editorial office:

> As you may recall, we corresponded previously relative to the entry in your encyclopedia on Jehovah's Witnesses. I have reviewed another entry, this one on Dwight D. Eisenhower, and again found the information incorrect. Eisenhower was not reared a Mennonite or River Brethren, but a Jehovah's Witness. The entire family were active in the Witnesses, even holding church meetings in their house for many years. Their mother Ida, and shortly there afterward her husband, converted when Ike Eisenhower was age five. This has all been well documented (see the enclosed article). The Britannica is not alone in making this error; many other reference books I have consulted have done the same. I have discovered once erroneous information becomes mainstream, it is very difficult to weed this information out.

On October 6, 1999, Anita Wolff, a special projects editor, responded to my letter as follows:

We will make the necessary corrections in our biography of Dwight Eisenhower. I have passed the brochure you sent on the Jehovah Witness's stance on saluting the flag to our religions editor. We appreciate your concern for the accuracy of our products, and we thank you for taking the time to comment.

The 2003 edition of the Britannica was rewritten, removing the River Brethren claim, stating only that Dwight was introduced to a "strong religious tradition at an early age."[1] Nothing was mentioned about the influence of the Witnesses or any other religious denomination.

POOR RESEARCH CONFRONTED

A review published on Amazon of Herald Gullan's book *Faith of Our Mothers: The Stories of Presidential Mothers from Mary Washington to Barbara Bush* highlighted the censorship concern.[2] One review of the book, titled "Poorly Researched," includes concerns commonly existing in books about Dwight. The anonymous reviewer noted he was a student of religious history and read Harold Gullan's book to determine if Gullan had the courage to write

> the truth about President Eisenhower's religious background, or whether he had regurgitated previously fabricated propaganda. Dwight Eisenhower was reared in the religious faith that later took on the name "Jehovah's Witnesses." However, Eisenhower biographers, American historians, and even the Watchtower Society (JWs) have worked in concert to distort that fact.

Dwight Eisenhower was a youth in the late 1890s and first decade of the 1900s. The reviewer notes Dwight's parents were involved in a religious group then known as "Bible Students," often derisively called by critics and opposers "Russellites" because

> they followed the teachings of Charles Taze Russell, the founder of the Watchtower Bible and Tract Society. This group eventually adopted the name "Jehovah's Witnesses" in 1931. The ruse that Ike's parents were "River Brethren" during his formative years and only briefly associated with JWs after Ike left home is an intentional effort to rewrite history so as to hide the fact that an American

---

1. See *Encyclopedia Britannica*, 2003 ed., vol. 4, 404.
2. Published on Amazon, dated July 6, 2002.

president, who also happened to be THE military hero of World War II, was reared in the religion which later became infamous for its theology which forbids members to participate in political and military activities.

This reviewer is not a Watchtower apologist, as is clear when he notes the claim this ruse was supported by the fact that the Watchtower

does not want to acknowledge such facts either, because to do so would require them to publicize to their current membership and potential converts the fact that their ever-changing theology once accommodated participation in military and political affairs. For example, in 1911, the year that Dwight Eisenhower entered West Point, the Chairman of the opening ceremonies at the then annual Watchtower Convention was General William Hall, a Congressional Medal of Honor winner from the western Indian Wars, who was named Adjutant General of the United States Army in 1912. (It is thus far an undocumented suspicion that Hall may even have played a role in Ike's West Point admission.)

The ruse is also assisted by the fact that at that point in the Watchtower Society's history, it had not yet become a totally separate denomination, and its "followers" often maintained membership ties with local churches, so long as the local church did not object to the member's promotion of Watchtower teachings (which at that time were not as objectionable as current). Ike and his parents may very well have remained members in the Eisenhower family's local "River Brethren" Church, but it is also a fact that Ike's parents' home was the local weekly meeting place for "Russellites" during Ike's formative years starting in 1896, and continuing even after he left home for West Point.

The reviewer concluded that after the first Watchtower president, Charles Taze Russell, died in 1916, his successor began initiating doctrinal changes including those relating to involvement in political and military affairs, adding at this time

Ike's father and siblings gradually separated themselves from the Watchtower Society. Ike's mother continued with the Watchtower Society, dying a loyal Jehovah's Witness. However, the rest of Ike's family (no doubt partially motivated by Ike's career), did everything they could to not only separate themselves from the Watchtower Society, but they even went to the extent of attempting to erase their past ties with such.

Unfortunately, the reviewer noted that, in general, "efforts to rewrite Ike's history have been successful. Regrettably, Gullan's lack of research has aided and abetted the fictionalization of an important part of American presidential history and likely will play "a role in the future perpetuation of rewritten history." This anonymous reviewer was obviously very knowledgeable about both the Watchtower's early history and Eisenhower's background.

An example of omission is that of Ambrose and Immerman, who stated only that "Ida organized meetings of the Bible Students of the Watchtower Society, which met on Sundays in the Eisenhower parlor."[3] They provided no hint of the extent or level of the Eisenhower family's involvement in the Watchtower.

Only the statements that the Eisenhower children were reared in "an atmosphere of religion, discipline, and love" and that Bible study was a central part of their upbringing are typically mentioned.[4] Often vague unexplained details, such as "no one was permitted to leave the dinner table until after Ida said, 'Amen,'" were added.[5] The only biography written of Ida mentions nothing about her Watchtower involvement and only a few sentences about her religious activities. It noted her Mennonite background only in passing.[6]

Dwight dearly loved his mother, the Bible, and God, but had ambivalent feelings about the Watchtower and his negative feelings about them surfaced at times. An extensive search of the major depositories of President Eisenhower's letters and papers indicates he wrote little about his feelings or experiences in the Watchtower, but wrote much about his faith in God.[7]

3. Ambrose and Immerman, *Milton S. Eisenhower*, 13.

4. Kinnard, *Ike 1890–1990*, 6.

5. D'Este, *Eisenhower: A Soldier's Life*. 30.

6. Duncan, *Earning the Right*, 7, 18, 28.

7. Keller, *Intellectuals and Eisenhower*.

Bibliography

Abrams, Ray H. *Preachers Present Arms: The Role of the American Churches and Clergy in World War I and II, with Some Observations on the War in Vietnam.* Scottsdale, PA: Herald, 1969.

"All the Presidents' Man." *Newsweek*, April 21, 1980.

Alley, Robert S. *So Help Me God: Religion and the Presidency.* Virginia: John Knox, 1972.

Ambrose, Stephen E. *Eisenhower: 1890–1952.* New York: Simon and Schuster, 1983.

———. *Ike: Abilene to Berlin; The Life of Dwight D. Eisenhower from His Childhood in Abilene, Kansas, through His Command of the Allied Forces in Europe in World War II.* New York: Harper and Row, 1973.

———. *The Supreme Commander: The War Years of General Dwight D. Eisenhower.* Garden City, NY: Doubleday, 1970.

Ambrose, Stephen E., and Richard H. Immerman. *Milton S. Eisenhower, Educational Statesman.* Baltimore: Johns Hopkins University Press, 1983.

American Bible Society. "Dwight Eisenhower's Bible-Based Legacy." *American Bible Society*, July/August, 1969.

American Civil Liberties Union. *The Persecution of Jehovah's Witnesses.* New York: American Civil Liberties Union, January 1941.

Anderson, Jack. "Is His Vote Record Related to Payroll?" *Detroit Free Press*, September 23, 1956, 16b.

Angelo, Bonnie. *First Mothers: The Women Who Shaped the Presidents; With a New Chapter on First Mother, Barbara Bush.* New York: Perennial, 2001.

Antrim, Doron. "Why the President Believes in Prayer." *Parade*, December 8, 1957.

"Atheist Morality: Was Hitler an Atheist?" 2005.

August, Melissa, and Harriet Barovick. "1 Million." *Time*, December 23, 2002, 21.

Azar, Larry. *Twentieth Century in Crisis.* Dubuque, IA: Kendall Hunt, 1990.

Ball, Harry W. "Ike to Get Honorary Messiah Degree." Associated Press, May 29, 1965.

Barna Research Group. *How Americans View Religious Groups.* Press release, March, 1990.

Beckford, James A. *The Trumpet of Prophecy: A Sociological Study of a Jehovah's Witness.* Oxford: Blackwell, 1975.

Bellah, Robert, and Philip E. Hammond. *Varieties of Civil Religion.* San Francisco: Harper and Row, 1981.

Bergman, Jerry. "The Adventists and Jehovah's Witnesses Branch of Protestantism." In *America's Alternative Religions*, edited by Timothy White, 33–46. Albany: State University of New York Press, 1995,.

Bibliography

———. "Dwight Eisenhower." Ch. 7 in *Religion and the American Presidency: George Washington to George W. Bush with Commentary and Primary Sources*, edited by Gastón Espinosa, 249–81. New York: Columbia University Press, 2009.

———. *Hitler and the Nazis Darwinian Worldview: How the Nazis Eugenic Crusade for a Superior Race Caused the Greatest Holocaust in World History*. Kitchener, ON: Joshua, 2012.

———. "The Influence of Religion on President Eisenhower's Upbringing." *Journal of American and Comparative Culture* 32:4 (Spring 2000) 89–107.

———. *Jehovah's Witnesses: A Comprehensive and Selectively Annotated Bibliography*. Westport, CT: Greenwood, 1999.

———. "Jehovah's Witnesses." In *The Encyclopedia of New York State*, edited by Peter Eisenstadt. Syracuse, NY: Syracuse University Press, 2005.

———. "Jehovah's Witnesses." In *The Encyclopedia of Religious Revivals in America*, edited by Michael McClymond. Westport, CT: Greenwood, 2006.

———. "The Jehovah's Witnesses' Experience in the Nazi Concentration Camps; A History of Their Conflicts with the Nazi State." *Journal of Church and State* 38:1 (Winter 1996) 87–113.

———. "Lying in Court and Religion: An Analysis of the Theocratic Warfare Doctrine of the Jehovah's Witnesses." *Cultic Studies Review* 1:2 (2002) 1. http://www.culticstudiesreview.org. German translation: "Lügen vor Gericht und Religion: Eine Analyse der Lehre der Zeugen Jehovas von der Theokratischen Kriegsführung."

———. "The Modern Religious Objection to Mandatory Flag Salute in America: A History and Evaluation." *Journal of Church and State* 39:2 (Spring 1997) 215–36.

———. "Steeped in Religion: President Eisenhower and the Influence of Jehovah's Witnesses." *Kansas History* 21:3 (1998) 148–67.

———. "Toledo Dentist Charles Betts and the Health Crusade Against Aluminum." *Ohio History* 118 (2011) 91–111.

Beschloss, Michael R. *Eisenhower: A Centennial Life*. New York: Harper Collins, 1990.

Bettelheim, Bruno. *The Informed Heart*. Glencoe, IL: Free Press, 1960.

Blanshard, Paul. *God and Man in Washington*. Boston: Beacon, 1960.

Blumenson, Martin. *Patton: The Man Behind the Legend, 1885–1945*. New York: William Morrow, 1985.

Boeckel, Richard A. "A Soldier Who Became a Preacher." *The Watchtower* 15 (1980) 24–29.

Boller, Paul F., Jr. "Religion and the U.S. Presidency." *Journal of Church and State* 21 (Winter 1979) 11–12.

Bonnell, John Sutherland. *Presidential Profiles: Religion in the Life of American Presidents*. Philadelphia: Westminster, 1971.

Bontecou, Eleanor, editor. *Freedom in the Balance*. Westport, CT: Greenwood, 1978.

Bradley, Omar N. *A General's Life: An Autobiography by General of the Army Omar N. Bradley*. New York: Simon and Schuster, 1983.

Brandon, Dorothy. *Mamie Doud Eisenhower: A Portrait of a First Lady*. New York: Scribner, 1954.

Branigar, Thomas. "No Villains—The David Eisenhower." *Kansas History* 15:3 (Autumn 1992) 168–79.

———. Letter to Jerry Bergman. August 9, 1994.

Brendon, Piers. *Ike: His Life and Times*. New York: Harper and Row, 1986.

Bibliography

Brinkerhoff, Merlin B., and Marlene M. Mackie. "The Applicability of Social Distance for Religious Research: An Exploration." *Review of Religious Research* 28:2 (December 1986) 151–67.

Broadwater, Jeff. *Eisenhower and the Anti-Communist Crusade.* Chapel Hill: University of North Carolina Press, 1992.

Brubaker, Jack. "Ike and the Brethren." *Lancaster New Era,* November 27, 1979.

Burns, Brian. *The Ike Files.* Kansas City: Kansas City Star Books, 2008.

Cannon, Marian. *Dwight David Eisenhower: War Hero and President.* New York: Franklin Watts, 1990.

Case, Shirley Jackson. *The Millennial Hope: A Phase of War-Time Thinking.* Chicago: University of Chicago Press, 1918.

Challener, Richard D. "John Foster Dulles: The Moralist Armed." *Soldiers and Statesmen: The Proceedings of the 4th Military History Symposium United States Air Force Academy October 22–23, 1970,* edited by Monte D. Wright and Lawrence J. Paszek. Washington, DC: Office of Air Force History and USAF Academy, 1973.

Chernus, Ira. *Apocalypse Management: Eisenhower and the Discourse of National Insecurity.* Stanford, CA: Stanford University Press, 2008.

———. *General Eisenhower: Ideology and Discourse.* East Lansing: Michigan State University Press, 2002.

Christendom or Christianity: Which One Is the Light of the World? New York: Watchtower Bible and Tract Society, 1955. See the section "Is a Christian a Pacifist?," 24–26.

Climenhaga, A. W. *History of the Brethren in Christ Church.* Nappanee, IN: E.V. Publishing, 1942.

Cochrane, Arthur C. *The Church's Confession under Hitler.* Pittsburgh, PA: Pickwick, 1976.

Cohen, Stan. *The Eisenhowers: Gettysburg's First Family.* Charleston, WV: Pictorial Histories, 1986.

Cole, Marley. *Jehovah's Witnesses: The New World Society.* New York: Vantage, 1955.

Cosmin, Barry A., and Seymour P. Lachman. *One Nation under God.* New York: Harmony, 1993.

Cox, Archibald. *The Court and the Constitution.* Boston: Houghton Mifflin, 1987.

Curry, Cecilia. "Class Prophecy." In *The Helianthus,* yearbook of Abilene High School, Abilene, Kansas, 1909.

Davis, Kenneth S. *Soldier of Democracy: A Biography of Dwight Eisenhower.* Garden City, NY: Doubleday, 1952, originally published 1945.

"Day of Jubilee." *New York Times,* January 20, 1953, 24.

Dershowitz, Alan M. *Chutzpah.* New York: Simon and Schuster, 1991.

D'Este, Carlo. *Eisenhower: A Soldier's Life.* New York: Henry Holt, 2002.

Dewhirst, Robert E. *Dutiful Service: The Life of Mrs. Mamie Eisenhower.* New York: Nova History, 2004.

DiCianni, Ron. *The Faith of the Presidents.* Lake Mary, FL: Charisma, 2004.

Dimont, Max I. *Jews, God, and History.* New York: New American Library, 1994.

Dodd, Gladys. "The Early Career of Abraham L. Eisenhower, Pioneer Preacher." *Kansas Historical Quarterly* 29, Autumn 1963.

———. Letter to Jerry Bergman. October 8, 1994.

———. "The Religious Background of the Eisenhower Family." BDiv thesis, Nazarene Theology Seminary, 1959.

Duncan, Kunigunde. "Christmas Prayers Go Out to Abilene." *Des Moines Tribune,* December 23, 1944, 14.

Bibliography

————. *Earning the Right to Do Fancy Work: An Informal Biography of Ida Eisenhower, the President's Mother.* Lawrence: University Press of Kansas, 1957.

"Dwight D. Eisenhower's Bible-Based Legacy." *Bible Society Record,* July/August, 1969. Reprint.

Eckhoff, H. Leonard, and N. Dean Eckhoff. *An Eckhoff Family History.* Manhattan, KS: Lyons Creek Associates, 1999.

Edgerton, Henry W. *Freedom in the Balance: Opinions of Judge Henry W. Edgerton.* Edited by Eleanor Bontecou. Westport, CT: Greenwood, 1978.

"Eisenhower Aides Join Him at Church." *New York Times,* January 21, 1953, 18.

Eisenhower, Abraham. "Eisenhower: Soldier of Peace." *Time,* April 4, 1969, 19–25.

————. "Life, Death." *Evangelical Visitor* 9 (July 1928) 4–7.

Eisenhower, Dwight D. *At Ease: Stories I Tell to Friends.* Garden City, NY: Doubleday, 1967.

————. Commencement address, Messiah College, May 29, 1965. Messiah College archives.

————. *Crusade in Europe.* Garden City, NY: Doubleday, 1948.

————. *Dwight David Eisenhower: A Bibliography of His Times and Presidency.* Edited by R. Alton Lee. Wilmington, DE: Scholarly Resources, 1991.

————. *The Eisenhower Diaries.* Edited by Robert H. Ferrell. New York: Norton, 1981.

————. *Ike's Letters to a Friend 1941–1958.* Edited by Robert Griffith. Lawrence: University Press of Kansas, 1984.

————. Letter to Paul L. Snyder. March 24, 1953.

————. *The Papers of Dwight Eisenhower—The War Years: II.* Edited by Alfred D. Chandler, Stephen E. Ambrose, Joseph P. Hobbs, Edwin Alan Thompson, and Elizabeth F. Smith. Baltimore: Johns Hopkins University Press, 1970.

————. *The Quotable Eisenhower.* Anderson, SC: Drake House, 1967b.

————. *Selected Speeches of Dwight David Eisenhower: 34th President of the United States.* Washington, DC: United States Government Printing Office, 1970.

Eisenhower, John. Letter to Jerry Bergman. September 15, 2001.

————, editor. *Letters to Mamie.* Garden City, NY: Doubleday, 1978

————. *A Personal Reminiscence.* New York: Free Press, 1996.

Eisenhower, Julie Nixon. *Special People.* New York: Simon and Schuster, 1997.

Eisenhower, Milton S. *The President Is Calling.* Garden City, NY: Doubleday, 1974.

Eisenhower, Susan. *Mrs. Ike: Memories and Reflections on the Life of Mamie Eisenhower.* Sterling, VA: Capital, 1996.

"Eisenhower's Faith: An Interview with Billy Graham." *The Link,* September 5–7, 1969.

Ellis, Richard. *To the Flag: The Unlikely History of the Pledge of Allegiance.* Lawrence: University Press of Kansas, 2005.

Elson, Edward L. *America's Spiritual Recovery.* Westwood, NJ: Revell, 1954.

————, editor. *Memorial Addresses and Other Tributes in the Congress of the United States on the Life and Contributions of Mamie Doud Eisenhower, 1896–1979.* Washington, DC: United States Government Printing Office, 1981.

————. "The President's Dedicated Home." *Christian Herald,* May 1959, 29–30.

Endacott, J. Earl. Records, Documentary Historical Series, box 4, Eisenhower Presidential Library, Abilene, KS.

Faber, Doris. *The Mothers of American Presidents.* New York: New American Library, 1968.

Bibliography

Fairbanks, James David. "Religious Dimensions of Presidential Leadership: The Case of Dwight Eisenhower." *Presidential Studies Quarterly* 12:2 (Spring 1982) 260–67.

"Faith of the Candidates." *Time*, September 22, 1952, 55–56.

Fecher, Charles, editor. *The Diary of H. L. Mencken*. New York: Knopf, 1989.

Ferrell, Robert H. "Eisenhower Was a Democrat." *Kansas History* 13:3 (1990) 134–38.

Field, Rudolph. *Mister American, Dwight David Eisenhower*. New York: R. Field, 1952.

Fleming, Helen. "Ike's Mom Jehovah Witness 50 Yrs., Say Group Leaders; Preacher from Door to Door in Abilene, Director Reports." *Chicago Daily News*, June 25, 1955, 1, 3.

Fox, Fredrick. "The National Day of Prayer." *Theology Today* 30 (July 1973) 258–60.

———. "Pro Ike." *Christian Century*, July 2, 1969, 907.

Franz, Frederick. *Jehovah's Witnesses: Proclaimers of God's Kingdom*. Brooklyn: Watchtower Bible and Tract Society of Pennsylvania, 1993.

Franz, Raymond, editor. *Aid to Bible Understanding*. New York: Watchtower Bible and Tract Society, 1971.

———. *Crisis of Conscience*. Atlanta: Commentary, 1983.

———. *In Search of Christian Freedom*. Atlanta: Commentary, 1991.

Freese, Arthur. "Man of the 20th Century." Interview with Milton Eisenhower. *Modern Maturity*, December/January 1975, 25–28.

Freudenheim, Milt. "The Religion of Ike's Parents." *Chicago Daily News*, June 23, 1955.

Fuller, Edmund, and David E. Green. *God in the White House: The Faiths of American Presidents*. New York: Crown, 1968.

Galambos, Louis. *Eisenhower: Becoming the Leader of the Free World*. Baltimore: Johns Hopkins University Press, 2017.

Gammon, Roland, editor. *All Believers Are Brothers*. New York: Doubleday, 1969.

Gerstenmaier, Eugen. "The Church Conspiratorial." Ch. 9 in *We Survived: Fourteen Histories of the Hidden and Hunted in Nazi Germany*, by Eric H. Boehm, 172–89. Boulder, CO: Westview, 2003.

Goodpaster, Andrew J. *For the Common Defense*. Lexington, MA: Lexington, 1977.

———. Personal interview. September 20, 2001.

Gowran, Clay. "Ike Sheds All Aloofness to Woo Delegates." *Chicago Daily Tribune*, June 9, 1952, 3.

Graham, Billy. "The General Who Became President." In *Just As I Am: The Autobiography of Billy* Graham, 188–206. San Francisco: Harper, 1997,.

Graves, William. "World's Last Salute to a Great American." *National Geographic* 136:1 (July 1969) 40–51.

Greene, Douglas. "I Like Ike: The Human Side." *The American Legion*, May 1983, 22–23, 50–52.

Griffith, Robert, editor. *Ike's Letters to a Friend, 1941–1958*. Lawrence: University of Kansas Press, 1984.

Grinder, Darrin, and Steve Shaw. *The Presidents and Their Faith: From George Washington to Barack Obama*. Boise, ID: Russell Media, 2011.

Gruss, Edmond. *The Jehovah's Witnesses and Prophetic Speculation*. Nutley, NJ: Presbyterian and Reformed, 1976.

Gullan, Harold I. *Faith of Our Mothers: The Stories of Presidential Mothers from Mary Washington to Barbara Bush*. Grand Rapids: Eerdmans, 2001.

Gunther, John. *Eisenhower: The Man and the Symbol*. Garden City, NY: Doubleday, 1951.

Gustafson, Merlin. "How a President Uses Religion and How It Uses Him." Unpublished Manuscript, n.d.

Bibliography

————. "The Religious Role of the President." *Midwest Journal of Political Science* 14:4 (November, 1970) 708–22.

————. "The Religion of a President." *Christian Century*, April 30, 1969, 6109–613.

Haldeman, I. M. *Millennial Dawnism: The Blasphemous Religion which Teaches the Annihilation of Jesus Christ.* New York: Charles Cook, 1910.

Harnsberger, Caroline Thomas, editor. *Treasury of Presidential Quotations.* Chicago: Follett, 1964.

Harrison, Barbara Grizzuti. *Visions of Glory: A History and Memoir of Jehovah's Witnesses.* New York: Simon and Schuster, 1987.

Hatch, Alden. *General Ike: A Biography of Dwight D. Eisenhower.* 1st ed. Chicago: Henry Holt, 1944. New enlarged edition, Cleveland: World, 1946.

————. *Young Ike.* New York: Julian Messner, 1953.

Haymann, Tom. *The Unofficial U.S. Census.* New York: Fawcett Columbine, 1991.

Hayward, Steven. *The Politically Incorrect Guide to the Presidents, from Wilson the Obama.* Washington, DC: Regnery, 2012.

Hefley, James, and Marti Hefley. *By Their Blood: Christian Martyrs of the Twentieth Century.* Grand Rapids: Baker, 1979.

Henderson, Jennifer Jacobs. "Hayden Covington, the Jehovah's Witnesses and Their Plan to Expand First Amendment Freedoms." PhD diss., University of Washington, 2002.

Hendon, David, and James Kennedy. "Civil Religion." *Journal of Church and State.* 39:2 (1997) 390–91.

Henschel, Milton G. Obituary, *Chicago Daily News*, June 25, 1955, 1, 3.

Henry, Patrick. "'And I Don't Care What It Is': The Tradition—History of a Civil Religion Proof-Text." *Journal of the American Academy of Religion* 49:1 (1981) 35–49.

Hertzler, John R. "The 1879 Brethren in Christ Migration from Southwestern Pennsylvania to Dickinson County, Kansas." *Pennsylvania Mennonite Heritage* 3:1 (January 1980) 11–18.

Hesse, Hans, editor. *Persecution and Resistance of Jehovah's Witnesses during the Nazi-Regime 1933–1945.* Bremen, Germany: Temmen, 2001.

High, Stanley. "Armageddon Inc." *Saturday Evening Post*, September 1940, 213f.

————. "What the President Wants." *Reader's Digest* 42:372 (1953) 1–4.

Hitler, Adolf. *Hitler's Secret Conversations.* Translated by Normal Cameron and R. H. Stevens. New York: Farrar, Straus and Young, 1953.

Holl, Jack M. "Dwight D. Eisenhower: Civil Religion and the Cold War." Ch. 6 in Mark Rozell and Gleaves Whitney, *Religion and the American Presidency*, 119–37. New York: Palgrave Macmillan, 2007.

————. "Dwight D. Eisenhower Religion, Politics, and the Evils of Communism." In *The Problem of Evil, Slavery, and the Ambiguities of American Reform*, edited by Steven Mintz and John Stauffer, 383–96. Amherst: University of Massachusetts Press, 2007.

Holt, Daniel D. "An Unlikely Partnership and Service: Dwight Eisenhower, Mark Clark, and the Philippines." *Kansas History* 13:3 (Autumn, 1990) 149–65.

Hopper, Paul. *Eisenhower Administration Project.* Columbia University, Dr. Edward L. R. Elson Oval History Research Office, January 11, 1968.

Hotchkin, Sheila. "Rare Documents from Nazi Trial Being Posted on Internet." *Bryan Times*, January 10, 2002, 3.

Hutchinson, Paul. "The President's Religious Faith." *Christian Century*, March 24, 1954, 362–69.

————. "The President's Religious Faith." *Life*, March 22, 1954, 150–67.

Bibliography

"I Chose My Way." *Time*, September 23, 1946, 27.

"Ike and Billy Talk Religion." *Evening News*, Harrisburg, PA, Wednesday, March 26, 1952, 18.

"Ike Will Invoke Divine Aid, Become President." *Omaha World-Herald*, January 20, 1953, 1.

"Ike's Faith." *Time* 60:12–13, August 18, 1952.

Irish, Kerry E. "Hometown Support in the Midst of War." *Kansas History* 25:1 (2002) 14–37.

Irving, David. *The War Between the Generals*. New York: Congdon and Lattés, 1981.

Jameson, Henry B. *Heroes by the Dozen*. Abilene, KS: Shadinger-Wilson, 1961.

———. "Ike Buried in Abilene; Massive Crowd for Eisenhower Funeral." *Abilene Reflector-Chronicle*, Memorial Edition, 1969.

———. *They Still Call Him Ike*. New York: Vintage, 1972.

Johnson, Eric A. *Nazi Terror: The Gestapo, Jews, and Ordinary Germans*. New York: Basic Books, 1999.

Johnson, George. *Eisenhower: The Life and Times of a Great General, President and Statesman*. Derby, CT: Monarch, 1962.

Jubber, Ken. "The Persecution of Jehovah's Witnesses in Southern Africa. *Social Compass* 24:1 (1977) 121–34.

Kaplan, William. *State and Salvation*. Toronto: University of Toronto Press, 1989.

Keim, Albert N. "John Foster Dulles and the Protestant World Order Movement on the Eve of World War II." *Journal of Church and State* 21 (Winter 1979) 73–89.

Keller, Craig Lee. Various interviews, 2000. (Keller was then a PhD candidate at George Washington University.)

———. "The Intellectuals and Eisenhower: Civil Religion, Religious Publicity, and the Search for Moral and Religious Communities." PhD diss., George Washington University, 2002.

Kershaw, Ian. *Hitler, 1936–45: Nemesis*. New York: Norton, 2000.

Kimball, D. L. *I Remember Mamie*. 1st ed. Fayette, IA: Trends and Events, 1981.

King, Christine Elizabeth. *The Nazi State and the New Religions: Five Case Studies in Non-Conformity*. Studies in Religion and Society 4. Lewiston, NY: Edwin Mellen, 1982.

———. "Strategies for Survival: An Examination of the History of Five Christian Sects in Germany 1933–45." *Journal of Contemporary History* 14 (1979) 211–23.

King, Kathleen, and Dennis E. Clayson. "Perceptions of Jews, Jehovah's Witnesses and Homosexuals." *California Sociologists*, Winter 1984, 49–67.

Kinnard, Douglas. *Ike 1890–1990: A Pictorial History*. Washington, DC: Brassey, 1990.

Knorr, Nathan H. "Appreciated Parents." *Awake!*, April, 1975, 22, 30.

———. "Conspiracy against Jehovah's Name." *The Watchtower*, June 1, 1957, 323–24.

———. "Eisenhower Book Stirs A Controversy: Conceals Fact that Parents Were Jehovah's Witnesses." *Awake!*, September 22, 1955, 3–4.

———. "Religion Void of Principle." *Awake!*, October 22, 1946. 7.

Kogon, Eugene. *The Theory and Practice of Hell*. New York: Berkeley Medallion, 1958.

Kornitzer, Bela. *The Great American Heritage: The Story of the Five Eisenhower Brothers*. New York: Farrar, Straus, and Cudahy, 1955.

Kotwall, B. J. "The Watchtower Society Encourages Lying."*Investigator Magazine* (Australia), 1997.

LaFay, Howard. "The Eisenhower Story." *National Geographic* 136:1 (July 1969) 1–39.

Larson, Arthur. *Eisenhower: The President Nobody Knew*. New York: Scribner, 1968.

Bibliography

———. "Eisenhower's World View." Chapter 14 in *Portraits of American Presidents*, edited by Kenneth W. Thompson, vol. 3, 39–62. New York: University Press of America, 1984.

Lasby, Clarence G. *Eisenhower's Heart Attack: How Ike Beat Heart Disease and Held on to the Presidency*. Lawrence: University of Kansas Press, 1997.

Lastelic, Joseph A. "Presidential Churchgoing Can Be an Ordeal."*Kansas City Star*, April 10, 1977.

Lee, R. Alton. *Dwight D. Eisenhower: A Bibliography of His Times and Presidency*. Wilmington, DE: Scholarly Resources, 1991.

———. *Dwight David Eisenhower: Soldier and Statesmen*. Chicago: Nelson-Hall, 1981.

Lenz, Johannes. *Untersuchungen über die künstliche Zündung von Lichtögen unter besonderer Berücksichtigung der Lichtobogen-Stromrichter nach Erwin Marx*. Braunschweig: Hunold, 2004.

Leroy Edwin. *The Conditional Faith of Our Fathers*. Washington, DC: Review and Harold, 1954.

Linder, R. D. "Eisenhower, Dwight David (1890–1969)." In *Dictionary of Christianity in America*, edited by Daniel Reid. Downers Grove, IL: InterVarsity, 1990.

Lingerfeldt, Clyde A. Correspondence to Jerry Bergman, September 23, 1995.

———. Interview, May 13, 2000.

Lipset, Seymour Martin. "The Sources of the "Radical Right." In *The Radical Right*, edited by Daniel Bell. Garden City, NY: Anchor, 1964.

Long, Vivian Aten. "Stalwart Faith of River Brethren in President's Religious Background." *Kansas City Times*, March 11, 1955.

Louderback-Wood, Kerry. "Jehovah's Witnesses, Blood Transfusions, and the Tort of Misrepresentation." *Journal of Church and State* 47:4 (2005) 783–822.

Lovelace, Delos Wheiler. *"Ike" Eisenhower: Statesman and Soldier of Peace*. New York: Thomas Crowell, 1961.

Lutzer, Erwin W. *Hitler's Cross: The Revealing Story of How the Cross of Christ Was Used as a Symbol of the Nazi Agenda*. Chicago: Moody, 1995.

Lyon, Peter. *Eisenhower: Portrait of the Hero*. Boston: Little, Brown, 1974.

Maddox, Robert. "Reflections on Surviving Morton Downey." *Church and State*, December, 1988, 21.

Magnani, Duane. *Danger at Your Door*. Clayton, CA: Witness Inc., 1987.

Mazur, Eric Michael. *The Americanization of Religious Minorities: Confronting the Constitutional Order*. Baltimore: Johns Hopkins University Press, 1999.

McCullun, John. *Six Roads from Abilene: Some Personal Recollections of Edgar Eisenhower*. Seattle, WA: Wood and Reber, 1960.

Miller, Francis Trevelyn. *Eisenhower, Man and Soldier*. Philadelphia: Winston, 1944.

Miller, Merle. *Ike the Soldier: As They Knew Him*. New York: Putnam, 1987.

Miller, William Lee. "The Liking of Ike." *The Reporter*, October 16, 1953, 20.

———. *Piety along the Potomac*. Boston: Houghton Mifflin, 1964.

———. "Religion, Politics, and the 'Great Crusade.'" *The Reporter*, July 7, 1953. 14.

Moore, James P., Jr. *One Nation under God: The History of Prayer in America*. New York: Doubleday, 2005.

"More about Eisenhower: A Soldier Recalls 'Why I Believe . . .'" *The Link*, September 1969, 8–10.

Morin, Relman. *Dwight D. Eisenhower: A Gauge of Greatness*. New York: Associated Press, 1969.

Bibliography

Morrow, Lance. "God Knows What the Court Was Thinking." *Time*, July 8, 2002, 96.

Muramoto, Osamu. "Recent Developments in the Care of Jehovah's Witnesses." *Western Journal of Medicine* 170:5 (1999) 297–301.

Mygatt, Gerald. *Soldiers' and Sailors' Prayer Book*. New York: Alfred Knopf, 1944.

Nannes, Caspar. "The President and His Pastor." *Colliers*, November 11, 1955, 29—31.

Neal, Steve. *The Eisenhowers*. Lawrence: University Press of Kansas, 1984.

———. *The Eisenhowers: Reluctant Dynasty*. Garden City, NY: Doubleday, 1978.

Nelson, C. Richardson. *The Life and Work of General Andrew J. Goodpaster*. New York, Rowman and Littlefield, 2016.

Nevin, David. "Home to Abilene." *Life*, April, 11, 1969, 24–34.

Newton, Merlin Owen. *Armed with the Constitution: Jehovah's Witnesses in Alabama and the U.S. Supreme Court, 1939-1946*. Tuscaloosa: University of Alabama Press, 1995.

Nussel, Donald. "Truth Connection to Eisenhowers Confirmed." *Bible Students Newsletter*, 26(3):7—10; 18, 1997.

Pach, Chester and Elmo Richardson. *The Presidency of Dwight D. Eisenhower*. Lawrence, KS: The University Press of Kansas, 1991.

"Pacifism and Conscientious Objection—Is There a Difference?" *The Watchtower*, February 1, 1951, 67–73.

Patterson, Bradley. Letter to Jerry Bergman, September 6, 2001.

Pearson, Drew. *Drew Pearson Diaries 1949-1959*. Edited by Tyler Abell. New York: Holt, 1974.

———. "Eisenhowers Seek to Clear Mother of Affiliation with Religious Sect." *Defiance Crescent News* 19, December 6, 1956.

Penton, M. James. *Apocalypse Delayed: The Story of Jehovah's Witnesses*. Toronto: University of Toronto Press, 1997.

———. *Jehovah's Witnesses and the Third Reich: Sectarian Politics under Persecution*. Toronto: University of Toronto Press, 2004.

———. *Jehovah's Witnesses in Canada: Champions of Freedom of Speech and Worship*. Toronto: MacMillan, 1976.

Perret, Geoffrey. *Eisenhower*. New York: Random House, 1999.

Picker, Henry, and Heinrich Heim. *Hitler's Table Talk, 1941-1944*. London: Weldenfeld and Nicolson, 1953.

Pickett, William. *Dwight David Eisenhower and American Power*. Wheeling, IL: Harland Davidson, 1995.

Pierard, Richard V. "Billy Graham—Preacher of the Gospel or Mentor of Middle America." *Fides et Historia* 5 (1973) 127–31.

———. "Billy Graham and the U.S. Presidency." *Journal of Church and State* 22:1 (Winter 1980) 107–27.

———. "From Evangelical Exclusivism to Ecumenical Openness." *Journal of Ecumenical Studies* 20 (1983) 425–46.

———. "On Praying with the President." *Christian Century*, March 10, 1982, 262–64.

———. "One Nation under God: Judgment or Jingoism?" In *Christian Social Ethics*, edited by Perry C. Cotham, 81–103. Grand Rapids: Baker, 1979.

Pierard, Richard V., and Robert D. Linder. *Civil Religion and the Presidency*. Grand Rapids: Academia, 1988.

Pinkley, Virgil. *Eisenhower Declassified*. Old Tappan, NJ: Revell, 1979.

"Prayer and Preparation." *Time*, January 26, 1953, 18.

Bibliography

"The President and His Church: What Senator Neely Says . . . Some Replies." *U.S. News and World Report*, , April 8, 1955, 50–52.

"President 'Stakes Down' His Faith." *Christian Century*, February 11, 1953, 155.

"The President's Prayer." *The Nation*, January 31, 1953, 91.

Pusey, Merlo. *Eisenhower: The President*. New York: Macmillan, 1956.

Raines, Ken. "Deception by J.W's in Court, OK with Judge?" *JW Research Journal* 3:2 (1996) 20.

Reed, David L. "Court Rules: Watchtower Booklet Recommends 'Untrue' Testimony under Oath." *Comments from the Friends*, Spring 1992, 10.

———. *Dictionary of "J.W.ese": The Loaded Language Jehovah's Witnesses Speak*. Assonet, MA: Comments from the Friends, 1995.

———. *Jehovah-Talk: The Mind-Control Language of Jehovah's Witnesses*. Grand Rapids: Baker, 1997.

"Remark Called Casual." *New York Times*, July 11, 1952, 10.

Reprints of the Original Watchtower and Herald of Christ's Presence. 12 vols. Chicago: Chicago Bible Students, 1981.

Reynaud, Michel, and Sylvie Graffard. *The Jehovah's Witnesses and the Nazis: Persecution, Deportation, and Murder, 1933–1945*. New York: Cooper Square, 2001.

Rogerson, Alan. *Millions Now Living Will Never Die: A Study of Jehovah's Witnesses*. London: Constable, 1969.

Roy, Ralph Lord. *Apostles of Discord: A Study of Organized Bigotry and Disruption on the Fringes of Protestantism*. Boston: Beacon, 1953.

Rozell, Mark J., and Gleaves Whitney. *Religion and the American Presidency*. New York: Palgrave Macmillan, 2007.

Russell, Charles Taze. "The Testimony of God's Stone Witness and Prophet, the Great Pyramid in Egypt." In *Studies in the Scriptures*, vol. 3, *Thy Kingdom Come*, 313–76. Allegheny, PA: Watch Tower Bible and Tract Society, 1904.

———. *Studies in the Scriptures*. Vol. 1, *The Plan of the Ages*. New York: Watchtower Bible and Tract Society, 1914.

Rutherford, Joseph. "The Altar in Egypt." *The Watchtower*, November 15, 1928, 333–45 (part 1); December 1, 1928, 355–62 (part 2).

———. *Riches*. New York: Watchtower Bible and Tract Society, 1936.

Schaaf, James Edward. *Mamie Doud Eisenhower and Her Chicken Farmer Cousin*. Whitehouse Station, NJ: Wilkie, 1974.

Seldes, George. *Never Tire of Protesting*. New York: Lyle Stuart, 1968.

Sellers, Ron. *How Americans View Various Religious Groups*. Barna Research Group, 1990.

Semonche, John E. *Religion and Constitutional Government in the United States; A Historical Overview with Sources*. Carrboro: NC: Signal, 1986.

"Should Christians Be Pacifists?" *Awake!*, May 8, 1997, 22–23.

Shribman, David. "Memorial Shows that America Still Likes Ike." *The Toledo Blade*, April 25, 2010, A5.

Sibley, Mulford Q., and Philip Jacob. *Conscription of Conscience: The American State and the Conscientious Objector, 1940–47*. Ithaca, NY: Cornell University Press, 1952.

Sinnott, Susan. *Mamie Doud Eisenhower, 1896–1979*. New York: Children's, 2000.

Slater, Ellis D. *The Ike I Knew*. New York: Ellis D. Slater Trust, 1980.

Slupina, Wolfram. "Persecuted and Almost Forgotten." In *Persecution and Resistance of Jehovah's Witnesses during the Nazi-Regime, 1933–1945*, edited by Hans Hesse, 266–93. Chicago: Berghahn, 2001.

Smith, F. LaGard. *ACLU: The Devil's Advocate; The Seduction of Civil Liberties in America*. Colorado Springs, CO: Marcon, 1996.

Smith, Gary Scott. *Faith and the Presidency: From George Washington to George W. Bush*. New York: Oxford University Press, 2006.

Smith, Jean Edward. *Eisenhower in War and Peace*. New York: Random House, 2012.

Smith, Kalmin D. "Civil Religion and the Presidency." Paper prepared for delivery at the 1975 annual meeting of the American Political Science Association, San Francisco, CA, September 2–5, 1975.

Smyth, Plazzi. *Our Inheritance in the Great Pyramid*. London: Daldy, Isbister, 1877.

Sorauf, Frank J. "Jehovah's Witnesses." In *Guide to American Law*, 333. St. Paul, MN: West Publishing, 1984.

Stark, Rodney. "The Rise and Fall of Christian Science." *Journal of Contemporary Religion*. 13:2 (1998) 189–214.

Starr, Isidore. *Human Rights in the United States*. New York: Oxford Book, 1964.

Sterling, Chandler W. *The Witnesses: One God, One Victory*. Chicago: Henry Regnery, 1975.

Stevens, Leonard. *Salute!: The Case of the Bible vs. the Flag*. New York: Coward, McCann and Geohegan, 1973.

Stevens, William Colt. *Why I Reject the Helping Hand of Millennial Dawn*. Nyack, NJ: Alliance, 1920.

Stevenson, W. C. *Year of Doom: 1975*. London: Hutchinson, 1967. Also published as *The Inside Story of Jehovah's Witnesses*; New York: Hart, 1968.

Stookey, Steven M. "In God We Trust?: Evangelical Historiography and the Quest for a Christian America." *Southwestern Journal of Theology* 42 (Summer 1999) 5–37.

Stringer, William H. "The President and the 'Still Small Voice.'" *Christian Science Monitor*, February 26, 1954.

Stroup, Herbert Hewitt. *The Jehovah's Witnesses*. New York: Columbia University Press, 1945; reprint, New York: Russell and Russell, 1967.

Summersby, Kay Morgan, and Barbara Wyden. *Past Forgetting: My Love Affair with Dwight D. Eisenhower*. New York: Simon and Schuster, 1977.

Taylor, Allan. Speech at Poughkeepsie, New York, June 26, 1948. Reprinted in *What Eisenhower Thinks*, edited by Allan Taylor. New York: Crowell, 1953.

"The Testimony of a Devout President." *Life* December 26, 1955, 12–13.

Thomas, Evan. *Ike's Bluff: President Eisenhower's Secret Battle to Save the World*. New York: Little, Brown, 2012.

Thompson, Kenneth W., editor. *The Eisenhower Presidency: Eleven Intimate Perspectives of Dwight D. Eisenhower*. Portraits of American Presidents 3. Lanham, MD: University Press of America, 1984.

Tonkin, R. G. "I Grew Up with Eisenhower." *Saturday Evening Post*, May 3, 1952, 18–19, 46, 48–49, 53.

Wallace, Chris. *Character: Profiles in Presidential Courage*. New York: Rugged Land, 2004.

Watchtower Society. Letter, April 16, 1999. Signed ECH:ECM.

Watson, Robert P., editor. *Laura Bush: The Report to the First Lady*. Huntington, NY: Nova History, 2001.

Whalen, William J. *Armageddon around the Corner: A Report on Jehovah's Witnesses*. New York: John Day, 1962.

White, Paul Dudley. *My Life and Medicine*. Boston: Gambit, 1971.

Bibliography

White, Timothy. *A People for His Name: The History of Jehovah's Witnesses and an Evaluation.* New York: Vantage, 1967.

Whitney, David C. *The American Presidents.* Garden City, NY: Doubleday, 1967.

"Why Jehovah's Witnesses Are Not Pacifists." *The Watchtower,* February 1, 1951, 73–81.

Wicker, Tom. *Dwight D. Eisenhower.* New York: Henry Holt, 2002.

Wickman, John E. "Ike and 'The Great Truck Train'—1919." *Kansas History* 13:3 (Autumn 1990) 139–48.

Wirt, Sherwood E. "The Faith of Dwight D. Eisenhower." *Decision,* July and August, 1965 (2 parts).

Witter, Ray. Interview by Walter Barbash, August 28, 1964. Transcript in Eisenhower Presidential Library, Abilene, KS. (Rev. Witter was the son of one of David's sisters and therefore was a cousin of Dwight Eisenhower.)

Yaffee, Barbara. "Witnesses Seek Apology for Wartime Persecution." *The Globe in Mail,* September 9, 1984.

Yaffee, Sallot, and Barbara Yaffee. "Secret Files Reveal Bigotry, Suppression." *The Globe in Mail,* September, 4, 1984.

Index

Index

Index

Index

Made in the USA
Monee, IL
10 July 2020